070.5026
Jon

AGANBI / EMAKPOSE MEMORIAL
REFERENCE LIBRARY
EKU, DELTA STATE
NIGERIA

£16.99

Publishing Law

Publishing Law is a comprehensive guide to the law as it affects the publishing process. Written by a publishing and copyright solicitor with many years experience of the publishing trade, this work will serve as a comprehensive handbook for all those who need a practical working understanding of where and how the law may apply, including publishers, authors, agents and many others.

Hugh Jones addresses a range of key legal issues in the publishing process: confidential information, copyright, moral rights, commissioning and contracts, editing and production, defamation, libel and other legal risks such as negligent mis-statement, obscenity and official secrets, defences such as fair dealing, trade marks and passing off, consumer law, data protection, advertising and promotion, merchandising, distribution and export. Advice is given on current copyright legislation and the integration of directives and regulations from the European Union. Legal points are explained with reference to important statutes, cases and relevant trade practices. A glossary of key terms and a list of useful addresses are provided.

Hugh Jones is a publishing and copyright solicitor at the City law firm of Taylor Joynson Garrett. He worked for fifteen years for the law publishers Sweet & Maxwell and the academic and reference publishers Macmillan. He is a member of the Publishers Association's Publishing Law group.

£16.99

AGANBI / EMAKPOSE MEMORIAL
REFERENCE LIBRARY
EKU, DELTA STATE
NIGERIA

REF No...........................

Publishing Law

Hugh Jones
Solicitor,
Taylor Joynson Garrett

A BLUEPRINT book
published by Routledge
London and New York

First published 1996
by Routledge
11 New Fetter Lane, London EC4P 4EE

Simultaneously published in the USA and Canada
by Routledge
29 West 35th Street, New York, NY 10001

The author has asserted his moral rights in accordance with
the Copyright, Designs & Patents Act 1988
© 1996 Hugh Jones

Typeset in Times by Laserscript Ltd, Mitcham
Printed and bound in Great Britain by
TJ Press (Padstow) Ltd, Padstow, Cornwall

All rights reserved. No part of this book may be reprinted or
reproduced or utilised in any form or by any electronic,
mechanical, or other means, now known or hereafter
invented, including photocopying and recording, or in any
information storage or retrieval system, without permission in
writing from the publishers.

British Library Cataloguing in Publication Data
A catalogue record for this book is available from the British Library

Library of Congress Cataloging in Publication Data
Jones, Hugh.
    Publishing law/by Hugh Jones.
    p. cm.
    "A blueprint book" – P. [4] of cover.
    Includes index.
    1. Authors and publishers – Great Britain. 2. Press law – Great Britain.
    3. Copyright – Great Britain. I. Title.
    KD1340.J66   1996
    343.4109'98 – dc20   96-24665
    [344.103998]   CIP

ISBN 0–415–15110–4 (hbk)
ISBN 0–415–15466–9 (pbk)

2 2 JAN 2003

TO HECTOR, AND FRIENDS

Contents

Preface

Contrary to the advertisements one sees in the Sunday newspapers ('Be a Writer!', 'Writing for Fun and Profit') writing a law book is not a whole bundle of fun, especially at 5 a.m., and my accountant, who knows how many beans make five, is sceptical about any profit. Compared with some other hobbies, however, it is at least *interesting*, and it has confirmed me in my long-held view that law is interesting too. How could law *not* be interesting? It is about real people, after all, usually having real disputes, and when those disputes are drawn from what we used to call the publishing trade I hope the end result will be of interest to all those involved in publishing too – authors, agents or publishers, and those working in associated occupations such as booksellers, librarians and printers. I have structured the book to reflect the whole chronology of publishing, from authors and ideas to sale and distribution, and I have tried to draw examples from publishing wherever possible so, whatever your involvement in publishing, this book is for you.

I assume no prior knowledge of English law – indeed, I have included as appendix A, an A–Z glossary of legal terms: words and phrases like 'plaintiff', or 'tort', or 'common law' that lawyers like me use every day, but which it occurs to me probably need explaining as we go along. So, if you are uncertain about EU Directives, or writs or injunctions, bear with me and refer from time to time to appendix A. I had originally intended to start the book off with a whole introductory chapter about English law, and how it operates in the UK and within Europe, but time ran out; it might anyway have looked just a little patronising. It would be interesting to know whether people would find such a general chapter of value in due course, and if so we might perhaps be able to incorporate it into any further editions. Since this kind of law book is a new enterprise, I know the publishers would be grateful for any comments or suggestions, and so would I.

I would never have got this far without the kind help and support of my many publishing friends, and my ever patient colleagues in law at Taylor Joynson Garrett, all of whom gave up what must have been many hours of their valuable time to reading, and commenting on, successive draft chapters and bore my constant nagging about the schedule with admirable fortitude.

Gill Davies, one of the most experienced commissioning publishers I know, reassured me that chapter 1 might not be an inappropriate way to start a book about law for non-lawyers, and Paul Mitchell, one of this country's best-known copyright lawyers, and head of the intellectual property department at Taylor Joynson Garrett, found the time not only to read chapter 2 on copyright, but also to look at chapter 4 on author contracts and chapter 3 on moral rights: the resulting chapters have all benefited greatly from his eye for detail and his many constructive criticisms, not only based on his lifetime's experience of the law but also on his practical experience as a co-author of another book on law: *Joynson-Hicks on UK Copyright Law*, which in its day was the definitive treatment of the 1988 Act and which is still much more useful to busy practitioners than many much larger works. Dr Jim Parker, Registrar of Public Lending Right, agreed at short notice to look at the PLR section for me, and made many helpful suggestions. Dr Ian McGowan of the Centre for Publishing Studies at the University of Stirling, and Paul Richardson at the School of Visual Arts, Music and Publishing at Oxford Brookes University, both read the whole of chapter 2 and made many helpful comments on the suitability of the work for publishing students and suggested a number of places where a little more explanation might not come amiss. Although this book was not written primarily for students, it is very much hoped that it will prove useful for their needs in understanding what are often very complex and unfamiliar legal concepts.

I was lucky enough to persuade Roger Palmer, of Roger Palmer Ltd (how nice it must be to be a limited company), one of this country's leading experts on publishing contracts, to read the whole of chapter 4 on contracts, and particularly on the all-important author–publisher agreement, and his unrivalled knowledge of current law and practice saved me from many errors and misjudgements – his own book on *Publishing Contracts* in the Blueprint Series will be eagerly awaited, as will his joint editorship with another long-suffering friend of mine, Lynette Owen, of Charles Clark's well-known *Publishing Agreements*. Lynette, who is justly famous not only in the UK but all round the world as Rights and Contracts Director of Longman (now Addison Wesley Longman), kindly went through the chapter from Hell: chapter 5 on other contracts, and gave me the benefit of her great knowledge of rights deals and particularly subsidiary rights.

James Shirras of Film Finances Ltd, and Gary Rogers of Channel 4 Television, both kindly commented on the film and TV rights section; Nainan Shah of Sony UK helped me immensely with the electronic and multimedia rights section and suggested the list of product categories and distribution media at p. 130. Richard Hayes of Imago Publishing Ltd found the time to look at the section on contracts with book packagers and made numerous detailed and helpful comments and ensured I kept my feet (more or less) on the ground. Neil White of Taylor Joynson Garrett kindly read the defamation chapter for me (chapter 7), and Deborah Stones also of Taylor Joynson Garrett read the whole of the copyright infringement chapter (chapter 8) for me – no mean feat, given the length and complexity of the topic. Alvin Deutsch of US attorneys Deutsch, Klagsbrun and Blasband very kindly undertook at very short notice (no notice at all, in fact) to give me his comments on the US law section, and made many helpful suggestions, greatly improving my understanding and coverage of that notoriously complex topic.

Many expert lawyers at Taylor Joynson Garrett found the time to look at my first draft chapters in areas where their expertise far exceeds mine: John Linneker gave me a number of helpful comments on chapter 9, on trade marks and passing off, and Charles Lloyd kindly read chapters 10 and 11 for me, on sales and marketing and advertising and promotion respectively. Jonathan Haydn-Williams put me right more than once on issues relating to the conflict of laws, and the difficult questions of the applicable law of contracts, and jurisdiction. Martin Baker commented *twice*, on two successive drafts of chapter 12 on distribution and export, and this chapter is infinitely the better for his great experience of UK and European competition law.

Any errors or inaccuracies which remain are, of course, my fault – not theirs. It would be a great help to know of any inaccuracies which slipped through the net, or even of any points which are unclear or potentially misleading: the law in this area moves so fast that keeping up-to-date is (literally) a full-time job. I have tried to account for most current developments, and to highlight forthcoming attractions like the EU Database Directive or the current Defamation Bill (which, by the time you are reading this, will probably be the Defamation Act 1996). It cannot be stressed too strongly that the law is stated as accurately as possible as at the date given below, when the proofs were returned. In the ensuing months and years, it is quite possible that much in UK and EU law will change, although I have tried to foresee at least the major likely developments. Meanwhile, I hope this little book will explain broadly where UK publishing law is now, and why, but it can only give a general view. For the most up-to-date legal advice, of course, there is no reliable substitute for a good lawyer.

Hugh Jones
London
24 July 1996

Ideas and original works I

Authors and ideas

1

On a wall in my office there hangs a poster, entitled 'How a Book is Made'. Published some time ago by The Bodley Head, it gave children (and lawyers) a simplified, and somewhat optimistic, explanation in pictures of how the publishing and production process worked in 1983. You can tell it is for children, because all the characters are cats. You know it is somewhat optimistic when you get to the bit when the buyer in a rather small bookshop – a suspicious-looking feline in a roll-neck sweater – says 'Great! I'll take a thousand' (a *thousand*?). The January picture, however, is a classic view of authorship: the author sits writing at a table at home alone, at night, rescued only by a cartoon bubble saying 'Inspiration at last!' With the possible addition of a PC, the first picture would be much the same today. That moment of inspiration is still the origin of every published work, and it is what this opening chapter is about.

ORIGINAL IDEAS

All published works start with an original idea, and all ideas have an author. *The Oxford English Dictionary* equates author with 'originator': in the classic publishing hierarchy, the inspiration of authors is the beginning, the process starts here. However, the person who goes on to write the final published work – the 'author' of the work, in both the colloquial and the legal sense – is not necessarily the same person as the person who had the original idea. Once it is put into concrete form, the final work can be protected by the law of copyright – as we shall see in chapter 2 – and in a number of other important ways, but is there any separate legal protection for the idea itself?

A good publishing idea, such as an idea for a children's story, may have immense commercial value – it may generate not only profitable individual works but entire series of profit-making publications as well as substantial other revenue, for example, from merchandising or film, TV or electronic exploitation. Even if the final finished works were written by others, none of what follows would have happened without the original idea. Despite this, it is not at all easy to protect original ideas as such; as a general rule, there is no copyright in an idea, and the less developed it is, the harder it will be to protect in any other way. However, more developed ideas, concepts, plots, scenarios or even characters might be capable of protection, particularly if the circumstances in which they were disclosed were clearly confidential.

CONFIDENTIAL INFORMATION

There is a general rule of equity in English law that a person who receives information in confidence has a duty to keep that confidence and not disclose the information to others. Lord Denning put it well (as usual) in a 1969 case when he said:

> No person is permitted to divulge to the world information which he has received in confidence, unless he has just cause or excuse for doing so. Even if he comes by it innocently . . . once he gets to know that it was originally given in confidence, he can be restrained from breaking that confidence.

How do you know, though, when information has been 'received in confidence'? Are publishers under a duty not to disclose or use information merely because it arrives on their desk in an envelope marked 'Confidential'? What if it is a completely unsolicited proposal – a fairly common publishing event – from someone they have never met? Well (as lawyers often say) that depends. It depends (in that particular case) on whether a *relationship* of confidence exists – or is created – between the person giving and the person receiving the information, so that its confidentiality would be understood and accepted on both sides. You do not make information confidential simply by stamping 'Confidential' on it. It must be accepted as such by both parties. It will only be confidential if:

- *there is a relationship of confidence*, as for example between husband and wife, or doctor and patient (or such a relationship can be implied); or
- *there is a contractual duty of confidentiality*, such as those included in many employment contracts, or consultancy agreements.

In the familiar circumstances of the unsolicited publishing proposal, neither of those two criteria are likely to apply (although they might). An author in such circumstances, with the good fortune to have had a new idea with commercial potential, might therefore consider entering into a short-term confidentiality agreement with the publisher concerned, if he or she wishes to protect the idea. However, this is only likely to provide short-term protection. Try as publishers might, it is very difficult to put a good idea out of their minds once it has been revealed to them, even if for some reason the author who brought it to them has to be turned down. Good ideas have a habit of re-appearing later in different forms and rejected authors might easily (and do) suspect that their ideas have simply been stolen. Given the economic realities of publishing, there is probably not a lot that can be done about this, and author–publisher confidentiality agreements are still comparatively rare.

OBLIGATIONS OF CONFIDENCE

What kinds of people might be under duties or obligations of confidence? Let us examine each category in turn:

CONFIDENTIAL RELATIONSHIPS

Clearly there are some close relationships, such as that between husband and wife, which the law will automatically regard as relationships of trust: the Duchess of Argyll found in a celebrated case in 1967 that information communicated confidentially to her by the Duke while they were married could not be published in later divorce proceedings. This duty of trust would probably extend to confidences disclosed in any sexual relationship, homosexual as well as heterosexual (unless 'grossly immoral'), and it has similarly been held to apply to secrets disclosed in other close, personal, professional or business relationships of trust, such as confessions made to a priest, information disclosed to doctors, solicitors or bankers, and secrets shared between partners of a firm or directors or shareholders of a company. It may well extend to ideas and other information disclosed by an author to his or her literary agent, but would not necessarily cover disclosures made to a publisher unless the author–publisher relationship was a fairly close or long-standing one. It would be unlikely to protect an unsolicited idea offered to a publisher by an author never previously dealt with: some other basis for protecting confidentiality would need to be found, such as a contractual agreement (see below).

IMPLIED CONFIDENTIALITY

A duty of confidentiality may be implied from particular circumstances, even though the relationship itself would not ordinarily be regarded as a confidential one. The question most often asked is: would a reasonable person, standing in the shoes of the recipient of the information, realise on reasonable grounds that the information was being given to him or her in confidence? In the leading case of *Prince Albert v. Strange* in 1849, the Prince Consort was granted an injunction preventing the publication of drawings and etchings by himself and Queen Victoria by an employee of their chosen printer: the employee concerned had been entrusted with the plates and other materials for a limited printing only, and clearly knew this – any further disclosure would have been a breach of trust. This would apply to any similar information improperly obtained, such as private letters. In a more recent Australian case adopting English law principles, the same implied duty of trust and confidentiality was held to apply to aboriginal tribal secrets disclosed to an anthropologist in the course of his research. The tribal elders showed him sacred sites, paintings and other objects, and shared secrets known only to male members of the tribe, and obtained an injunction limiting his right to publish them later in a book. The outcome might have been different if it had been clear to them from the outset that he was researching the information for publication in a book, but then he might not have been given the information.

CONTRACTUAL AGREEMENTS

Duties of confidence may be entered into contractually, for example, as part of a consultancy agreement, or covering disclosures of trade secrets made prior to a possible joint venture: clearly those seeking commercial backing for an exciting new idea will need to disclose at least some details of the idea in order to interest their potential partners, but they will only want to do so in circumstances of agreed confidentiality. A specific contractual undertaking is therefore usually recommended – and is fairly common – in these circumstances.

The most common contractual obligations of confidentiality, however, arise out of contracts of employment. The relationship of employer and employee (lawyers used to call it master and servant) has always been regarded as a relationship of trust, particularly where the employee is relatively senior and has regular access to the employer's trade secrets. The general rule is that employees may not disclose confidential information acquired during the course of their employment, or use it for the benefit of others, either while they are employed or (usually more importantly) after they have left. The test most usually adopted is: would people of ordinary honesty and intelligence recognise the information as the property of their employers and not their own to do with as they like?

The kind of confidential publishing information covered would include lists of customers, contacts or suppliers, advance price lists, pricing structures or mark-ups, contract terms, royalties or other financial information, and (of course) future publishing plans. This would include documents as well as more general information, but they need not be taken away in physical form – an employee who memorised a list of customers for use in a future job might still be prevented from disclosing that information later. All kinds of publishing employees may be covered, including editorial, marketing, production and finance staff, particularly those at senior levels. To reinforce the general rule, confidentiality clauses are often specifically written into their employment contracts.

For many employers, the greatest risk of disclosure of trade secrets comes when senior employees – such as marketing or other directors – leave to go to other jobs, or to set up on their own. For this reason, employment contracts for such staff often include restrictive covenants preventing the use of the firm's confidential information in the future, or for a limited number of years. Such covenants restricting future behaviour need to be very carefully drafted, however

– the wider and more restrictive their terms, the more likely it is that a court might find them to be void as being in restraint of trade (see later, chapter 12). In the first place, the terms of such clauses will be strictly and narrowly construed, against the person seeking to enforce them: so that, for example, an agreement not to 'disclose' company information will be just that, and may not prevent the employee from 'using' the information. Secondly, the information protected must truly amount to a trade secret of the firm's: no employee can be prevented from using his or her general 'know-how' (often called 'life skills') in future jobs, even though that expertise will inevitably have been picked up in earlier employments. This is only reasonable: otherwise, as one judge put it, 'no servant could ever advance himself'.

KINDS OF CONFIDENTIAL INFORMATION

PLOTS OR SCENARIOS

According to one school of thought, there are only a very few truly original plots – most 'new' works of fiction, or plays, are simply adaptations or re-workings of familiar themes. This probably fails to do justice to many fine authors and playwrights, but remarkably similar plots and scenarios do often re-appear, and there is often a very strong smell of plagiarism. However, similar plots can often be created quite independently and innocently, as some leading authors have found: when the plot of one novel seems to copy the plot of an earlier novel it often becomes clear after initial argument that the earlier idea has not been copied after all, and that both plots in fact are remarkably similar to something even older.

In other cases, however, a plot or scenario may be protected if it was only revealed in confidential circumstances. W. S. Gilbert obtained an injunction in 1894 to prevent unauthorised publication of the plot of his new play *His Excellency*, which was then in rehearsal but had not yet opened, on the grounds that the people seeking to publish it knew it had been obtained in breach of confidence. Publishers would similarly be prevented from re-using themselves the key elements of a scenario – plot, characters, dramatic ideas – which had been submitted to them, but rejected, if it could be established that it had been submitted in confidence and accepted as such at the time. There may also be an action for breach of copyright in the case of more developed material – we will look at this in chapter 2, and in more detail in chapter 8.

DEVELOPED CONCEPTS

What if an idea is less than a completed plot or scenario, but is developed to the point where it is more than a mere idea? Hughie Green, in a famous case, failed to protect the general ideas and format behind his game show *Opportunity Knocks* because so little of his own format had actually been put into fixed or developed form, or even written down: there were, for example, no scripts as such. However, in the more recent case of *Fraser v. Thames T.V.* (1983) a much more developed concept – about a female pop group – was successfully protected by an action for breach of confidence, on the basis that several important criteria had been met:

- the concept was clearly identifiable, and had some originality (was not, for example, public knowledge);
- it had been developed to a point where it was capable of being realised in practice, and had some real commercial potential;
- it had been disclosed in confidential circumstances, which were agreed as such by both parties.

UNPUBLISHED MANUSCRIPTS

Once original ideas are put into concrete written – or retrievable – form, they will normally attract copyright protection as copyright works: we will deal with this important form of protection more fully in chapter 2. This will apply even to incomplete first drafts, provided that they display the necessary elements of originality for copyright protection to apply. In addition, (or if for some reason copyright protection did not apply), there is probably still a general equitable duty of confidentiality which would restrain a publisher (or anyone else) from publishing a manuscript, if it had been submitted to them in confidential circumstances. Where the circumstances suggest otherwise, however – as with articles sent to a magazine, or Letters to the Editor – there may be a strong implied licence to publish.

CHARACTERS

An idea for a new character (like Peter Rabbit or Superman) may have huge commercial potential, but the idea itself is unlikely to attract copyright protection (although original drawings or artwork might) and is unlikely to be protected by a duty of confidentiality unless there is a clear relationship, or circumstances, of confidence (or a specific confidentiality agreement). A better form of legal protection is to register any character with that kind of potential (or names or logos) as a trade mark – we will deal with trade marks in chapter 9.

OTHER INFORMATION

Many other kinds of information may be protected by a duty of confidentiality, including confidential reports or surveys and confidential data stored on computer programs, provided that they are confidential, and have been confidentially acquired. Even news information as routine as results of horse races can be confidential, particularly if it is understood to have commercial value (as the judge in one case put it: 'By the expenditure of labour and money the plaintiffs had acquired the information and it was, in their hands, valuable property in this sense – that persons to whom it was not known were willing to pay, and did pay, money to acquire it.')

STATE SECRETS

Although former cabinet ministers and civil servants – particularly those employed in the security services – may often be subject to the Official Secrets Acts, actions for breach of confidence may also be possible in relation to government information. We shall deal with government secrets more fully in chapter 7. Such actions are not always successful, as the government found in the *Spycatcher* and *Crossman Diaries* cases, but there remains a general duty of confidentiality, particularly where profits are being made: in *Attorney-General v. Jonathan Cape* (1976), it was accepted as a general rule that 'a man shall not profit from the wrongful publication of information received by him in confidence'.

ACTIONS FOR BREACH OF CONFIDENCE

In order for an action for breach of confidence to succeed it will be necessary to prove:

- that the information is confidential in nature (for example, trade secrets rather than 'life skills', and more than 'trivial tittle-tattle'); and
- it was communicated in circumstances imposing an obligation of confidence.

There is no need to prove specific damage or loss as such, although that will strengthen any later award of damages. Since breach of confidence is an equitable jurisdiction, injunctions are often possible, to prevent breaches taking place, provided that there is some evidence an unauthorised disclosure is about to take place, and provided also that the terms of the injunction are reasonably specific, so that the defendant knows what it is that he or she may not disclose. If disclosure has already gone ahead, an award of damages may be given, together with delivery up of unauthorised material and an account of profits – on the general equitable principle that no-one should be allowed to gain from their own wrongdoing.

DEFENCES

A defence to any action might be available if:

- the information has already become public knowledge, and is therefore no longer confidential;
- there is a public interest in disclosure (at least as strong as – or stronger than –

the public interest in protecting confidences: for example, to expose a crime or tax fraud, or public health hazard).

SUMMARY CHECKLIST: PROTECTING IDEAS

- Is this a pure idea, or has anything been put into concrete form (for example on paper or disk)?
- If any written text or illustrations exist, can they be protected by copyright? Are they original?
- Are there any names, or characters or logos, which could be registered as trade marks?
- Is the information confidential in nature?
- Was it communicated in conditions of confidentiality?
- Is there a specific confidentiality agreement (for example relating to an individual idea, or more generally as for a consultant or employee)?
- If not, is there a general relationship of confidence – or can one be implied from the circumstances? Would a reasonable person realise that the information was being given in confidence?

Copyright

2

INTRODUCTION

We saw in chapter 1 that there is no copyright in an idea. However, there might be copyright protection for some kinds of more developed material, once something is put into concrete form or given tangible expression. Clearly, copyright law will not protect you just for having a good idea, but it may protect you for doing something positive to express it – in effect, for putting it into a form where it can be shared with the rest of the world. The law recognises that doing this requires an investment of time and effort, and also some skill. It also carries with it a serious risk: once expressed in tangible, physical form, an idea can be copied by others. This has always been true – even before Gutenberg – but it is particularly true in an age of computers. So the law provides protection against copying for those who make that investment and take that risk, and thus an incentive for them to invest their efforts in more ideas in the future. This is one of the most important truths to grasp about copyright, and UK copyright in particular. Although it protects authors and their works – quite rightly – it is not a reward for authorship, but a protection for investment. This explains why UK copyright law has developed in the way it has over the centuries, and it is unlikely that the UK's worldwide publishing business in its present form could exist without it.

What is copyright then, and why is it so important to publishing?

COPYRIGHT AND INTELLECTUAL PROPERTY

Copyright should, literally, be the right to copy; in fact in legal terms it is better to think of it as the right to *control* copying by others. Put a little more precisely, copyright in the UK is the exclusive statutory right, given (usually) to those who create original works, to exercise control for a specified period of time over the copying and other exploitation of those works. It therefore gives creators two different, but matching rights:

- an exclusive, positive right to copy and exploit their own works, or license other people (such as publishers) to do it for them; and
- a negative right to protect anyone else from doing so without their consent, coupled with powerful legal remedies for copyright infringement if they do.

Under UK copyright law, the emphasis is very much on the second, negative, right: UK copyright is primarily a right to prevent other people from doing things. (We will look at copyright infringement, and the various restricted acts under UK law, in chapter 8.)

Copyright may thus be grouped with the protection given to the owners of patents and the proprietors of registered trade marks, which (together with registered and unregistered designs and confidential information) traditionally make up the area of law known as 'intellectual property'. This term is not very precise, or very accurate (not every right is strictly speaking a right of property, for example), but it is a useful label for the increasingly important legal protection given to products of the mind: intellectual creations which, when applied commercially or industrially, are of some value to society, and worth protecting legally. In today's technological, computerised society, intellectual property (sometimes called 'industrial property') is an increasingly important form of national and international legal protection for trade in all kinds of goods, not only for books and CDs, but for films, videos, computer software, distinctive trade brands, new drugs and other inventions. Countries wishing to trade with each other – developed, as well as developing – increasingly ask what the others will do to protect the intellectual property rights of their authors and inventors. It is a key issue for all trading countries, and for trading blocs such as the EU, and intellectual property is normally fairly near the top of the agenda in international trade negotiations. The Uruguay Round of GATT was an excellent recent example (for more on GATT, see p. 218), and the new World Trade Organisation is firmly supportive of international copyright protection.

Before looking at modern copyright law in detail, it might be helpful to explain how we have got to this point, and how copyright law has developed over the centuries to meet the challenges of a fast-moving technological society.

FROM SCROLLS TO SCREENS: A BRIEF HISTORY OF COPYRIGHT

Although authors had a limited form of moral rights in the ancient world (plagiarism being punishable in Ancient Greece, for example) the general lack of literacy, and the slow and labour-intensive nature of copying by hand then and throughout the Middle Ages, meant that most copying was only undertaken for religious, legal or government purposes under circumstances which were fairly easy to control. Authors and playwrights had very little (if any) commercial interest in the copying of their works, and were either wholly dependent on patronage by the court and the aristocracy, or the Church or guilds, or earned a living independently (like Shakespeare, as an actor/manager). Copyright only really started to develop as an organised system of legal protection in Europe when commercial copying first became possible in the fifteenth century with the invention of the printing press. In England, this happened effectively when William Caxton started his printing operation in 1476. Richard III first sanctioned the printing – and importing – of books in a statute of 1483, and for a while printing flourished, and the Guild of Stationers – until then largely scholarly booksellers – began to include a new kind of printer/entrepreneur: the first modern publishers.

THE GUILD OF STATIONERS

Like today's publishers, fifteenth-century stationers had their profitable back lists (usually of classical or biblical texts), but they also invested their own risk capital in printing, advertising and selling the works of new authors, either purchasing them from the authors for an outright fee or sharing any profits. A powerful business partnership was thus born: the authors contributed their time and creative skill in writing the work, and the stationers – the publishers – invested their money and business acumen in printing and promoting it. The new printing process – the most efficient means of copying yet known – was effectively under the control of the Stationers Guild, and like all medieval guilds it protected its rights well. By 1533 Henry VIII had been persuaded to repeal Richard III's statute and protect English stationers by banning the importation of foreign books. The Tudor monarchs, always short of money and beset by intrigue, found that they could raise useful revenue by granting printing licences, but they also found that they could thereby control who was printing what. In other words, royal licensing quickly became linked with royal censorship. Indeed, when the Stationers Company's first Royal Charter was granted by the Catholic Queen Mary in 1556, the main concern of the Crown at the time was the suppression of heresy rather than the propagation of literature or learning. All lawfully printed books had to be registered by the Stationers Company, and a succession of decrees from the Court of Star Chamber provided extensive powers to search out and destroy those which were not.

THE LICENSING ACTS

This useful form of royal licensing continued under Elizabeth I and the Stuarts, and even after the Star Chamber was abolished in 1640, Parliament felt it necessary to make its own ordinances prohibiting the printing and importing of unlicensed works. The first Licensing Act was passed in 1662, after the Restoration, giving the representatives of the King and the Stationers Company power to seize unlicensed or pirated books, and impose fines – to be divided equally between the Crown and the authorised licensee, who was often referred to as the 'owner'. The owner of a limited government Licence was thus gradually coming to be recognised as the owner of an independent property right, and before long 'copy-right' was being bought, sold and bequeathed – like any other valuable property.

The royal licensing system was finally swept away after James II was exiled in the Glorious Revolution and in 1694 Parliament refused to renew any further Licensing Acts. This suited the new mood of Parliamentary supremacy following the Bill of Rights, but it left the Stationers without any clear legal basis for their publishing activities, and no effective protection against unauthorised copying. They therefore lobbied Parliament vigorously for a new Act, and as a result the first Copyright Act was passed, the Statute of Anne of 1709.

THE STATUTE OF ANNE

Under the 1709 Act, authors and their assigns – who included publishers – were given 'the sole right and liberty' of printing books for a period of 14 years from first publication: if the author was still alive at the end of that period, it was renewable for a further 14 years. Books already in print when the Act came into force in 1710 were given one single term of 21 years, but in both cases, the right could not be enforced without registering the work with the Stationers Company first. Thus a fixed, statutory copyright was created, based on previous publishing custom and enforceable – as before – by confiscation and fines. The protection it gave lasted, however, for a comparatively short period of time, and when the first statutory copyrights started to expire there was renewed pressure for a continuing common-law copyright, covering unpublished as well as published works. The question continued unresolved throughout the eighteenth century, until the House of Lords decided the matter once and for all in the historic case of *Donaldson v. Beckett* in 1774: there was indeed a common-law copyright, their Lordships decided, but only in unpublished works – once published, copyright protection for all works was determined, and limited, by statute. Copyright was therefore primarily a statutory, not a common-law, right and was intended to expire after a fixed number of years: this is substantially the position today (common-law copyright was finally abolished by the 1911 Act).

WIDER PROTECTION

During the eighteenth and nineteenth centuries, new Acts were passed to extend the new statutory copyright to cover new technologies, and to works other than books: engravings were covered in 1734, after lobbying by Hogarth, among others, sculpture in 1814, performing rights in music and drama in 1842 and paintings, drawings and photographs in 1862. The period of copyright protection itself was also increased gradually from the original 28-year maximum, despite opposition from Macaulay, who argued that longer protection, particularly beyond the author's life, would be an unreasonable tax on future generations of readers. The period was extended in 1814 to 28 years from publication or the rest of the author's life, whichever was the longer, and in 1842 to 42 years or 7 years after the death of the author, again whichever was the longer. This was something of a compromise, and there were many who felt that it still penalised unfairly the widows and children of authors who died young – as many of them then did. The idea of a copyright which might last long enough to protect authors' heirs had to wait much longer, and when it came it was as a result of international, rather than domestic, pressure.

THE BERNE CONVENTION

While Britain was pragmatically creating statutory copyrights, primarily to protect the investment of entrepreneurs, many of our European trading partners were more consciously protecting the creative act of authorship. Their copyrights, tellingly called Author's Rights, included not only copyright as we know it, but also neighbouring rights, such as performing rights, and moral rights relating to the work itself which were personal to the author and could never be alienated, (some of which are now included in UK law: see chapter 3). The different traditions met at an inter-governmental conference in Berne in 1885, designed to deal with international piracy of the sort suffered by Dickens and Gilbert & Sullivan and establish an international regime of mutual copyright protection. The Berne Convention of 1886 was the result: still in force over a hundred years later and now acceded to by over a hundred nations, it is probably the most successful international treaty ever signed. The signatory states agreed between them to grant mutual copyright protection to each other's copyright works, on the basis either that the author was a national of one of the member states, or that his or her works were first published there. Protection was to be equivalent to 'national treatment' – in other words, French authors should expect the same copyright protection for their works in England that English authors received themselves. With one or two exceptions, this has remained a fundamental principle of the Berne Convention ever since.

THE 1911 ACT

Three further basic principles of Berne were agreed when the powers next met in Berlin in 1908:

- copyright protection should arise automatically on creation of the work, without any registration formalities;
- works protected must however display some 'originality'; and
- protection would last for the rest of the life of the author, plus a further 50 years after that. (This was thought long enough to protect not only the author, but two generations of his or her heirs.)

These international principles involved substantial revisions to UK law, which were brought about in the 1911 Copyright Act. Typically, there were a number of compromises: the ban on any formalities meant that the requirement of registration at Stationers Hall finally had to be abolished – but registration still continued on a voluntary basis (and it can still prove useful today as evidence of first publication in the UK). The new continental term of copyright of life plus 50 years was also introduced – but, after a period of 25 years from the author's death had elapsed, subject to licences of right on payment of a 10 per cent royalty, and reversion of any assignments by authors for longer than 25 years to the author's heirs, (to protect authors' estates from unwise disposals). This reversionary right only applied to assignments by authors and then only when the author was the first owner of the copyright. So, for example, if the author was an employee, and the employer was the first owner of the copyright (see p. 32), there would be no reversion. There was continued provision for new technology: sound recordings were given copyright protection for the first time.

THE 1956 AND 1988 ACTS

Technology, and international events, moved on, and after the end of the Second World War, and the involvement of the USA and developing countries in the establishment of the Universal Copyright Convention in 1952, (see chapter 8), the UK passed the 1956 Copyright Act, extending copyright for the first time to films as works in their own right, and to broadcasts, and establishing a new 'typographical copyright' in published editions, and a new Performing Right Tribunal.

Computer programs were given statutory protection (as 'literary works') in 1985 and a 'Topography Right' was created in semiconductor products in 1987, followed finally by the current UK Copyright Act, the Copyright Designs & Patents Act 1988. This Act consolidated existing law and introduced, among other things, a rental right for certain works and – for the first time in English law – the moral rights for authors required by Berne. We will deal with the 1988 Act more fully in the rest of the chapter: suffice it to say here that EU harmonisation and new technology are already requiring further amendments. With the Uruguay Round of GATT, however – of which copyright and other intellectual property was such an important feature – and the new World Trade Organisation's support for Berne, international copyright has indisputably come of age.

COPYRIGHT WORKS

INTRODUCTION: TYPES OF WORKS

We are accustomed to speaking about copyright in books, but in fact 'a book' is not a copyright work as such, under modern UK copyright law. It used to be, and initially, as we have seen (above, p. 14) copyright *only* extended to books and other printed matter: 'book' was defined in the 1842 Copyright Act as 'every volume, part or division of a volume, pamphlet, sheet of letter-press, sheet of music, map, chart, or plan separately published', and this definition may occasionally still be relevant for works created before 1 July 1912. However, the world has moved on since then, and definitions based on traditional packages such as 'books' are not specific or flexible enough for modern publishing, where individual creations – such as text, graphics, or sound recordings – may now need to be re-used and adapted in different combinations and in different forms (such as films or multimedia). Each original element may also be created and owned by quite different people, who may wish to exploit them in different ways: it is important therefore to identify who owns the rights in each constituent part and keep those rights separate. For this reason, it is better to think of books, journals or CD-ROMs not as 'works' at all but as packages or bundles of works, which are developing and changing all the time.

What copyright works, then, does UK law protect? Not every creation counts as a work. The works which may currently be protected are set out in section 1(1) of the Copyright Designs & Patents Act 1988 (referred to throughout the rest of this book as 'the 1988 Act'). Three general categories of works may be protected:

1 original literary, dramatic, musical or artistic works;
2 sound recordings, films, broadcasts or cable programmes; and
3 the typographical arrangement of published editions.

There may also be in due course a separate publication right in previously unpublished works (see below, p. 27).

If you want to secure copyright protection for a work in the UK, therefore, the first thing you will need to do is make sure that it falls into one of the above categories. There are other qualifying criteria which each individual work will also need to fulfil (see below, p. 34), but these three categories are the essential starting point. Many of the categories have been defined quite widely over the years – so that literary works, for example, now include computer programs and compilations – and we will examine each of the categories most relevant to publishing in turn. As will become obvious, a modern publication may contain several different copyright works.

LITERARY WORKS

Of all copyright works, literary works are still the most important for authors and publishers, although others (such as artistic works) are important too as we shall see. Under section 3 of the 1988 Act, a 'Literary Work':

- means any work (other than a dramatic or musical work) which is written, spoken or sung;
- includes a table or compilation and a computer program;
- must be recorded, 'in writing or otherwise'.

'Written, spoken or sung'

A work does not need to be 'literary' in the colloquial sense in order to be a literary work, as long as it is written, spoken or sung. Some very un-'literary' written matter indeed has been given copyright protection in the past, such as business letters, football coupons, trade advertisements and examination papers: indeed, it is possibly more useful to think of 'literary' in the broadest context of sales 'literature' or business 'literature' than as having any necessary connection with Dickens or Proust. It merely needs to be written (or spoken or sung). There is no requirement for written matter to be written in any particular language or notation, or even to use words at all: mathematical symbols and equations, or scientific formulae will be equally protected. Under section 178 of the 1988 Act 'writing' and 'written' include any form of notation or code, whether by hand or otherwise, and regardless of the method or the medium used.

Tables and compilations

Tables and compilations have been given copyright protection as literary works since the 1911 Act, and may be of considerable commercial value in published works today – in many cases (such as databases) forming the whole or virtually the whole of the work. Examples are TV listings, railway timetables, professional or trade directories, street directories, guides to selected retail outlets, trade catalogues, book or price lists, or even – given sufficient originality in the selection (see p. 19 below) – schemes of chapters or sequences of topics or headings. Databases stored electronically are equally protected whether or not printed out or published in written form. UK copyright law recognises that an original compilation is more than the sum total of individual entries (which may or may not be literary or other works in their own right) and protects the selection and arrangement of those items as a separate copyright work. This new compilation may have value as much for what is omitted, as for what is included: however, there does need to be some evidence that some skill and judgement has gone into the selection and arrangement – we will consider this below, under originality (p. 19).

Copyright protection for databases in the UK is likely to be significantly reduced when the EU Database Directive is implemented (see below, p. 20).

Computer programs

Computer programs are specifically protected as literary works, having been given statutory protection for the first time by the Copyright (Computer Software) Amendment Act 1985. They are not defined in the 1988 Act, but would probably include any sequence or set of instructions in machine-readable form which are capable of causing a computer to perform a particular task or function. This would extend to programs held in most current forms, as long as they could be said to be held in notation or code and therefore 'written': this would clearly include print-outs, but equally computer chips, magnetic tapes, disks and recordings. Design material created in preparation for computer programs is now also protected as a literary work under the Copyright (Computer Programs) Regulations 1992.

'Computer-generated works' are also protected under the 1988 Act, and are defined as works generated by a computer 'in circumstances such that there is no known author of the work'. This difficult philosophical concept is probably best left to the experts: we will consider it again (briefly) under ownership (see p. 30).

Recorded in writing, or otherwise

A literary work will not be protected unless it is put into some permanent, or material, form or, in the case of electronic information, a retrievable form. The means of recording used is very widely defined: 'in writing, or otherwise' could include almost any form of record, and specifically extends to non-written media. This means that a speech or lecture will be protected as a literary work even if delivered without a text or notes, provided that someone (not necessarily the speaker) makes a record of it at the time: for example, makes a tape recording, or keys it into the memory of a lap-top computer. The same might be true of an interview, provided what was said had enough originality to qualify as a copyright work at all (see below).

It does not matter who makes the recording, and in fact there is no requirement that it should even be made with the speaker's consent. In many cases two quite separate copyrights will be created at the same time – copyright in the spoken (and recorded) words as a literary work, and a separate copyright in the recording either as a new literary work or as a sound recording. Even a verbatim report of a speech has been given separate copyright protection – in the famous case of *Walter v. Lane* in 1900 – where special skill is needed to write it down. As we shall see later, although such parallel copyrights may be dependent on each other, they may be owned by different people.

Originality

Copyright protection under the 1988 Act is not given to all literary works, but only to 'original' literary works: dramatic, musical and artistic works must also be original. The requirement does not extend to any other works, but since literary (and artistic) works in particular play such a central role in publishing, establishing originality in appropriate cases is clearly of great importance. So: what is 'original'?

For the purposes of copyright law, all that original means is that the work concerned should originate from the author: in other words, that he or she should not have copied it from anywhere else. Any evidence that you have saved yourself time and effort by copying slavishly from someone else will rob your work of its originality and thus of its copyright protection. However, it does not need to display what we may think of colloquially as original thought, in the sense of unique perception or insight which no-one else has contributed to the subject before. It is quite permissible to base your work entirely on common sources and existing material (provided you do not copy them) – the originality which is required is not so much original thought as original effort: an independent work which (however mundane or derivative) you have used your own time and effort, and your own faculties and skills to create. (What in America they used to refer to as 'sweat of the brow' – however following the 1991 US case of *Feist Publications Inc. v. Rural Telephone Service*, mere sweat is not now enough under US law. It may also not now protect databases in the EU – see below.)

On this basis, it is easy to see how English law grants copyright protection to railway timetables and football coupons, as well as to great works of literature. It also means that two or more very similar – or even identical – works could be created independently by different people, provided that each of them has expended their own skill and effort. Thus two photographers might take virtually identical photographs of the same scene, and two novelists may write strikingly similar stories: provided no copying had taken place, each one may constitute a separate copyright work.

Some copyright works are, by their very nature, bound to be similar, if not identical. Published mathematical tables are the classic example, since any two authors working them out properly are bound (one hopes) to arrive at the same result. A compilation such as a directory of professional names and addresses is bound to be very similar to another directory covering the same profession, but both will be protected if both are the result of independent skill and effort. Copying does occur, of course, and we will consider 'originality' again later on, under infringement of copyright (chapter 8). Many directory publishers include deliberate minor errors in their databases in order to expose copying: it is stretching coincidence a bit far to claim that while expending your own skill and effort, you still nevertheless happened to reproduce exactly the same errors as someone else.

Copyright protection for databases in the EU is likely to be more difficult to obtain after member states implement the Database Directive – due by 1 January 1998. At the time of writing, it has not yet been implemented in the UK. The Directive provides that copyright will only protect databases which 'by reason of the selection or arrangement of their contents, constitute the author's own intellectual creation' – an intellectual standard that would rule out many commercially valuable databases currently protected in the UK, particularly those merely consisting of alphabetical listings. A new 'unfair extraction right' to prevent unauthorised extraction or re-use of the database's contents, will be available to the producer, but this will last only for 15 years. Each substantial revision of the database will however start a fresh 15-year period running, so there could be perpetual protection for a database under the Directive, if it is updated sufficiently regularly and substantially.

New editions, and even possibly revised reprints, will often contain enough originality to be protected as separate copyright works, provided that there is sufficient that is new. (In the 1870 case of *Black v. Murray and Son* it was said that it will not be enough to create a new copyright in a new edition 'merely to make a few emendations to the text, or to add a few unimportant notes. To create a copyright by alterations in the text, these must be extensive and substantial, practically making a new book'.)

Abridgements may also be protected, including abstracts of articles (but abstracts may often be copied under section 60 of the 1988 Act).

Translations have always been given separate copyright protection in view of the obvious skill involved, even though – by definition – derived entirely from an existing work.

It is very unlikely that the title of a book would have enough originality to be protected as a literary work in its own right – unless it was unusually long. Indeed, it may not be a 'work' at all, and it may also not be a substantial part of another work (see chapter 8, p. 189). However, titles may in appropriate cases be protected as registered trade marks, given the necessary distinctiveness, or in some cases by the law of passing off (see chapter 9).

SUMMARY CHECKLIST: LITERARY WORKS

To summarise briefly so far: in order to be protected under UK copyright law as a literary work, a work must display the following features, among others:

- It must be written, spoken or sung (this includes tables, compilations and computer programs).
- It must be recorded, in writing or otherwise.
- It must be 'original'.

There are other qualifying requirements which apply to all copyright works, as we shall see (below, p. 34) but a work must fulfil at least the above three criteria if it is to be protected as a literary work at all.

ARTISTIC WORKS

Artistic works are defined in section 4(1) of the 1988 Act to mean:

1 a graphic work, photograph, sculpture or collage, irrespective of artistic quality;
2 a work of architecture being a building or a model for a building; or
3 a work of artistic craftsmanship.

'Artistic' is not defined but, like 'literary', it is more a generic grouping than any particular cultural yardstick. As the definition shows, artistic quality is not required at all for graphic works, photographs etc., which are protected 'irrespective of artistic quality', but a specific artistic element does seem to be required for works of artistic craftsmanship: we will look at this further when we consider those works (below, p. 23).

Remember also that artistic works, like literary works, must be 'original' in order to be protected under the 1988 Act: a slavish copy would be unlikely to be given copyright protection. It is arguable, however, that a professional (or at least a skilful) copy of a painting might constitute a new copyright work, even though it was an exact replica, and re-origination of old illustrations by a new computer process might also create new copyrights if sufficient skill and judgement were involved.

The artistic works most relevant to publishing and printing are graphic works, photographs and works of artistic craftsmanship.

Graphic works

Graphic works are defined in section 4(2) of the Act as including:

- paintings, drawings, diagrams, maps, charts or plans;
- engravings, etchings, lithographs, woodcuts or similar works.

All such works are protected irrespective of artistic quality, so judges (fortunately, one may think) are not required to make value judgements about 'art'. Together with photographs (below), this wide definition of graphic works must cover most if not all illustrations which may currently be contained in published works, or which are relevant to publishing, for example, the design of a new typeface. Note also that diagrams and charts are included, so that small and relatively mundane technical illustrations within the text, such as graphs, may be given copyright protection as artistic works just as much as more obvious pictures, provided they display sufficient originality.

Strangely, unlike many other works, there is no requirement under the 1988 Act that graphic works should be fixed in any permanent (or retrievable) physical form, although this is probably implied. In the case of a painting, however, there is some authority for saying that it must be put on to some permanent (or at least fairly fixed) surface: in a celebrated and rather unsatisfactory judgment in 1983 (decided under the 1956 Act) the pop singer Adam Ant was denied copyright protection for his distinctive face make up on the grounds that paint without an independent surface of some kind could not be a 'painting' for copyright purposes (his face being an insufficiently permanent surface since presumably even pop singers need to wash from time to time).

Photographs

Section 4(2) of the 1988 Act defines a photograph as:

a recording of light or other radiation on any medium on which an image is produced or from which an image may by any means be produced, and which is not part of a film.

Films are separately protected, and a single frame of a film would therefore now be protected as part of a film and not as a photograph, although the position was different before the 1956 Act came into force: the date the photograph was taken may therefore be highly relevant, to ownership, to whether or not any 'originality' is required, and also to how long copyright protection lasts, (see p. 40).

The Act makes no distinction between negatives and positive prints: negatives, as the master copy, would certainly be protected, and prints may well be protected separately if they displayed sufficient originality. However, a straightforward photocopy would not qualify as an original copyright work.

Works of artistic craftsmanship

Original works of craftsmanship, such as furniture or ceramics, may be protected as registered designs under the Registered Designs Act 1949, or (since the 1988 Act) as unregistered designs: however, they may also in some circumstances be entitled to copyright protection as works of artistic craftsmanship if they are more than merely functional, and display some 'artistic' element. It is not clear how significant this artistic element needs to be, or what relationship it needs to bear (if any) to the function of the item in question. A prototype for a suite of mass-produced furniture was denied copyright protection in one case on this basis, but works with a more obvious artistic element, such as hand-painted ceramics, inlaid cabinets, stained glass, specialised printing and hand-tooled bookbinding would almost certainly be protected.

SUMMARY CHECKLIST: – ARTISTIC WORKS

To be protected under UK copyright law:

- All artistic works must be 'original'.
- Graphic works (paintings, drawings etc.), and photographs, must be original, but need not display any particular artistic quality.
- Paintings must be fixed on to a surface.
- Works of artistic craftsmanship must have an 'artistic' element.

DRAMATIC AND MUSICAL WORKS

Dramatic works

When dramatic works were first given separate statutory protection under UK law, in the Dramatic Copyright Act 1833, they were defined as including 'any tragedy, comedy, play, opera, farce or other dramatic piece of entertainment'. Now, under the 1988 Act, they are not defined at all, other than to specify (in section 3(1)) that they include a work of dance or mime. A dramatic work probably, however, needs to be capable not only of being performed in some way, but also of being acted, and hence needs to have an essential and coherent dramatic structure of its own: TV personality Hughie Green (as we saw in chapter 1) failed to prevent the New Zealand Broadcasting Corporation in 1989 from producing their own game show using elements very similar to *Opportunity Knocks*, since no actual scripts seemed to exist and what was taken had no dramatic structure or coherence of its own, being not much more than a collection of gags and by-lines and one or two props such as the famous clapometer. Similarly, a singer giving a recital in the Wigmore Hall, although clearly performing, would be unlikely to be performing a dramatic work, unless a significant amount of action was involved.

Like literary and musical works, dramatic works must be recorded 'in writing, or otherwise'. They must also be 'original'.

Musical works

The 1988 Act, at section 3(1), helpfully defines a musical work as 'a work consisting of music'; it does however go on to tell us that such a work is distinct from any words or action intended to be sung, spoken or performed with it. Thus, lyrics of a song or the libretto of an opera would not be part of the musical work itself, but would normally be separate literary works, and choreography or other action would be a dramatic work: quite often these works would have been created and thus will be owned by different people.

Musical works, to be protected by copyright, must be recorded, in writing or otherwise – this may be by means of written scores or by being recorded onto tapes, or by being fixed by any other means. The recording itself will be a separate copyright work (probably either a literary work or a sound recording).

Finally, as with other copyright works in this group, all musical works must be 'original'. As has been seen with literary and artistic works, this implies no more than some significant creative effort and skill, and an absence of copying: it is not necessary to be Mozart. However, an original musical work must be more than a mere interpretation.

SOUND RECORDINGS, FILMS, BROADCASTS OR CABLE PROGRAMMES

Sound recordings

Sound recordings were given separate copyright protection under UK law by the 1911 Copyright Act, as a response to the growing sale of phonographs and perforated rolls. The recording industry is now a major international industry and the opportunities for digital as well as mechanical copying are considerably more sophisticated.

Sound recordings continue to be protected in the UK as separate copyright works under the 1988 Act, and are now defined (in section 5A(1)) as meaning:

(a) a recording of sounds, from which the sounds may be reproduced, or

(b) a recording of the whole or any part of a literary, dramatic or musical work, from which sounds reproducing the work or part may be produced, regardless of the medium on which the recording is made or the method by which the sounds are reproduced or produced.

Thus, two separate kinds of sound recording are protected – those which are recordings of pure sounds (such as birdsong), and those which are recordings of other copyright works, such as recordings of famous actors reading books (literary works), or reciting plays (dramatic works), as well as – of course – recordings of music.

Modern film soundtracks are now protected not only as part of the films which they accompany (under section 5B(2)) but also as sound recordings separately from the films themselves (although the position may be different for soundtracks created before 1989).

In addition to copyright, the 1988 Act also introduced a limited rental right for sound recordings (and for films and computer programs) – we will deal with this later, when we look at the restricted acts which only a copyright owner may do (below, p. 188). There is, as yet, no blank tape levy in the UK.

There is no requirement that a sound recording should be original (unlike literary, dramatic, musical or artistic works). However copyright will not protect a sound recording which is merely a copy of a previous sound recording (section 5A(2)).

Films

A film is a separate copyright work, defined in section 5B(1) of the 1988 Act as meaning 'a recording on any medium from which a moving image may by any means be produced'. This definition is wide enough to cover videos.

Film soundtracks are now protected both as part of the films concerned, and independently as sound recordings (see above). In addition, a typical film will include many other copyright works, and the relevant rights will need to be acquired (or licensed) from the respective owners in order to make the film: these rights are collectively referred to in the film business as the 'underlying rights'. These might include, for example, the screenplay and the book or script (dramatic and literary works), the score (a musical work), graphics, cartoons or set designs (artistic works), as well as the soundtrack (sound recording). Individual frames or stills from a film are protected as part of the film, and not as photographs (see above, p. 23). This may be significant, since (for example) a photograph (as an artistic work) must be original, whereas the film need not be. Films like sound recordings do not need to be original: however, section 5B(4) of the 1988 Act provides that a film which is merely a copy of a previous film will not be protected by copyright.

Broadcasts and cable programmes

Broadcasts include not only traditional radio and TV broadcasts, but also (since the Cable and Broadcasting Act 1984) direct broadcasting by satellite. The wide definition of broadcasts (in section 6 of the 1988 Act) effectively includes all transmissions which are not sent via fixed, land-based routes (such as cable): broadcast means 'a transmission by wireless telegraphy of visual images, sounds or other information' which can lawfully be received by the public or which is sent for public presentation. Note: (1) that broadcasts may consist not only of pictures and sound but also of 'other information' – such as teletext; and (2) that an encrypted transmission is only regarded as being lawfully received by the public if they have access to authorised decoding equipment.

Cable programmes, under section 7 of the 1988 Act, are any items 'included in a cable programme service': a cable programme service is a service which consists exclusively or mainly in sending pictures, sounds or other information via a telecommunications system and not via broadcasts. Cable services must be sent for reception at two or more places or for general public presentation.

Cable programme services do not include 2-way services, in which 2-way information exchange (rather than 1-way reception) is an essential feature of the service, or services run purely for internal business or domestic purposes, and not linked to any other telecommunication system.

TYPOGRAPHICAL ARRANGEMENTS

There is a separate copyright in the UK in typographical arrangements of published editions. It lasts only for 25 years from the end of the year of publication, and is owned by the publisher: the purpose is to protect the publisher's skill and investment in the composition and typesetting, so a separate copyright is given to the visual appearance of the printed page itself, as well as to its contents. This means that, on a typical printed page (like the one you are reading at the moment) there are likely to be several copyrights: a literary copyright in the text, and possibly in any compilation, artistic copyright in any photographs, charts or illustrations, and a separate typographical copyright, owned by the publishers, in the arrangement of the page itself. This protects a publisher of a public domain edition, say of Shakespeare or Milton: although the text is long since out of copyright there may still be an enforceable copyright in the publisher's edition.

Typographical arrangements do not need to be 'original' as such (unlike the artistic copyright which may exist in a new typeface) but they will not be protected if they merely reproduce the typographical arrangement of a previous edition. A publisher cannot therefore perpetually extend typographical copyright beyond 25 years simply by re-issuing the last edition.

PUBLICATION RIGHT IN PREVIOUSLY UNPUBLISHED WORKS

In addition to typographical copyright it is likely that there will be before very long a new publication right, also lasting 25 years from publication, and also owned by the publisher, in previously unpublished works. This is as a result of EC Directive 93/98 (the Duration Directive, p. 37). The UK has not at the time of writing implemented this part of the Directive, but it is likely to do so in the Copyright and Related Rights Regulations 1996.

The right, when implemented in the UK, should protect EEA publishers of original literary, dramatic, musical and artistic works and films in which copyright has expired but which were never previously published during their copyright terms in the UK or any other EEA state.

The new right will benefit many editions of previously unpublished works in EU and EEA member states which do not have typographical copyright, but in the UK it will overlap extensively with existing rights, both typographical copyright, and the final stages of perpetual copyright in unpublished works which is not due to expire finally until 2039: we will look at unpublished works in more detail below (p. 41).

SUMMARY CHECKLIST: COPYRIGHT WORKS

It should be clear by now that a modern publication such as a book or a CD is unlikely to be a single copyright work, but a bundle of several different works. Before we go on to consider who *owns* each copyright, it may be useful to remind ourselves which works may most often be relevant:

BOOKS

May contain:

- original text (literary work). The plot – if any – may be a dramatic work;
- quoted text from other sources (separate literary works);

- index, prelims, tables or compilations (literary works);
- illustrations/photographs (artistic works);
- overall compilation (particularly in the case of collective works such as encyclopaedias (literary works);
- typographical arrangement (typographical copyright);
- jacket text and illustrations (literary and artistic works).

CD-ROMS

May contain:

- original and quoted text (literary and possibly dramatic works);
- tables or compilations (literary works);
- illustrations/photographs (artistic works);
- overall compilation (literary work);
- computer programs/software (literary work);
- accompanying manual/booklet (literary and artistic work and typographical copyright).

MULTIMEDIA CD

May contain:

- all works in a CD-ROM (see above);
- animations/graphics/cartoons (artistic works);
- video and film (films);
- music (musical work);
- lyrics (literary works);
- drama/plays (dramatic works);
- recordings of music, speech or other sounds (sound recordings);
- performances of works (rights in performances).

Moral rights of authors may also now be relevant in relation to many of the above works – on moral rights generally, see chapter 3.

OWNERSHIP OF COPYRIGHT

Who owns all these different copyrights, and connected rights? Given the variety of copyright works which UK law protects, it might be thought that working out who owns which rights would be a complete nightmare – but in fact, in most cases, the underlying principle of copyright ownership is very simple. There are (of course) some exceptions (such as employee works) which we will come to, but, subject to those, the general rule is stated in section 11(1) of the 1988 Act:

The author of a work is the first owner of any copyright in it.

The search for a copyright owner is therefore in most cases the search for the author. And who, then, is the 'author'? Section 9(1) tells us: the author is the person who creates the work. As a general rule, therefore, the creator of a work usually owns the copyright in it.

It should not be forgotten that the rules governing who is the author of a work and who owns copyright in it vary according to when the work was made. In the notes which follow, we will focus on the current law, but for pre-August 1989 works it will often be necessary to refer back to the 1956 or 1911 Acts, or even earlier.

'AUTHORS'

As we saw in chapter 1, there is no copyright in ideas, so the author or creator of a novel or a play is not necessarily the person who had the original idea, but the person who first put that idea into concrete form. These may be one and the same person, of course, or they may have worked on the project together (in which case they may be joint authors) but they may also be completely different people. The law tries to find the real creator – the person who actually executed the work, the person who made it.

Someone who was merely putting a literary (or artistic) work onto paper at the instruction of someone else – a secretary writing a letter, or an amanuensis helping to take down a book, for example – would not be regarded as the author of that work. But where the work is not merely dictated, but is ghost written, then the ghost writer will own the copyright, because it is the ghost writer who has created the work which appears on the page. Appropriately enough (for ghosts) this was held in a 1927 case to protect the writings of a spiritualist medium, despite claims that the real 'author' resided in another world. And, in the same way, a reporter writing up a report of a speech (even, in one famous case, a verbatim report) would probably be regarded as the 'author' of that report and would own the copyright in it (although copyright in the speech itself would still be owned by the speaker).

Joint authors

In some cases, it may simply not be possible to identify separate copyright works, and say that X wrote this bit and Y wrote that. Where it is possible (for example where contributors write distinct chapters of a book or entries in an encyclopaedia) each one will own a separate copyright. Where it is *not* possible, but more than one person clearly contributed (as, for example, where a scientific research team publishes their findings) they are treated as joint authors.

In many cases, it will be a question of degree, whether what is created is a collection of separate works, or whether it is truly a joint work. Under the 1988 Act (section 10(1)) a work of joint authorship is:

a work produced by the collaboration of two or more authors in which the contribution of each author is not distinct from that of the other author or authors.

Each of them must be authors, however: someone who contributed ideas and suggestions but took no part in the actual writing, would be unlikely to be considered a joint author. This would be the case even if they made minor revisions, unless their revisions were unusually original.

Joint authors usually own the copyright as 'tenants in common' – under section 173(2) of the 1988 Act, no single joint copyright owner can publish or license the work without the consent of the others, and when a joint copyright owner dies the same rights and duties will pass to his or her heirs.

Collective works

In a collective work such as an encyclopaedia or dictionary, there is likely to be a copyright not only in the individual entries – normally owned by the respective authors – but also in the overall compilation of the collective work as a whole. The 'author' of that compilation is usually taken to be the person who was responsible for assembling it, and whose selection and arrangement it is. This might be one person, such as a General Editor, or one or more of the contributors (who might then be joint authors of the compilation) or even possibly the publisher.

Photographs

Under the current, 1988, Act the author of a photograph is the person who creates it – usually the photographer. This means that copyright in all photographs taken after 1 August 1989 will be owned by the photographer, unless there is an agreement to the contrary or one of the exceptions applies (see below). For photographs taken between 1 June 1957 and 1 August 1989, however, the 1956 Copyright Act defined the author as the person who, at the relevant time, owned the material on which the photograph was taken – it may therefore be important to find out when the photographs were taken, in order to find out who owns the copyright. There may also be special provision for commissioned photographs under the 1956 Act (see below, p. 31).

Software and computer-generated works

Copyright in a computer program which is created by an identifiable human being will normally be owned by that person, as with any other literary work. In a case of a computer-generated work, however – generated in circumstances such that there is no human author – section 9(3) of the 1988 Act provides that the 'author' is the person who undertook the arrangements necessary for the creation of the work.

Typographical arrangements

Copyright in typographical arrangements of published editions is owned by the publisher.

Sound recordings and films

Under the 1988 Act, the author of a sound recording or a film is the person by whom the necessary arrangements for making it were made. In many cases this might be several people, but is most likely to be a record or film production company. In the case of a film, the Duration Directive, and 1995 Regulations made under it (see p. 37), have specified that copyright protection shall be calculated from the death of one of four possible categories of authors, but the authorship roles under the 1988 Act have not yet been changed.

The soundtrack of a film is now not only treated as part of the film concerned but is also protected as a separate copyright work (as a sound recording) and copyright may thus be separately owned.

As pointed out at the beginning of this section, pre-1989 ownership may be different, and the complex provisions are beyond the scope of this book. In cases of doubt, specialist legal advice should be sought.

Broadcasts and cable programmes

The author of a broadcast under the 1988 Act is the person who transmits the programme (provided he or she has at least some responsibility for its contents, and is not – like BT – simply a common carrier). Where more than one person is involved in making the broadcast, it is to be taken as being a work of joint authorship.

The author of a cable programme is the person providing the cable programme service in which it is included.

Commissioned works

There are no special provisions in the 1988 Act relating to commissioned works, so for works created after 1 August 1989 the general rule of copyright ownership applies, and the author will normally own the copyright, not the commissioner (unless there is a contract providing otherwise). In fact (despite popular beliefs to the contrary) even before 1989 there has never been any general rule of law that if you commissioned a work you would automatically own the copyright in it. There were three very limited exceptions under the 1956 Copyright Act, covering certain kinds of commissioned artistic works, but these never extended to literary or other works. The exceptions were:

• commissioned photographs;

- commissioned portraits (painted or drawn);
- commissioned engravings.

A person commissioning such works after 1 June 1957 but before 1 August 1989 might own the copyright, if the work was made in response to the commission, and if he or she paid for it (or at least agreed to). There were similar provisions under the 1911 Act. Otherwise, the artist or photographer, like authors of literary works, would probably own the copyright in the normal way. For most commissioned works, therefore, unless one of the limited exceptions above applies, or unless there is an agreement to the contrary, it is likely that the author or artist, not the commissioner, will own the copyright.

WORKS BY EMPLOYEES

There is one major exception to the general rule that authors own copyright in their works, and that concerns works created by employees. Under section 11(2) of the 1988 Act:

> where a literary, dramatic, musical or artistic work is made by an employee in the course of his employment, his employer is the first owner of any copyright in the work subject to any agreement to the contrary.

The position was broadly the same under the 1956 and 1911 Acts. There are two particular points to note.

'Employees'

The terms 'employee' and 'employment' refer to employment under what the law calls a contract of service or apprenticeship – in other words, someone employed under a contract of employment, rather than a self-employed person such as a freelancer. The contract of employment does not need to be full-time, or permanent, so part-time and temporary employees would be covered, but as Lord Denning said in one case, the person concerned does need to be 'employed as part of the business'. One traditional test, in cases of doubt, used to be the degree of control exercised by the employer – if the people concerned have little or no discretion over the way the work is done they are probably employees (although there are exceptions: directors, for example, may have considerable discretion but might still be regarded as employees for copyright purposes). It is usually reasonably easy to tell: in the 1916 case of *University of London Press Limited v. University Tutorial Press Limited* two external examiners were held *not* to be employees of London University, since they were not exclusively employed by London University, and prepared the papers in their own time, for a one-off fee: they therefore owned the copyright, not the university.

'In the course of his employment'

For the employer to own the copyright, the employee must have created it *in the course of* that employment, not merely while employed. A night security guard who wrote a novel while on duty would probably therefore own the copyright in it, since writing novels would be unlikely to feature anywhere in his (or her) job description. In other cases, such as lecturers preparing teaching manuals, or academic or scientific researchers publishing research papers, the position may be less clear-cut. Even where the work is done outside official working hours, it may still be in the course of employment.

Before 1989, under the 1956 Act (and earlier law) employers might also have owned the copyright in works of their employees which were created for publication in a newspaper, magazine or similar periodical. This only applies, however, to pre-1989 works.

MANUSCRIPTS AND ARTWORK

Before we leave the subject of ownership, it is important to remember that ownership of copyright in something is not the same as physical ownership of the documents or artwork, or other materials such as disks or tapes, on which it is recorded. Although ownership of physical materials might still be relevant to establish copyright in some older works – such as photographs created before 1989 – for most purposes now the two things are completely separate. An author delivering a manuscript, print-out or disks, or an artist delivering original artwork or photographs, will therefore continue to own those physical materials, and be entitled to their (reasonably) safe return, even if he or she does not own the copyright or subsequently assigns it to someone else. Since busy publishing offices are not always the best places to store valuable materials, many publishers in the delivery clauses of their contracts expressly disclaim any liability for loss or damage to manuscripts and other materials submitted to them – however, publishers are probably under a general duty at least to take reasonable care of an author's materials.

SUMMARY CHECKLIST: COPYRIGHT OWNERSHIP

- As a general rule, for modern works, the author of a work owns the copyright in it
- Is the person concerned really the 'author'?
- Are there joint authors? If so, do all the copyright owners agree?
- Is there a separate copyright in any compilation?
- Have any computer-generated works, sound recordings or films been created?
- If so, who made the necessary arrangements?
- Were any photographs taken before or after August 1989?

- Were any commissioned photographs, portraits or engravings created before August 1989?
- Was the author an employee?
- Did the author create the work in the course of that employment?

QUALIFICATION FOR COPYRIGHT PROTECTION

Although it is no longer necessary to register copyrights at Stationers Hall (or anywhere else), the work will not qualify for copyright protection under UK law unless it meets certain qualifying criteria. Works may qualify by virtue of:

- the author, or
- the country in which the work was first published.

These two 'points of attachment' for copyright protection are common to most Berne member countries: it does not matter whether it is the author or the place of first publication which qualifies for copyright protection, but one or other of them must. Often, of course, a work will qualify on both counts.

QUALIFICATION BY REFERENCE TO THE AUTHOR

A work qualifies for copyright protection in the UK if the author was at the material time a 'qualifying person'. A qualifying person is defined in section 154 of the 1988 Act and includes:

- a British citizen, or a citizen of a British Dependent Territory;
- a British National (Overseas), or a British Overseas Citizen;
- a British subject or a British protected person;
- a person domiciled or resident in the UK (or another country to which the 1988 Act extends or has been applied);
- a body incorporated under UK law (or the law of another country to which the Act extends or has been applied);
- a citizen or subject of a foreign country to which the 1988 Act has been applied or extended by Order in Council (or who is domiciled or resident there).

Most of these terms are defined further in the British Nationality Act 1981. For most practical purposes, an author will qualify, at least as 'resident', if at the material time he or she lived at a home address in the UK, or the relevant foreign country. Foreign countries are periodically added by Order in Council, in accordance with the UK's Berne, UCC and other treaty obligations (see chapter 8, pp. 217–20).

The 'material time' is:

- for unpublished works, when the work was made;
- for published works, the date of first publication.

(If the author dies before publication, the material time is immediately before his or her death.)

COUNTRY OF FIRST PUBLICATION

If for some reason copyright protection does not attach to a work by virtue of the author's nationality or other qualifying status, it may still do so if it was first published in the UK, or another qualifying country to which the 1988 Act extends or is applied.

What is 'first publication'? Indeed, what is 'publication'?

Publication

Publication, under the 1988 Act, takes place when copies of the work are issued to the public with the licence of the copyright owner. This would cover most publishing, but not for example the delivery of a speech or lecture, or the exhibition of a painting (unless copies were subsequently issued). Note that copies, in the plural, must be issued, although making most works available via an electronic retrieval system will count as publication. It is not necessary that works should be issued for commercial sale: private or free circulation would probably count as publication. The work will not be 'published', however, if publication is a purely token gesture and 'not intended to satisfy the reasonable requirements of the public' – what the 1988 Act describes as 'merely colourable'.

First and simultaneous publication

First publication, although not defined, simply means what it says: the first time authorised copies are issued to the public. So, if a copyright owner, or his or her licensee, first issues copies of a work to the public in the UK, that work will qualify for copyright protection under UK law, irrespective of the nationality of the author. Works of (say) US authors would therefore have qualified for copyright protection under UK law if they were first published here, even before the USA joined the UCC or Berne Conventions.

Publication also counts as first publication, even if simultaneous publication takes place somewhere else: 'simultaneous publication' for these purposes means publication within 30 days. So, a US work simultaneously published in New York and London with a gap of no more than 30 days between publication dates, would count as first published in the UK. (Under the 1911 Act, the simultaneous publication period was only 14 days – this shorter period continues to apply to works first published before 1 June 1957.)

SUMMARY CHECKLIST: QUALIFYING WORKS

- Was the author a Qualifying Person at the material time?
- If the author does not have a relevant British qualification (such as nationality or residence) is the author a citizen or subject of a qualifying foreign country?
- For a published work, did the author qualify at the date of first publication?
- For unpublished works, did the author qualify when the work was made?
- If the author is not a qualifying person, was the work first published in the UK (or another country to which the 1988 Act applies)?
- If not first publication, was there 'simultaneous' publication within 30 days?
- Did publication satisfy the reasonable expectations of the public?

DURATION OF COPYRIGHT

AUTHORS' LIVES

As we have seen, copyright in the UK is primarily a statutory right, and ever since the first Copyright Act of 1709 it has had a fixed term, or duration. After that, it expires and the protection ends. Although the first statutory copyrights only lasted for 14 years, they could be renewed for a second term if the author was still alive at the end of the first one, so from the outset the length of copyright protection has been linked to how long the author managed to stay alive. After various increases, the Berne Convention countries meeting in Berlin in 1908 (see p. 15) agreed each to adopt the same minimum term of copyright protection for literary and artistic works, starting from the moment of creation of the work and lasting until 50 years after the death of the author (sometimes – a little unnecessarily – referred to as 50 years 'post mortem auctoris', or '50 years pma'). In 1908 this was thought sufficient to protect two generations of the author's heirs (on the assumption – presumably – that each generation produces an heir at the average age of 25) and seemed a suitable compromise between those who argued that free access to literature required a shorter fixed term and those who felt that copyright should benefit the author's estate in perpetuity. It is not a perfect formula, but during the course of the twentieth century the Berne period has gained widespread international acceptance. Countries belonging to the Universal Copyright Convention (see p. 219), adopted a shorter minimum period of 25 years pma, but the Berne period is now the more common.

For convenience and certainty, since the exact date of authors' deaths is often hard to prove, the 50-year period of copyright is deemed to run, not exactly from the 50th anniversary of the author's death but 50 years from the end of the calendar year in which the author died. So, in an appropriate case, if an author died on 1 July 1945, copyright in the author's works would expire on

31 December 1995. It is important to remember this: for authors who die in January this can mean virtually a whole year's extra copyright protection.

EU HARMONISATION: LIFE PLUS 70

This widespread international standard did not, however, provide a level enough playing field for the European Commission, since it only provided a minimum, and some EU member states (such as Germany and Spain) provided longer terms. In addition, some countries like France gave longer protection to certain works, and in certain cases to account for the war years of both world wars.

The cross-border difficulties all this might create came before the European Court of Justice in the *Patricia* case in 1989, which decided that goods which had come out of copyright in Denmark, but which were still protected in Germany (which had a longer period of protection than Denmark) could not lawfully be put on sale in Germany despite the free movement of goods provisions of the Treaty of Rome (for more on free movement of goods and parallel imports, see chapter 12). The EU attempted to deal with this lack of harmony in 1993 by Directive 93/98/EEC – variously called the Duration Directive, or the Term Directive – which provided for the copyright term for literary, artistic and other works to be harmonised upwards to 70 years pma throughout the EU and EEA. The Commission took the view that the EU could not harmonise *downwards*, since that would deprive some right holders of existing rights, so it decided to harmonise *upwards*, to the longest (German) term. It also advanced the highly questionable argument that the period of copyright in Europe should be increased anyway, since we all now live longer. No evidence was ever produced to support this assumption and it seems highly unlikely that the present generation of authors' heirs seriously expect to live a whole 20 years longer than its grandparents did. However, member states were required to implement the necessary changes to their domestic laws by 1 July 1995, and the increased term now applies to all EEA-origin works which were protected in at least one member state on that date. The UK implemented the Directive (late) by means of the Duration of Copyright and Rights in Performances Regulations (1995).

THE 1995 REGULATIONS

Because the Duration Directive extended protection for works protected at 1 July 1995 'in at least one member state', each member state's implementing measures had to provide not only for *extensions* of copyright periods which were still running, but also for *revivals* of copyright in works which had gone into the public domain in their own country during the previous 20 years, but which might still be protected in, for example, Germany or Spain. Following the *Phil Collins* decision of the European Court of Justice in 1993, this was especially true if the author was (or would have been) an EU national. In the UK, this means that works by authors such as Thomas Hardy, John Buchan or Rudyard Kipling will have come back into copyright, having previously been in the public domain. The needless confusion and uncertainty caused by this retrospective law is likely to continue for several years to come. In addition, the much-vaunted harmonisation is unlikely to result for some time, since it was left to each member state to decide several crucial questions, each in their own way:

• who should *own* the revived or extended copyright?
• what – if any – royalties would the new owners be entitled to?
• what protection or compensation would be available for those publishers (and others) who had exploited previously public domain works in good faith?

The UK's 1995 Regulations, came into force on 1 January 1996. As well as longer protection for newly created works, they provided for:

1 *extensions of copyright* for relevant works in which copyright still subsisted in the UK at 31 December 1995; and
2 *revivals of copyright* for works whose terms of copyright expired before 31 December 1995 in the UK but which were still protected by copyright in another EEA member state on 1 July 1995.

The 1995 provisions did not apply to Crown or Parliamentary copyright, or to computer-generated works. The introduction of the so-called Publication Right, relating to works not published until after copyright has expired, was postponed, but has now been reintroduced (see p. 27).

Extensions

The owner of an extended copyright is generally the person who owned the copyright immediately before commencement (1 January 1996).

In addition, any copyright licence, any term or condition of a copyright agreement, or any waiver or assertion of moral rights which existed immediately before commencement, and which was for the (then) full period of copyright, will continue to apply during the period of extended copyright (subject to any agreement to the contrary).

Revivals

Following the *Phil Collins* decision of the European Court of Justice (see above), this is now likely to cover the works of all EU and EEA authors who died between 1925 and 1945, provided they were protected in another EEA state (most probably Germany) at 1 July 1995. Depending on the year of the author's death, the revived copyright may last for anything from a year or so to an extra 20 years.

The new owner of any revived copyright is generally the person who owned copyright immediately before it expired. This is at least even-handed between publishers and authors: the last owner may have been a publisher, or equally a literary estate. If the former owner has died (or, in the event of a company, ceased to exist) the author or his or her estate will acquire the right – however, there may be some problems in tracing rights ownership.

Any waiver or assertion of moral rights in force immediately before copyright expired will continue to apply during the period of revived copyright: there are now detailed provisions for exercise of moral rights after an author's death.

Acquired rights

The Directive required member states to protect acquired rights of third parties: although it was not entirely clear exactly what this meant, it was the only express provision protecting those, like publishers, who had invested in good faith in editions of public domain works, only to find themselves potentially infringing a new, revived copyright. The 1995 Regulations now protect such publishers in relation to revised copyrights in two ways:

1 *Non-infringing acts.* After commencement (1 January 1996), it is not an infringement of any revived copyright to do anything in pursuance of 'arrangements made' before 1 January 1995, or to issue to the public copies of the work made before 1 July 1995 (in both cases, at a time when the work was in the public domain). There are similar provisions relating to anthologies or adaptations, although these are slightly unclear.
2 *Licences of right.* There is considerable comfort for publishers of previously public domain works: 'any acts' (including copying, or issuing copies to the public) will be treated as licensed by the new owner of the revised copyright, subject only to payment of 'such reasonable royalty or other remuneration as may be agreed' (or, in the absence of agreement, arbitrated by the Copyright Tribunal). The acts will be treated as licensed from the outset (even though any royalty is not agreed or arbitrated until later), but the publisher must give reasonable notice to the new copyright owner of an intention to do – or (presumably) continue to do – the acts concerned.

Previous exclusive licensees will find that they may be in competition with any number of non-exclusive licensees of right under the above provisions, but on the other hand there does seem to be a reasonable basis for protection for those who seek to exploit (or continue to exploit) previously public domain works in good faith. The new requirement to give notice may, however, cause publishers some difficulty, particularly where the identity of the new copyright owner is not immediately obvious. And how the Copyright Tribunal – not thus far very much involved in publishing arbitrations – will arrive at a definition of 'reasonable royalties' remains to be seen.

DURATION OF COPYRIGHT IN INDIVIDUAL WORKS

In addition to harmonising – or attempting to – the period of copyright protection for literary and artistic works, the Directive also contained important provisions for duration of copyright in other works such as films, and for certain neighbouring rights. We shall deal with these and the relevant UK provisions in turn below, when we look briefly at each kind of work.

Literary, artistic, musical and dramatic works

Previously 50 years pma: increased in the UK from 1 January 1996 to 70 years pma (that is 70 years from the end of the calendar year in which the author died (see above, p. 37)). Photographs benefit from the 20-year extension, like other artistic works: this is a double extension for pre-1989 and pre-1957 photographs which were calculated from the year of first publication, and from the year the photograph was taken, respectively: for all photographs the term is now 70 years from the end of the year of the photographer's death.

Works of joint authorship

The Directive and the 1995 Regulations re-inforced the existing UK position, under which the term of copyright (now increased to 70 years pma) is calculated from the year in which the last surviving (known) author dies.

Anonymous and pseudonymous works

Under the 1995 Regulations the term is increased to 70 years from the year it was made, or (if it was published during that period) 70 years from the end of the year in which the work is made available to the public. However, this only applies when the author is truly unknown – when the pseudonym adopted leaves no doubt as to the author's identity (or the author's identity is revealed) the term of copyright will be 70 years pma, as in literary, artistic, musical and dramatic works above.

Computer-generated works

The 1995 Regulations exclude computer-generated works from the provisions of the Directive: the term of copyright in the UK is still the term provided in the 1988 Act, that is, 50 years from the end of the calendar year in which the work was made.

Posthumously published works, and publication right

Under the 1956 Act, copyright in literary and artistic works ran for 50 years from the year of first publication. With effect from 1 August 1989, the 1988 Act provided a fixed period of 50 years from 1 January 1990 for unpublished works in existence at 31 July 1989. Works created on or after 1 August 1989 enjoy the normal copyright period, calculated in relation to the author's life, whether they are published or not. These periods are unchanged by the 1995 Regulations.

Where posthumous first publication in the UK or elsewhere in the EEA took place after the then period of copyright protection had *expired*, Article 4 of the Directive provided for a new publication right. This right is to be owned by the first publisher of the work, and last for 25 years from the end of the year in which the work is first made available to the public. The UK may implement these provisions in the Copyright and Related Rights Regulations 1996.

Unpublished works

Unpublished works were at one time protected in the UK by a perpetual common-law copyright, but this was abolished by the 1911 Act. The transitional provisions of the 1988 Act provided that works which were still unpublished when the 1988 Act came into force (1 August 1989) should be protected for 50 years from the end of that year – that is, until 31 December 2039. They still are.

Typographical arrangements

Copyright in the typographical arrangement of published editions is unaffected by the 1995 Regulations, and continues to last for 25 years from the end of the year in which the edition was first published.

Sound recordings and films

Under the 1988 Act, copyright in both sound recordings and films expired 50 years from the end of the year in which they were made (or, if they were released before then, 50 years from the year of release). Following the Directive and the 1995 Regulations, there are two significant changes:

1 for sound recordings, the 50-year period remains the same, but the definition of 'release' now includes any (authorised) first publication or playing in public, broadcast or inclusion in a cable programme service;
2 for films, the period of copyright is increased dramatically to 70 years from the end of the year in which the last known of four persons connected with the films dies:
   (a) the principal director;
   (b) the author of the screenplay;
   (c) the author of the dialogue;
   (d) the composer of the music (if it was created specifically for the film, and actually used).

If the identity of *none* of these people is known, copyright expires 70 years from the year the film was made, or (if it was made available to the public before then) 70 years from the year it was made available.

In the (unlikely) event that no-one falls into the categories (a)–(d) above at all, then the Regulations provide that the extension will not apply and copyright will expire 50 years from the year the film was made.

Broadcasts and cable programmes

Copyright – owned by the relevant broadcasting organisations – continues to last 50 years from the end of the year in which the first transmission was made, whether by wire or over the air, by cable or satellite.

Copyright in a repeat broadcast or cable programme expires at the same time as copyright in the original broadcast or cable programme.

Crown and Parliamentary copyright

The Crown claims copyright in every Act of Parliament, and in all works created either by the Queen personally, or by an officer or servant of the Crown in the course of his or her duties: this is called 'Crown Copyright'. Crown Copyright is largely controlled and administered by HMSO. Under the 1988 Act (unchanged by the 1995 Regulations) Crown copyright lasts for 125 years from the year the work was made, if the work remains unpublished commercially. Official papers are often never published commercially, but simply available for inspection after 30 or more years. If the work is published commercially within 75 years of its making, copyright lasts 50 years from the year of first publication.

Parliamentary copyright exists in Bills, and other works made under the direction or control of either House: it lasts for 50 years from the end of the year in which the work was made. A similar copyright is owned by certain international organisations. These also are unaffected by the 1995 Regulations.

Universities' copyright

The universities of Oxford and Cambridge, Edinburgh, Glasgow, St Andrews and Aberdeen, and the Colleges of Eton, Westminster and Winchester secured perpetual copyright in 1775 in works printed by them, in which they had been given or bequeathed the copyright. This perpetual copyright was limited by the 1988 Act, and any such copyrights will now expire at the end of 2039. The works concerned may of course qualify for copyright protection on other grounds, in which case longer terms of protection may apply.

Peter Pan

J. M. Barrie's famous play went out of copyright at the end of 1987, but the 1988 Act contained special provisions to enable the trustees of the Great Ormond Street Hospital to continue to collect royalties in perpetuity in respect of certain uses of the play. Following the 1995 Regulations, it is likely that all Barrie's works, including *Peter Pan*, came back into copyright in the UK as from 1 January 1996, and will continue in copyright until the end of 2007: presumably the hospital will continue to receive royalties during this period (unless some other arrangement is agreed) and after 2007 the provisions of the 1988 Act will continue.

SUMMARY CHECKLIST: DURATION OF COPYRIGHT

- UK copyright is a statutory right, and now always has a fixed term of years.
- That term may vary, depending on the work, and it may be calculated in relation to the date of the author's death, or to creation or first publication of the work, or to the year it was 'released' or first made available to the public.
- The Berne Convention international minimum for literary and artistic works is 50 years from the end of the year in which the author died.
- Within the EU, the term of copyright in literary and artistic works has now been harmonised upwards by the Duration Directive to 70 years pma.
- The new 70 year term applies to all EEA-origin works which were protected in at least one member state on 1 July 1995.
- Within the UK, this meant that some existing copyrights were extended, but also that some works will have come back into copyright, having previously been in the public domain.
- For the current UK position, it is necessary to check the relevant provisions of the 1995 Regulations (and the 1988 Act, as now amended).

Other rights of authors: moral rights and PLR

3

MORAL RIGHTS

INTRODUCTION

In addition to copyright, authors now have in the UK personal statutory rights relating to their works and their reputations, called moral rights. They are quite separate from the copyright itself, and remain attached to the author personally, or the author's estate, even if the copyright is later assigned to someone else, such as a publisher. They cannot be sold or assigned to anyone else (although they can be inherited) but they can be waived: we will consider waiver further, below.

The idea of authors having personal moral rights is (relatively) new to UK law, although *droit moral* has been well-established in France, and elsewhere in Europe, for some time: indeed, the continental view of copyright itself is primarily as an author's right (*droit d'auteur*) – quite different from the pragmatic economic right which has developed in the UK. With our different mercantile traditions, we have tended to regard such things as authors' moral rights as dangerously romantic and suspiciously foreign. In so far as UK law has bothered about the honour and reputation of authors, and the integrity of their works, at all, it has tended to look first for any breach of contract, and failing that leave them to uncertain remedies such as defamation actions, or actions for malicious falsehood, or passing off. This has provided remedies in some extreme cases, but has fallen some way short of Britain's commitments under the Berne Convention, and arguably still does.

Article 6 bis of Berne

Moral rights as a species come in all shapes and sizes: consider, for example, the thought provoking *droit de repentir*, which – in countries where it applies (not the UK) – allows an author to have second thoughts entirely and insist on withdrawing a work, even after publication (there is usually provision for compensation). Only two moral rights, however, are specifically written into the Berne Convention (at Article 6 *bis*): the right to claim authorship of the work (the right of paternity), and the right to object to distortions, mutilations or other derogatory treatments of the work which would prejudice the author's honour or reputation (the right of integrity). All member countries are obliged to provide for protection of these two key rights.

The 1988 Act

The Whitford Committee, which preceded the UK's current Copyright, Designs and Patents Act 1988, recommended that the two moral rights of paternity and integrity at least must be incorporated expressly into UK law, together with two others, all of which we will look at in more detail below. The 1988 Act now provides for four statutory moral rights:

- The Right of Paternity.
- The Right of Integrity.
- The Right to Prevent False Attribution.
- The Right to Privacy of Certain Photographs or Films.

They are, however, severely hedged about with restrictions, as we shall see.

THE RIGHT OF PATERNITY

Section 77 of the 1988 Act gives the author of a copyright literary, dramatic, musical or artistic work, and the director of a copyright film, the right to be identified as the author or director of the work. In the case of commercial publication, this means that the author has the right to be identified in (or on) each copy or, if that is not appropriate, in some other way 'likely to bring his identity to the notice of a person acquiring a copy'. This might require careful consideration if the information is only available electronically. The identification must be 'clear and reasonably prominent' – this probably means not necessarily on the spine or even on the title page (if in printed form), but not hidden away in 8-point type either. The author may specify a pseudonym, or some other form of preferred identification (for example, initials). The right lasts for as long as the work remains in copyright.

Although this new statutory right now complies with the UK's Berne obligations, it is accompanied by a number of restrictions, some of them quite significant:

The work must be in copyright

The paternity right only applies to 'copyright' works: the works must meet the various criteria for copyright protection in the UK (see chapter 2), and the period of copyright must still be running. It also only applies to copyright literary, musical, dramatic or artistic works, or films – sound recordings, broadcasts and cable programmes, and typographical arrangements are not covered.

Publication must be commercial

In the case of a book or similar publication, before the author's right of paternity comes into effect the work must be published 'commercially' (or be performed in public or broadcast, or included in a cable programme service or in copies of a film or sound recording issued to the public). This therefore rules out token or nominal publication (described in the Act as 'merely colourable') or anything that is not intended to satisfy the reasonable requirements of the public. By implication, the book must be reasonably widely advertised to its intended market, and be available in quantities capable of fulfilling a likely minimum of orders. Authors wishing to acquire an enforceable right of paternity should consider whether their publishing contract binds the publisher to commercial publication as defined in the 1988 Act. Availability via an electronic retrieval system counts as publication.

The right must be asserted

The right of paternity is the only moral right that needs to be expressly 'asserted' by the author before it can be enforced. Joint authors must each assert independently. Many commentators have argued that this formal requirement seriously weakens the right's effectiveness and may even be contrary to the Berne Convention (which normally bans formalities of any kind). In steering the 1988 Act through Parliament however, the UK government relied on the actual wording of Article 6 *bis*, which does not require any absolute right of paternity but only a right to 'claim authorship': Section 78 of the 1988 Act therefore requires assertion.

The assertion may be included:

- in an assignment of copyright (which must be in writing) or;
- via some other written document signed by the author.

The former method binds not only the person to whom copyright is assigned but also all those whose claims stem from theirs – whether they personally knew about the assertion or not. The latter method binds only those 'to whose notice the assertion is brought', which is why many author contracts now provide not only that the publishers themselves will credit the author but also that a similar contractual obligation will be written into any sub-licences.

The author must therefore assert his or her right positively and in writing. Some early correspondence in *The Bookseller* suggested a quasi-religious ceremony, along the lines of a christening, with the new-born book being sprinkled with holy water before the proud author signs a formal assertion of paternity, but this – alas – came to nothing. What most often now happens is that a form of assertion is printed on each copy of the work, this being seen as the most practical method for an author to put the world generally on notice of a new right. Note that it is *only* the paternity right which needs to be asserted: all-embracing phrases such as 'the author's moral rights are hereby asserted' go further than is strictly necessary.

Assertion is not retrospective – so if an author allows a work to be published without asserting his or her right of paternity, and later decides to assert, the publisher cannot be sued in respect of books already sold. Once the publisher is on notice of the author's assertion, however, all stock subsequently sold must thereafter identify the author in accordance with the Act. In theory, this would include stock already in the warehouse but not yet sold, but where there is no good reason for the author's delay in asserting, the Act allows a court to take this into account, and it is unlikely a publisher would be penalised in such circumstances.

The right does not apply to every work

No right of paternity attaches to authors of certain works. The following are the most important:

- computer programs, computer generated works, or typeface designs;
- works created in the course of employment (where the copyright is originally owned by the employer and the employer has authorised the publication complained of);
- works made for the purpose of reporting current events;
- works written for publication and published in a newspaper, magazine or similar periodical.
- works written for publication and published in a 'collective work' such as an encyclopaedia, dictionary or year book.

The last exception seems at first sight to cover all major (even multi-volume) works of reference, and even perhaps some multimedia works, but it must surely be a question of degree. Where individual articles or entries are significant contributions to the literature in their own right, it will probably still be advisable to identify the author in accordance with the Act – unless one of the restrictions applies (for example, that the right has not been asserted, or has been waived).

The author may consent, or waive the right altogether

Under section 87 of the 1988 Act, none of the author's moral rights will be infringed if he or she consented to the acts concerned. This is perhaps only reasonable; however, section 87 also goes much further and provides that all the author's moral rights, including the right of paternity, may also be *waived*, partially or completely. This is in sharp contrast to the continental position – in France, for example, the author's *droit moral* is 'perpetual, inalienable and imprescriptible' – and has been strongly criticised as a further serious weakening of the author's rights in the UK.

Under the 1988 Act a waiver may be general and unconditional, or it may be limited in some way: it may apply only to certain works, or kinds of works, or it may apply only in certain circumstances, for example, as in some contracts, only in so far as necessary to exploit subsidiary rights, such as film or book club rights. It may also be conditional, and it may be made subject to revocation.

Unconditional and irrevocable waivers may not always make sense, either from the author's or the publisher's point of view, since a right waived absolutely is a right lost forever. (We shall consider waivers more generally in the context of particular contracts, in chapters 4 and 5.)

Waivers do not have to be in writing, and section 87 (4) specifically allows for informal waivers (implied by the author's conduct, for example) under general common law principles. However, such implied or informal waivers may be difficult to prove, and if a reliable waiver is needed it is probably advisable to take the hint in section 87(2) that moral rights 'may be' waived by a written document signed by the author.

SUMMARY CHECKLIST: THE RIGHT OF PATERNITY

- Is the work a relevant copyright work? Is it one of the excluded categories of works?
- Has it been published commercially, or otherwise exploited?
- Has the right been asserted?
- Has the author consented, or waived the right?

THE RIGHT OF INTEGRITY

If the right of paternity is the Berne Convention's primary moral right of authors, the second key right enshrined in Article 6 *bis* is almost as important: the right of authors to object to 'derogatory treatment' of their work. This is usually referred to informally as the Right of Integrity. The right is now set out in section 80 of the 1988 Act, which provides that authors of copyright literary, dramatic, musical or artistic works, and directors of copyright films, have the right, in specified circumstances, not to have their work subjected to derogatory treatment. Like the Paternity Right, the Right of Integrity lasts for as long as the work remains in copyright.

Derogatory treatment

What, one may ask, is 'derogatory treatment'? Does it cover what publishing contracts often refer to as reasonable editorial changes?

There are in fact now two separate questions:

- Do the particular acts complained of amount to a 'treatment' at all?
- If so, is that treatment 'derogatory'?

The Act gives some assistance, but there have been virtually no decided cases on moral rights in the UK since the 1988 Act and in order to find the answers it may often be necessary to refer to earlier case law for guidance.

'Treatment'

The 1988 Act defines treatment to include any of the following things done to a work:

- Adding to it;
- Deleting from it;
- Altering it;
- Adapting it.

Specifically excluded from this list however are translations, or musical arrangements, or transcriptions which amount to no more than a change of key or register. The exclusion of translations might seem hard to justify, given their frequency, and the ease with which a bad translation can ruin an author's reputation, but ministerial statements prior to the 1988 Act suggest that those may ironically have been the very reasons for exclusion – coupled perhaps with the fact that contractual remedies are usually available in such circumstances, under the translation rights contract (see chapter 5).

What if the work is entirely untouched and unchanged, but is placed in an unflattering or unfortunate context (perhaps next to racist or indecent material)? Under the 1988 Act if none of the four positive acts listed above had occurred, the placing of the work in that context would not amount to a 'treatment' at all, and could not therefore infringe the integrity right. So, a composer whose music was faithfully played and recorded could not complain of a breach of the integrity right if that recording then featured in the sound track of a documentary film condemning the political regime under which the composer lived and worked (as Shostakovich and a number of other Soviet composers found in a celebrated US case after the Second World War).

'Derogatory'

The 1988 Act (section 80) provides that:

> The treatment of a work is derogatory if it amounts to distortion or mutilation of the work or is otherwise prejudicial to the honour or reputation of the author or director.

'Distortion' and 'mutilation' are strong words. 'Prejudicial to . . . honour or reputation' also implies an objective standard, similar in strength to the various definitions of defamation (see chapter 7). It seems likely, therefore, that it will not be the author's opinion (or injured feelings) alone which will provide the yardstick for what is or is not prejudicial to their honour or reputation: authors will have to produce objective evidence that their honour or reputations have actually suffered, or are likely to.

Derogatory treatment will clearly include complete mutilation or emasculation of a work, or a complete misrepresentation of the author's real views or philosophy. Indeed, if the treatment is that serious there would probably also have been an action for defamation anyway, as some early cases showed: in the 1908 case of *Humphreys v. D.C. Thomson*, an author succeeded in persuading a jury that a newspaper serialisation that cut much of her background text, added other lower grade material at the beginning and end of extracts, and changed ('simplified') names of characters, all without her consent, so lowered her reputation in the eyes of right-thinking members of the public that it amounted to defamation. This could still be true in similar circumstances today, and it would almost certainly now amount to derogatory treatment too.

Editorial 'improvements' in general are therefore now highly unsafe, particularly where the risk of breaching the author's right of integrity is accompanied by the risk of defamation, or breach of contract. In the case of breach of contract this will particularly be so where the contract is an informal one, with no express provisions allowing the publishers to make 'reasonable' (or any other) changes. Consider, for example, the unusual case of Mr Joseph, in *Joseph v. National Magazine Company* (1959). Mr Joseph was a successful Knightsbridge antiques dealer, who was something of an expert on jade carvings. He agreed to advertise two of his latest acquisitions in the prestigious magazine *The Connoisseur* for a reduced fee, on the basis that he would also submit a signed article on jade to appear on the facing page. His article was not however printed as submitted, but was sent for editing and revision without his knowledge to a freelance journalist, the editor having decided he did not care for its style. What came back was radically changed, with numerous stylistic 'improvements' and 23 new errors of fact.

Mr Joseph refused to allow the article to be published under his name in such an emasculated form and sued (successfully) for breach of contract. Mr Justice Harman said in the High Court:

> I can see no justification for the contention that an editor may alter the matter and manner of a signed article in this way. Style is, I suppose, a matter of taste. [The editor] said that the plaintiff's article was not in The Connoisseur manner and he preferred [the journalist's] production. For myself, I think it was greatly inferior, being written in the kind of journalese which alters the words 'before burial' to 'prior to interment'. However that may be, the plaintiff was entitled to write his own article in his own style, expressing his own opinions, and was not bound to submit to have his name published as an author of a different article expressing other opinions in a different style.

Although there was a clear breach of Mr Joseph's contract, the circumstances of that contract were somewhat untypical, since there was no more than a verbal agreement, which arguably only gave the publishers a limited licence to publish his article exactly as he wrote it – especially since it was a signed article for which he had paid. In a more standard publishing agreement, it is likely that there will be some provision for reasonable alterations, and if the alterations made broadly comply with the terms of the contract it is unlikely that a claim of derogatory treatment will succeed, since the author will have consented – via the contract – to the changes made (see below).

Where alterations go *beyond* any contract, however, an action for breach of contract is likely to succeed and there may also now be derogatory treatment. In the above case there might also be an issue of false attribution.

'Bad Boys Megamix'

Although a music case, the injunction granted to George Michael in 1991 is still instructive as one of the few reported occasions so far, since the 1988 Act, on which an issue of derogatory treatment was considered by the UK courts. Michael complained that five of his early tracks, recorded in the days when he was a performer with Wham!, had been used without his consent in a 'Megamix' medley: the tracks (he alleged) had been edited, some words had been changed, and fill-in music from elsewhere had been added. Clearly, a 'treatment' of the works had taken place, since there were both deletions and alterations (and possibly additions also – although 'filler' music linking separate tracks might not strictly speaking 'add' to the tracks themselves) – but was the treatment 'derogatory'? Michael argued that the megamix 'completely alters the character of the original compositions'. The judge, adopting a somewhat cautious approach, first pointed out that:

> It is not, in my judgment, self-evident that taking parts of five different works and putting them together necessarily involves a change of character or modification.

However, on the arguments before him he took the view that it was at least 'arguable that such treatment amounts to distortion or mutilation within Section 80(2)(b) of the 1988 Act', and therefore granted Michael's application for an injunction.

That particular case went no further: we still await a fully decided case on derogatory treatment and the author's moral right of integrity under the 1988 Act. Until that comes along – it surely cannot be far away – the decisions set out above may be a helpful guide to the likely approach of UK law (and, perhaps equally important, UK judges).

Limitations on the right of integrity

As with the right of paternity, the author's Right of Integrity will only apply if:

- the work is a copyright work;
- the work is published commercially (other uses may also suffice: see above).

The Integrity Right does *not*, however, need to be 'asserted'.
The right does not apply to the following works among others:

- computer programs or computer-generated works;
- works made for the purpose of reporting current events;
- Works written for publication and published in a newspaper, magazine or similar periodical;
- works written for publication and published in a 'collective work' such as an encyclopaedia, dictionary or year book;
- works created in the course of employment (where the employer owns the copyright, authorises the treatment concerned and – where the author is identified – provides a 'sufficient disclaimer').

Most of the above exceptions are similar to the list of exceptions to the right of paternity (above, p. 47), apart from the provision for a disclaimer in employee works, and the omission of typeface designs from the list – the Paternity Right does not apply to such designs, but the Right of Integrity *does*.

The Right of Integrity also does not apply to anything done to avoid the commission of an offence, or complying with a statutory duty, or (as with the BBC) to avoid anything which offends against 'good taste or decency or which is likely to encourage or incite to crime or lead to disorder or to be offensive to public feeling'. This last exception now provides a let-out for the BBC even where alterations are significant structural changes – although it was decided in a 1967 case that deletion even of two (crucial) words from a play could be 'structural', it would not now amount to derogatory treatment if (as in that case) the BBC's cuts were motivated by a desire not to offend public feeling. As with employee works, however, there must be a 'sufficient disclaimer' (if the author is identified).

Finally the Right of Integrity will not apply:

- To anything done with the author's consent or;
- If the author has waived the right.

SUMMARY CHECKLIST: THE RIGHT OF INTEGRITY

- Is the work a relevant copyright work? Is it one of the excluded categories of works?

- Has it been published commercially, or otherwise exploited?
- Has any 'treatment' of the work taken place?
- Has the work been added to, deleted from, altered or adapted (except by translation)?
- If so, was the treatment 'derogatory'?
- Did it distort or mutilate the work?
- Was it otherwise prejudicial to the author's honour or reputation?
- Did the author consent, or waive the right?

FALSE ATTRIBUTION

Authors not only have a moral right of paternity – to be credited as the author – but also have its converse: the right *not* to be credited with things they did *not* write. This is known as the right to prevent false attribution, and is now contained in section 84 of the 1988 Act. Of the four moral rights contained in the 1988 Act, it is the only one to have existed before in statutory form: there was a very similar right in section 43 of the 1956 Act.

The right applies to literary, dramatic, musical and artistic works, and to films and (unlike the paternity and integrity rights) can be exercised by any 'person' – they do not have to be authors.

The attribution complained of may be express or implied, and the right will be infringed wherever a false attribution:

- is included in copies of a work issued to the public or;
- is in (or on) an artistic work exhibited to the public.

The right may also be infringed by false attributions contained in public performances or showings, broadcasts, or cable programme services, but only where the person concerned knew or had reason to believe that the attribution was false. There are also secondary offences of possession, or dealing with, copies of works containing such attributions, but again where the presence of the attribution was known, and was known to be false.

The right is an entirely personal right, allied to a person's reputation rather than to any copyright works he or she may have created – it does not therefore last for the full term of copyright, like other moral rights, but only for 20 years after the person's death.

As with other moral rights, it often overlaps with other legal remedies – in this case with the existing laws of passing off, and defamation. Indeed, where other, more traditional, remedies exist it may well be that judges will prefer to use those and will pay less attention to specific statutory moral rights. The damages awarded to the singer Dorothy Squires in *Moore v. News of the World* (1972) may be instructive: for a report of a newspaper interview falsely attributed to her as her own writing ('How My Love for the Saint Went Sour by DS talking to WT') the jury awarded £4,300 for libel but only a nominal £100 for false attribution under the 1956 Act. This may have had something to do with the judge's guidance:

> Nobody suggests that if she is entitled, it should be a shilling or something contemptuous; but it should be a very much more modest amount than you would give for libel if you find the damages for libel have to be assessed . . . I cannot suggest a figure, but something small . . . some gentle, gentle amount for a rather technical cause of action.

THE RIGHT TO PRIVACY

Some countries – the USA for example – have significant and substantial laws protecting personal privacy, but no general privacy law yet exists in the UK. This limited right to privacy, contained in section 85 of the 1988 Act, is not really a moral right at all, and applies only to certain photographs and films which are commissioned for private and domestic purposes (such as wedding photos).

Under the 1956 Act, the person who commissioned such photos (usually the happy couple) owned the copyright in them, and could thus control the use made of them. Under the 1988 Act, however, this rule was changed (see p. 31) and the author (that is, the photographer) now owns the copyright. This would have meant that professional photographers could make unlimited copies of wedding photos they had taken and could, for example, sell them to national newspapers if the bride or groom subsequently became newsworthy. It was to prevent this limited, but very real, danger that section 85 was passed. Those commissioning such photos or films can now prevent:

- copies being issued to the public;
- the works being exhibited in public or;
- the works being broadcast or included in a cable programme service.

The right lasts for as long as the work concerned remains in copyright.

REMEDIES FOR INFRINGEMENT OF MORAL RIGHTS

Section 103 of the 1988 Act provides that an infringement of a moral right:

> Is actionable as a breach of statutory duty owed to the person entitled to the right.

Damages may be awarded, and an injunction may be granted in appropriate cases. There is also express provision for a disclaimer, to be approved by the court, 'dissociating the author or director from the treatment of the work'.

PUBLIC LENDING RIGHT

After vigorous lobbying by authors such as Maureen Duffy and Brigid Brophy, a Public Lending Right for authors (PLR) was established in the UK by the Public

Lending Right Act 1979, and came into effect in 1982. The first payments were made in 1984, and payments have been made annually ever since: payment is entirely out of central government funds. The scheme is administered by a Registrar of Public Lending Right and a small staff, supported by an advisory committee representing interested bodies, including the responsible government department, the Department of National Heritage.

The PLR scheme provides for authors (and others, such as illustrators) to receive payments in proportion to the number of times their books are borrowed from public libraries in the UK: borrowings are recorded from a sample of 30 library authorities around the UK and the results grossed up annually to arrive at an estimate of the national loans of each book.

No author may currently get more than £6,000 per annum – only 104 authors received the maximum amount in the financial year 1995/96, and most of the 24,000 authors currently registered for PLR (it is necessary to register in advance) will receive less than £100. The total government funding for the PLR scheme in 1995/96 was under £5 million for the second year in succession (a reduction on the 1993/94 figure) – working out at a rate per loan of exactly 2p.

In order to participate in the PLR scheme, and benefit from any modest annual payments which may be on offer, it is necessary to register with the PLR Registrar (his address is set out at appendix B). Those entitled to register include not only authors, but other persons who have contributed to the text or illustration of a published book: this would include illustrators, photographers, editors and translators, who will receive a share of any PLR payment generated by loan of the book. Those registering must be resident either in the UK or in Germany (there is currently a reciprocal scheme with Germany).

Payment continues for 50 years after the death of the author or contributor. There are no plans at present to increase the UK PLR period to 70 years after the author's death, in line with EU harmonisation of the term of copyright (see p. 37).

The EU Directive on Rental and Lending Right requires EU member states to recognise the rights of authors to license or prohibit the public lending of their works, or alternatively ensure that they receive remuneration for such lending: the right to remuneration cannot be waived. It is understood that the current UK Public Lending Right scheme will remain unchanged.

Commissioning: publishing contracts

II

Author contracts 4

HOW A CONTRACT IS MADE

In this chapter we will look at contracts generally – what they are, legally, and how they are made – and then examine in some detail the contract which is in many ways the most important contract in publishing – the publisher's initial contract with the author. This will raise a number of important issues, such as ownership and control of rights, which we will need to come back to again and again, so we will spend some time on these. In the next chapter, chapter 5, we will go on to look at some other key publishing contracts, such as contracts with contributors, and co-publishing and subsidiary rights deals.

WHAT IS A CONTRACT?

A contract is an agreement that the law will enforce. That sounds rather simple, and it is: contracts are in essence very simple things. You do not need to sign a 20-clause standard form document in order to have a binding contract with someone – indeed in most cases you do not need any writing at all. The 20-clause document may be important later on, in granting rights and confirming your agreement on a number of detailed points, and we will look at such important details in the second half of this chapter. But you may well find you have an agreement that the law will enforce long before you get to that stage. There are two separate elements to consider:

1 *'An agreement'*. There must actually be an agreement between the parties concerned; all that this means is that the parties:
   - must have reached a clear agreement on a specific matter, and
   - must have intended 'to enter into legal relations' – in other words, make a binding legal commitment to each other on the matter.
2 *'That the law will enforce'*. The agreement must be legally enforceable – so the parties must be capable of entering into binding contracts (which will not,

for example, be declared void because one of them is under age, insane, or incapable through drink), the bargain must not itself be illegal or contrary to public policy, and must either be under seal or in writing (for certain types of contract) or – more usually – must be supported by some 'consideration': something (almost anything) of value must be given or promised in return for the promises made.

We will look at these various criteria below, but assuming that most authors and publishers are over 18, not insane or (completely) drunk, and that their agreement is (on the whole) legal and decent, the most important requirements for an enforceable publishing contract are likely to be these:

- a clear agreement
- an intention to be legally bound by it;
- some valuable consideration to seal the bargain.

We now know, following the 1991 decision of the Court of Appeal in *Malcolm v. OUP* (see below, p. 62) that these simple key requirements can be met long before a formal written contract is signed, or even discussed, and that a publisher may become bound contractually to publish a book, even during what have traditionally been thought of as mere 'pre-contract negotiations'.

CLEAR AGREEMENTS: OFFER AND ACCEPTANCE

For a contract to exist, a clear agreement must be reached, with no significant misunderstandings: the parties must not be at cross-purposes. One side must make an offer in clear terms, and the other side must accept that offer on basically the same terms, otherwise no contract can come about. Let us suppose that Routledge makes an offer to an author (who shall be nameless) to publish at a (fairly) reasonable royalty a 288-page book by him on publishing law, to be delivered by 1 March 1996. That is a fairly clear 'offer'. If accepted, they clearly intend it to be legally binding, and the provision for a royalty means there will be valuable 'consideration'. Suppose then, however, that the author (who has been under a lot of stress recently) replies: 'Thank you for your offer; I am happy to confirm that I will write a 1,288-page loose-leaf text, including precedents, on Publishing Law on the terms you have set out.' Is there a contract? No – because the offer, to write a 288-page book, has not been accepted: what has happened is that the author (who is *clearly* under stress) has made a counter-offer, to write something altogether different and more ambitious. Routledge may like this new offer, and decide to accept it, or the parties may continue negotiating, and reach agreement sooner or later, either on the original terms or on revised terms, but until they do no contract exists.

ACCEPTANCE BY CONDUCT, AND OFFERS TO TREAT

Silence does not imply acceptance (even if the offer attempts to provide that it will) but offers may be accepted by *conduct* as well as by written or spoken words. Suppose that an author and publisher are discussing a draft contract but for one reason or another never actually sign it. The basic terms of the offer contained in the proposed contract may still be accepted or confirmed by either of them if they start to act on the basis of those terms – for example, by delivering the book on time, or by commencing production. If publisher and author both continue to 'perform' the terms of the contract, even though it was never signed, it will increasingly bind them, on those terms. However, if it is left unsigned, and there is no separate agreement on these points, the publisher may well find that it has no more than an implied licence to publish (and perhaps deal with certain subsidiary rights) on a non-exclusive basis, and would not have been granted an assignment of copyright, or any exclusive publishing licence (both of which must be in writing, and signed).

Does a bookshop make an offer when it displays a book in the window at a certain price? Suppose the price label is out of date: can a customer 'accept' the offer and claim there is a binding contract at the old price? No – because shops in those circumstances are not making binding offers, but merely offers to come in and enter into negotiations – what the law calls 'offers to treat'. So if our canny customer takes the book to the till and offers the old price, it is then open to the bookseller to reject that offer and instead make a counter-offer to sell it at the correct price.

INTENTION TO BE LEGALLY BOUND

Both parties must intend to enter into legal relations, and intend that their agreement will bind them legally. An agreement to meet in the Festival Hall Bar at 7 p.m. is *not* usually intended to be legally binding, and if one party is late and as a result they both miss the first half of the concert (because the late one has the tickets) there may be a serious row but there will be no breach of any contract. An agreement to share in National Lottery winnings, however, or an agreement by an author to deliver a manuscript on disk to a publisher by a specified date *are* both normally intended to be contractually binding. It will be a question of fact in each case.

If one or other party wishes to negotiate, but avoid any binding legal commitment for the time being, it is possible to achieve this by marking all correspondence 'Subject to Contract', so that it is clear that the necessary intention to conclude a contract is not yet present.

CONSIDERATION

So that there is no doubt that the parties mean what they say, an agreement is not generally binding under English law unless:

- it is signed (and witnessed) as a Deed, or made under seal (for some formal assignments, or certain transactions involving land); or
- it is supported by some valuable 'consideration'.

For most publishing contracts therefore – even informal, verbal ones – this means that there must be consideration – either consideration now, or a promise of future consideration to come. An upfront fee or an advance would be present consideration – an undertaking to pay future royalties would count as future consideration. Sometimes of course both exist, but both are equally valid in the eyes of the law.

Although money normally features somewhere, 'consideration' does not actually need to be in the form of convertible currency, provided it is of some economic value. It also does not have to represent an adequate commercial price – it can be purely nominal, for example £1. A promise by a magazine publisher to publish in book form articles by the athletes Harold Abrahams and Eric Liddell (later made famous in the film, *Chariots of Fire*) for a payment of '4d per copy' was held by the Court of Appeal in 1922 to be sufficient consideration to form the basis of a binding publishing contract, even though virtually no other details had been settled. Despite the reservations of the court ('I cannot but wonder that publishers and authors enter into agreements as indefinite as this'), '4d per copy' is perfectly clear, and sufficient, consideration.

Mutual promises can be good consideration for each other, provided that both of them have an economic value to the party to whom they are made: arguably a publishing agreement which is not signed as a Deed and which makes no mention of fees or royalties or anything else of economic value – even free author's copies – might well lack the necessary consideration to be binding, even if it contains a firm commitment to publish, since although the act of publishing will cost the publisher money it may not in itself convey anything of economic value to the author. Most publishing agreements, however, are quite clearly of economic value to the author.

MALCOLM V. OUP

At this point, let us pause for a moment and look at a relatively recent (1991) publishing case in which the Court of Appeal reconsidered these very issues. Its confirmation that a publisher can be bound by even a purely verbal agreement provided it has the necessary ingredients listed above has important implications for all authors and publishers, and all who deal with publishing contracts.

Mr Malcolm submitted a manuscript to Oxford University Press. Their in-house editor, a Mr Hardy, and an outside reader, both liked it, but thought it too long, and Mr Hardy suggested substantial cuts. Now, Mr Malcolm had had a number of unsatisfactory experiences with other publishers at this 'pre-contract discussion' stage, and made it clear to Mr Hardy he was looking for a firm publishing commitment before embarking on any more revisions, which he estimated could well take up to six months' work. There followed two telephone calls from Mr Hardy, both of which Mr Malcolm – with unusual foresight – tape recorded. In the second telephone conversation Mr Hardy made some crucial remarks, which should be required reading in every editorial department:

- '. . . we would like to do it. That is to say, I mean I know you want a commitment sufficient to take you through the last stage of revision and that's what I am offering'.
- 'I will be getting in touch again when I have done the costs and cast off and so forth and then we can, er, talk about some sort of contract.'
- 'It seems to me that because it's such a risky venture I am not going to be terribly generous financially, erm . . . I mean what I think we should agree is that you have a fair royalty.'

The next day the editor sent the author an 'Author's Publicity Form' to complete and ended his letter by saying 'I am pleased we are going to do your book'. The author made the agreed revisions, but OUP subsequently changed their minds, and declined to publish. Mr Malcolm sued for breach of contract.

The Court of Appeal – reversing an earlier decision by the High Court – found that in these circumstances all the necessary elements were present to create a binding contract, and therefore found that OUP's refusal to publish after all was indeed a breach of contract.

The court made a number of important findings:

- No special formalities are required for publishing contracts, and it does not matter if contract details such as exact royalty terms, print number or format are all left to be agreed later; an agreement is not incomplete in law simply because it calls for further agreement on some key points later on, as long as the parties have settled the essential elements of the bargain.
- In this case, there was a clear agreement – that Mr Malcolm would deliver, and OUP would publish, a specific book (indeed the author was busily revising it to OUP's own specifications).
- There was a sufficiently clear intention on both sides to enter into legal relations: Mr Malcolm had made clear his determination to have a firm commitment before doing any more work and Mr Hardy had offered that commitment. As Lord Justice Leggatt put it:

  'It is difficult to know what was meant by "a firm commitment" other than an intention to create legal relations . . . to suggest that Mr Hardy intended to induce Mr Malcolm to revise the book by giving him a valueless assurance would be tantamount to an imputation of fraud.'

- There was also sufficient 'consideration' for the contract, in the shape of Mr Hardy's promise to pay a 'fair royalty'. This vague phrase is not a recommended method of settling consideration for a contract, but it is (just) sufficient in law. '4d per copy' was sufficient consideration in 1922 (see above p. 62) and 'a fair royalty' appears to be equally sufficient today.

On this basis Lord Justice Leggatt and a majority of the court concluded that OUP did enter into a binding contract to publish Mr Malcolm's book, for a fair royalty ('it follows that in my judgment when Mr Hardy used the expressions "commitment" and "a fair royalty" he did in fact mean what he said and I venture to think it would take a lawyer to arrive at any other conclusion').

A final – equally important – finding by the court was that specific performance of a publishing contract might be ordered in appropriate cases – in other words, that the publisher should be ordered to publish the book – and it is important to bear this in mind. In most cases, however, courts will avoid making such orders, since they will be difficult if not impossible for the court to enforce. If (as here) an award of damages for breach of contract is a viable alternative, courts will normally prefer to award damages (on damages generally, see chapter 8).

PARTICULAR CONTRACTS AND LEGAL CAPACITY

CONTRACTS WHICH NEED WRITING

Although verbal contracts are binding in most publishing situations, there are some kinds of contracts which must be in writing. Others do not need to be in writing themselves, but some written evidence must exist to support them. In addition, some specific assignments or grants or licences must be written.

Contracts which must be in writing

- Bills of exchange, promissory notes, and bills of sale;
- Regulated consumer credit agreements;
- Hire purchase and consumer hire agreements.

Contracts for which written evidence must exist

- Marine insurance contracts;
- Contracts of guarantee;
- Contracts for the sale (or other disposition) of an interest in land.

Assignments or grants which must be written

- Assignments of copyright (under section 90(3) of the 1988 Act);
- Grants of Exclusive Licences (under section 92 of the 1988 Act).

(in both of these last two cases, the assignment or grant must not only be in writing, but also *signed* by, or on behalf of, the copyright owner. If it is not, it will be unenforceable as a legal right (although an equitable interest might in some cases exist).

ILLEGALITY

The law will not enforce a contract to do something which is legally wrong, such as the commission of a crime, or a tort (such as a libel), or which is otherwise contrary to public policy. Thus contracts which promote sexual immorality or which pervert the course of justice are void and unenforceable, as are certain kinds of gaming and wagering contracts. Contracts to finance other people's litigation in return for a share in the proceeds (formerly an offence known as 'champerty') are unenforceable (although if the US contingency fees system is ever introduced into the UK this may have to change).

Also illegal are contracts in restraint of trade, and contracts the purpose of which is to procure the breach of an existing contract: so that publisher B wishing to entice an author away from publisher A, cannot sign the author up to a more attractive deal knowing it to involve the breach of the author's existing contract – the new contract will be unenforceable, and publisher B will probably be liable to an action in tort from publisher A for procuring a breach of contract.

INCAPACITY OF THE PARTIES

Not everyone is legally capable of entering into binding contracts. Those who might *not* have the necessary legal capacity at the relevant times, and whose contracts would therefore be liable to be declared void, include the following:

Minors

The age of legal capacity was reduced from 21 to 18 by the Family Law Reform Act 1969 (so those of us who were 19 or 20 when the Act came into force all missed out on coming of age parties). Until people have reached their 18th birthday, they are not fully capable of entering into binding legal contracts – they are known as minors (previously 'infants'). This is designed to protect the young from unwise contracts – particularly from contracts which (as in the case of many young pop singers or athletes) might involve very large sums of money and which would significantly restrict their future freedom. On the other hand, those who do business with minors in good faith may also need protection – if for example they supply valuable goods to them on credit, or pay them advances. In order to balance these two objectives, the law will as a general rule uphold minors' contracts if they are for 'necessaries', or are otherwise – on the whole – for the minors' benefit. In a well known publishing case in 1966 (*Chaplin v. Leslie Frewin (Publishers) Limited*) Charlie Chaplin's son – who was then a minor – was held to be bound by a book publishing contract under which he had already been paid significant advances, since the contract was itself for his benefit and also enabled him to make a start as an author; equally, it would have been unfair to deprive the publisher of the opportunity to recoup his advances.

Mental patients

If you are insane, you are considered by the law to be 'incapable of intelligent consent'. However, insanity is not always a permanent state and those suffering from insanity often have lucid intervals during which they are quite capable of entering into rational agreements. A contract made by a mental patient is therefore not void from the outset, but may be declared void by the patient later, if it is not for his or her benefit, particularly if the other party knew of the insanity and took advantage of it. Equally, a beneficial contract made while insane can be *affirmed* later on.

Drunkards

Rather like the insane, those who enter into contracts while their faculties are completely incapacitated through drink may plead their extreme drunkenness as a defence in any subsequent actions under those contracts. But they may do this only if:

- their drunkenness completely prevented them from understanding the transaction; and
- the other party knew this.

Most publishing lunches nowadays would be unlikely to have the necessary effect. In any event, if the drunkard ratifies the contract later on, when sober, he or she will become liable in the normal way.

Those acting beyond their authority

Companies which enter into contracts for activities which are not within the company's objects as set out in its Memorandum and Articles of Association may well be acting *ultra vires*, or beyond their authority, and such contracts may be open to challenge, for example by the shareholders. For this reason, most Memoranda and Articles are drafted as widely as possible, but something clearly *ultra vires* may still be declared void. One way of avoiding this risk is to provide that the object of the company is to carry on business as 'a general commercial company' – since 1991 this authorises a company 'to carry on any trade or business whatsoever'.

Similarly, partners may not always have authority to bind a partnership in contracts unconnected with the partnership – such contracts may need to be ratified later on.

Employees who are allowed regularly to negotiate contracts – such as publishing directors, or commissioning editors – may however often be considered to have apparent authority to do so, and a contract made in good faith with such employees may well bind the company. Publishers should therefore bear in mind that if they give employees business cards describing them as 'Publisher' or 'Commissioning Editor' and send them off to Frankfurt and Bologna and on commissioning tours around universities, they may well be bound by any apparently reasonable contract they may make (however strenuously the board or publishing committee may object later on).

Similarly agents – such as commercial or literary agents – may in some circumstances also go beyond the scope of their authority, but (depending on their particular terms of appointment) most agents will have considerable implied authority to enter into reasonable contracts on behalf of their principals.

Finally, contracts entered into by bankrupts may not always be enforceable, unless affirmed by their trustee in bankruptcy. However, a contract – such as a royalty agreement – which produced *income* for a bankrupt (or his or her creditors) would almost certainly be affirmed.

SUMMARY CHECKLIST: BINDING CONTRACTS

- Are both parties legally capable of entering into contracts?
- Has a clear agreement been reached between them?
- Has a specific offer been accepted (in substantially the same terms)?
- Did both parties intend the agreement to bind them legally?
- Is there valuable 'consideration' (however nominal)?
- Is the contract one which needs to be in writing (for example, if it is to include an assignment of copyright)?
- Might it be illegal, or against public policy?
- Might it be voidable, for example if entered into by a minor or someone acting beyond their authority?

AUTHOR–PUBLISHER AGREEMENTS

STANDARD FORM AGREEMENTS

After all the discussions and pre-contract negotiations (and, possibly, the lunch) there will come a point of decision, yes or no: either the author or the publisher (or both) will decide they do not wish to take the idea any further after all, or both of them will decide that they are ready and willing to go ahead, and to commit themselves to do so by signing a formal publishing contract. They may already have agreed the basis of a deal (indeed, as we have seen above, they may already have a binding contract) but now they will want to confirm in legally binding terms what they have already agreed, and settle a number of other detailed matters at the same time. They will want an agreement that enables them to do two key things:

- to make mutual undertakings to each other (I will write the book if you publish it);
- to acquire rights (in the publisher's case, all the rights it needs to publish and exploit the work, and in the author's case the right – amongst other things – to a reasonable share in the proceeds).

They may sit down with a large blank sheet of paper and prepare a contract from scratch; this form of reinventing the wheel is not generally recommended, and can miss vital points. What more often happens is that one or other of the parties will have been here before, and will produce a standard form contract.

Most publishers with any experience will have some kind of standard author agreement; in the case of a large publishing company it is likely to be a detailed printed or word-processed document of 20 or more clauses. It will however reflect that publisher's own experience: every clause will be there for a good reason, but it will – of course – be drafted from the publisher's point of view. This does not necessarily mean that it is unfair or unreasonable, but authors need to bear its origins in mind. Equally, most major literary agencies have their own standard author–publisher contracts, which not surprisingly are drafted much more with the author's interest in mind: for example, fewer rights are normally granted to the publisher, and the financial terms to the author are usually better. Whose version is used depends entirely on the relative negotiating strengths of the parties. A literary agent representing a successful author is likely to be in a strong position to deal on its own standard terms, whereas a publisher taking the risk of publishing an unknown author will prefer to use its own standard contract initially.

In recent years, Minimum Terms Agreements have been agreed between several publishing houses and the Society of Authors and the Writers Guild on behalf of their members: these are more author-centred and either involve the grant of a more limited publishing licence, or (more often) a review after perhaps 10 years, so that more control is kept in the author's hands.

Even so, dealing on the other side's standard terms can still represent a serious negotiating disadvantage, especially if detailed terms are not properly explained or understood. If in doubt, ask. If no satisfactory explanation is forthcoming, get a second opinion from your professional body, or from an independent lawyer with experience of publishing contracts. And, when dealing with any standard form contract, bear the following points always in mind:

- The law will enforce most reasonable agreements which reflect what both parties want (for the few exceptions, see above, pp. 64–7)
- From a legal point of view, most clauses of most contracts are therefore fully negotiable

THE STANDARD AUTHOR–PUBLISHER AGREEMENT

Most good publishing contracts deal with the same basic points, although sometimes in a different order and sometimes (as we have seen) from very different points of view. In the rest of this chapter we will follow the sequence of topics in the standard author–publisher agreement which is probably in most widespread use, the first precedent in Charles Clark's admirable source book, *Publishing Agreements* (fourth edition, 1993 – a fifth edition is believed to be on the way). Comparisons with other versions, such as agent's contracts or Minimum Terms Agreements, will be made as we go along. You may find it useful to refer to your own version at the same time.

THE PREAMBLE: THE PARTIES, AND THE WORK

It may sound rather obvious, but it is a good idea to say clearly right at the beginning of any publishing contract who you are and which precise publication you are talking about. Both sides are taking on significant legal obligations, so it is necessary to know who it is exactly who will be bound by those obligations. It is also essential to know how far those responsibilities extend, so 'the Work' needs to be clearly defined; it is often sensible to set out a precise specification (word-length, format, number of illustrations etc.) in a separate appendix at the end. Finally, although strictly speaking it is not legally necessary, if the contract is not already pre-dated it is highly desirable if the last person to sign the contract also *dates* it clearly so that everyone knows when the rights and obligations start to run (and, in some cases when they finish). There might be difficult problems of evidence later on, otherwise.

The Parties

The Parties need to be carefully defined. In the case of 'the Author' (sometimes the 'Proprietor', for example where there is a literary estate) it is normal for the term to be defined to include the Author's executors and (sometimes) administrators, where the Author dies or becomes incapacitated, and also his or her 'assigns': we will deal with assignments in a moment.

In the case of 'the Publisher' it is customary to include the Publisher's successors in business, should the company be taken over (as has been known) and often also other related publishing imprints, so that a publisher will retain the option to publish the work under another imprint if that seems more appropriate at the time, but limited (usually) to subsidiaries, or imprints elsewhere in the same group.

'Assigns' and assignment

The parties are often defined to include their respective 'assigns'. As a general rule, either party to a contract may freely assign their rights under that contract (unless there is a specific provision in it to the contrary) but not their *duties*. The person to whom the rights are assigned (called 'the assignee') may take over the entire benefit of the contract from the person doing the assigning ('the assignor'): it is also possible, of course, to assign specific rights separately, such as the copyright.

The Author may wish to assign the benefit of the contract to a spouse or relative, or to a separate company (perhaps for tax reasons). Equally the publisher may wish to assign copyrights or publishing licences under individual contracts, or whole lists of contracts, as part of a sale to another publisher in due course. If this is envisaged – or might be – it is important to make sure that the wording of the contract allows for this: the definition of both parties should include their respective 'assigns', and there should be no ban, or undue restriction, on assignments later on in the contract, unless this is what both parties want.

Any continuing *duties* and obligations of either party may *not* generally be assigned without at least the implied consent of the other – particularly in a contract involving continuing skill and judgement on both sides, as with many publishing contracts. Either party may quite justifiably have reservations about the possibility of future assignment of continuing obligations by the other. The Publisher may be unhappy about the Author assigning any remaining personal obligations – for example to keep a reference work up to date – to a third party, or a company, less able to meet these obligations, and may require a letter of inducement from the Author beforehand by way of reassurance. The Author may have equal fears that any continuing obligations of the Publisher – to promote and exploit the Work effectively, for example, and pay royalties – may be assigned to a different company altogether, with less feel for the market or the Work concerned and about which the author quite possibly has strong views. Where such personal obligations remain, it is always advisable to obtain the express consent of the other party before any assignment, if this is possible. In many cases – such as the sale of a list – it may be advisable to arrange for relevant contracts to be 'novated' (newly executed, and signed by the new parties), so that:

- the relevant rights are re-affirmed;
- the new publisher clearly takes over both the benefit and the burden of the contract.

Some agent's contracts include non-assignment clauses, usually towards the end of the contract, banning assignment by the Publisher without the prior written consent of the Author, sometimes with a proviso that such consent shall not unreasonably be withheld. And a typical Minimum Terms Agreement might provide that the Author shall be consulted in advance on all in-company assignments from one imprint to another, and outlawing assignments to outside third parties altogether (unless they are acquiring a substantial part of the company's business or at least an entire imprint). This can make sense, but both parties should think carefully whether such restrictions on their future activities are in their long-term interests, particularly if the proposed restriction is not mutual, but affects only one side.

Acquisition of an entire company – usually by a purchase of shares – will not normally involve any individual assignments, and will therefore probably not be prevented by non-assignment clauses in individual author contracts.

RIGHTS GRANTED

From a publisher's point of view, one of the main objectives of an author contract is to acquire rights. By far the greatest part of a typical publisher's business consists in exploiting other people's copyright works, and that exploitation may cover many languages, forms and media and involve publishing activities in all corners of the globe: it is essential therefore that it should all be clearly licensed by the copyright owner. Every author contract should therefore make it clear who owns the copyright, and what publishing rights that owner grants to the publisher. This will ensure:

- that author and publisher (and the rest of the world) clearly know who controls which rights;
- that the publisher can safely sub-license individual rights to others;
- that rights can effectively be assigned or transferred;
- that all licensed activities can be protected legally against copyright infringers (around the world if necessary).

There are two ways for a publisher to acquire the publishing rights it needs:

1 by obtaining an assignment of the entire copyright from the copyright owner, or
2 by being granted a publishing licence – in terms wide enough to cover all the publishing activities envisaged.

Full copyright or a licence?

It is more common for authors to retain their copyrights and for publishers to be their exclusive licensees, but there may be some kinds of publishing where an assignment of the full copyright makes sense if both sides agree – such as major works of reference or multimedia works, often with hundreds of different contributors, where the publisher will want to retain overall long-term control. In most other cases, however, a sole and exclusive publishing licence, drafted in wide terms if necessary, will probably meet most publisher's needs. It has been likened by a number of commentators to taking a lease of a house rather than buying the freehold – a long lease for all practical purposes will probably be just as valuable. Although the image is helpful, the analogy is not entirely accurate, since a freehold should last forever whereas copyright in most cases expires 70 years after the author's death. While the copyright lasts, however, a full assignment of it is the closest to a freehold a purchaser can get. And an assignment is generally irrevocable, while a licence can usually be revoked (for example for breach of its terms).

If a full assignment of copyright is needed, remember that in order to be effective under the 1988 Act it must be *in writing*, and *signed* by or on behalf of the copyright owner. Do not assume that just because an assignment letter has been sent off to the author a valid assignment has somehow magically taken place – it hasn't. Copyright will not be assigned until the author or their representative actually signs the document.

Sole and exclusive licences

If you grant someone the 'sole' right and licence to do something you are undertaking not to grant a similar licence to anyone else but you are not necessarily ruling out the possibility that you may continue to do it yourself (although this has usually been implied). An 'exclusive' licence, on the other hand, is now defined under the 1988 Act and clearly excludes not only other potential licensees but also the person granting the licence. An author granting both a sole and an exclusive licence to a publisher is therefore granting complete control of all the publishing activities listed. It is by far the most powerful right to have, short of a complete assignment, and under the 1988 Act gives such licensees the same rights and remedies against copyright infringers as if they were full assignees (we will look at remedies further in chapter 8). Like assignments, however, exclusive licences must be in writing and signed by or on behalf of the licensor.

Scope of the licence

The activities licensed

In the process of publishing, the publisher will need to do a number of things which UK law treats as 'restricted acts', and which may only be done with the copyright owner's licence or permission. We will look at restricted acts more fully in chapter 8, but for present purposes a publishing licence needs to include at least:

- the right to 'produce' (which would cover copying); and
- the right to 'publish' (perhaps self-evidently – this would cover issuing copies to the public)

and also the right to sub-license others to do the same. The right to make an 'adaptation' may also be needed, if for example translation rights are included. It is important that the licence should cover not only the Work as a whole, but also any 'substantial part' of the Work since otherwise this may also be a copyright infringement. Again, we will discuss this more fully in chapter 8.

There are other restricted acts, such as public performance and broadcast of the work which are normally covered – if appropriate – under subsidiary rights (see below, p. 84).

Formats

The licence may cover 'all forms and media', which although not very specific at least makes the intention clear, or it may be restricted to 'volume' form only. 'Volume' rights normally include all the publisher's own hardback and paperback editions, including promotional, mail order and premium sales and book club sales, together with royalty inclusive export sales of bound copies or sheets. Although there is no unanimously agreed definition of volume rights, the term quite probably also includes anthology, digest book condensation, and picturisation book rights, and may include other rights too which relate to exploitation of the book as a whole. One-shot periodical rights were expressly held to be included under a grant of volume rights in *Jonathan Cape Ltd v. Consolidated Press Ltd* (1954), where a substantially complete work was published in a single issue of *The Australian Women's Weekly* without the consent of the publisher, Jonathan Cape, who owned the volume rights. If the entire work is published, the fact that it appears in non-book format does not of itself prevent publication from being in 'volume' form.

Volume rights do not include subsidiary rights such as serial rights or electronic or film rights, but these are often the subject of additional specific grants of rights under the royalties and subsidiary rights sections (see below, pp. 82 and 84). It is absolutely crucial to make sure that all the forms and media in which publication is envisaged are included somewhere and that the parties agree who has the right to exploit the work in which formats; translation rights may be vital to travel books, for example, and merchandising rights to childrens' books – neither of these are included in volume rights. Publishers with experienced rights managers are normally quite capable of exploiting such rights, but many agents prefer to retain them; it will be for the parties to decide who is best placed to control these rights. If in doubt, seek advice, or refer to Lynette Owen's indispensable guide: *Selling Rights*.

Languages

Licences often cover the English language only, or sometimes all languages. The restriction to English only would deprive the publisher of the right to publish (or more likely license) translations, unless translation rights are granted later on (see below, p. 86). As in 'formats' above, this should be clearly agreed.

Territories

Licences may be granted to publish worldwide (or preferably 'throughout the Universe', not in order to secure the Venusian and Martian rights – although doubtless that will come – but in order to remove any doubts about satellite broadcasting); alternatively they are often limited to specific territories of the world (often listed in a Schedule). It is entirely for the parties to agree who is best placed to exploit the Work in each part of the world – many publishers will have the capacity to exploit internationally, or the author or agent may prefer to retain some rights (for example North American or US rights) for themselves. Note, now, that exclusive UK rights are no longer exclusive if the rest of Europe (specifically, the EU and EEA) are open territories shared with other publishers: under the Free Movement of Goods Provisions in Article 30 of the Treaty of Rome (see chapter 12, p. 284) a US edition lawfully on sale in (say) Belgium cannot be prevented from entering the UK. There may be other territories whose local copyright laws might make exclusivity difficult to enforce, such as Australia: if these territories are likely to be important to you, it may be worth taking further advice.

Duration

Finally, it is very important to specify clearly for how long the licence granted lasts. Many publishers will seek a licence for the full term of copyright (now, in the EU, increased to 70 years after the author's death), and in the case of some works, especially textbooks or major reference works, the publishers may well need the life of several editions before the Work will truly come into profit. If the full term of copyright is agreed, it is advisable to include not only the current term, but also any extensions, renewals and revivals (on Duration generally, see chapter 2, p. 36).

Some Minimum Terms Agreements provide for a shorter licence period of, say, 20 or 30 years: 10-yearly reviews are fairly common. Again, it will be for the parties to agree what suits them (and that particular Work) best, but a publisher accepting a licence for a limited period should be aware of the risks of investing heavily in establishing a Work (and perhaps an author) only to find that the licence, or part of it such as the paperback rights, terminates after 10 or 20 years.

DELIVERY, APPROVAL AND ACCEPTANCE

Delivery of the Work is the author's primary responsibility under the contract, so the publisher will want to make sure:

- that it is actually delivered, and more or less on time;
- that, when it arrives, it accords with the contract;
- that any necessary revisions and improvements can be made, or – failing that – the contract can be terminated on a reasonable basis.

Equally, the author will want to see a fairly clear commitment to publish the Work if it is delivered substantially as per contract, and that if things do go wrong there is a reasonable agreement about any advances, and (particularly) that the rights can be reclaimed.

There are a number of other important considerations to bear in mind: not least, what amendments might be 'reasonable' in the light of what was agreed, and the author's moral rights, and how both author and publisher can disentangle themselves from the contract if the Work as originally agreed clearly isn't going to happen. We will explore all these tricky issues – and some possible solutions – in more detail in chapter 6, but when considering the contract wording itself, these are the points to bear in mind:

- In the event of a dispute, it is the wording of the contract which will prevail – so make it as clear and unambiguous as possible.
- Agree clearly the time and method of delivery (for example on disk) and what happens if it is late.
- If time is of the essence, say so: otherwise it is unlikely the publisher will be able to terminate the contract simply because the Work is not in bang on time.
- Agree in advance any acceptance criteria. Refer if possible to known yardsticks: a requirement that the work 'shall conform to a reasonable extent to the specifications set out in the Appendix' (or possibly the synopsis) is fairly easy to pin down in any subsequent dispute, but beware generalised phrases like 'of a standard which might reasonably be expected' (by whom?), or other question-begging adjectives such as 'acceptable' or 'satisfactory'.
- Agree a specific procedure and a timetable for any revisions, and do not forget that the author may have a moral right of integrity (see chapter 3, p. 48).
- Consider the effects of terminating the contract: will the publisher retain an option, and what happens to any advance? It is also advisable to make it clear if (and how) the rights are to revert to the author; reversion is implied when a contract containing a licence is terminated, but the rights will not necessarily revert where there was an assignment, unless there is clear provision for this (probably by means of a formal re-assignment).

COMPETING WORKS

Many publishers' contracts contain non-competition clauses under which the author promises as long as the contract lasts not to undertake any other works which might reasonably be considered either to compete directly with the contract Work or to 'affect prejudicially' its sales or other exploitation. These are often expressed to cover not only directly competing works, but also abridgements or expansions of the same material, if done without the publisher's consent. Such restrictions may be an understandable way of protecting the publisher's investment, particularly in the case of STM or professional textbooks or services, but they must not be drafted so widely that they would amount to a total ban on any further writing in the area: that would almost certainly be an unreasonable restraint of trade (see p. 269), which the courts would refuse to enforce. This will particularly be the case where the author is an acknowledged expert in the area concerned: such a ban might prevent the author not only from developing his or her reputation and career, but quite possibly from earning a living.

WARRANTIES AND INDEMNITIES

In publishing a work, a publisher takes a number of significant legal risks. If the Work contains statements defamatory of other people, the publisher will be liable legally for publishing them just as much as the author; equally, if any material is obscene, it is the publisher who will be prosecuted, for publishing an obscene article. There are a number of other legal risks, which we will discuss fully in chapters 7 and 8, and for this reason the publisher will normally require certain warranties and indemnities from the author to protect against them. This does not mean that the publisher should become complacent about the need for in-house vigilance and, if necessary, outside legal advice (such as libel reading), or the need for adequate insurance cover, but it is generally thought to be reasonable that the author (who after all knows the work better than anyone else) should either disclose any known risks or else warrant that the Work is safe to publish.

Which warranties are sought, and which are given, is of course a matter for the parties to agree. Many publishers' standard contracts contain full lists of warranties – an agent's contract may contain only one or two. However few or however many there are, they should all be taken seriously. Breach of a warranty will probably not entitle the publisher to terminate the contract altogether (see p. 238), but it will provide an action for damages, so together with the indemnities which are usually required each warranty should give the author pause for thought.

The warranties most commonly given are these:

That the author has full power to make the agreement

Not everyone has full legal capacity to enter into binding contracts – for example the mentally ill, children under 18, or those acting beyond their authority (for a full treatment see above, pp. 65–7). The author's warranty on this point will give the publisher some protection against the risk of the contract subsequently being declared void.

That the author is a qualifying person

Following the 1988 Act it is now common to seek a warranty that the author is at the material time a 'qualifying person' under section 154 of the Act. As we saw in chapter 2 (p. 34) the Work may qualify for copyright protection in the UK either on the basis of first publication here or in another qualifying country, or alternatively on the basis of the author's nationality or other status. Clearly, the place of publication is outside the author's control, but the author may be able to warrant that he or she is (for example) a British citizen or British subject, or domiciled or resident here, or a citizen of another EU member state: the full list of nationality and status qualifications is set out at pp. 34–5. For authors unfamiliar with section 154 (which is probably quite a few) it is often helpful to put the warranty in context by phrasing it thus: 'The author warrants that he/she is a British citizen, or is otherwise a qualifying person under section 154 of the 1988 Copyright Designs and Patents Act.'

That the author is the sole author of the Work, and owns the rights granted

It is important for a publisher that the author owns all the relevant rights, and that there are no rival claimants such as joint authors. As a general rule, you cannot grant rights you do not own (see p. 239).

That the Work is original to the author

A literary or artistic work will not be protected as a copyright work unless it is 'original'. Under UK law the standard of originality required is not very high (see chapter 2, p. 19), but there must be some evidence of skill and judgement, and individual effort. The author will not own the copyright unless that effort is his or her own effort – if anyone else's effort is involved there may be joint authors, or possibly a claim for copyright infringement (see below).

That the Work has not previously been published, or any of the rights previously assigned or licensed

As we saw in chapter 2, first publication can be one basis for copyright protection, so it is important to know that there will be no rival claims from any previous publications. The warranty against previous publication is usually limited to the territories covered by the agreement, and often to the specific formats covered (such as volume form) although sometimes it covers any forms.

It will also be important to the publisher to know that an assignment or exclusive licence has not previously been diluted by the grant of some particular rights elsewhere: for example US rights or French language rights. Such previous grants or licences will normally survive any new agreement, and the new publisher's licence will be subject to them. So if it turns out that US rights have already been granted elsewhere, the new publisher will not have worldwide rights after all, but only worldwide rights minus the US rights previously granted. Authors (and agents) are usually therefore asked to warrant that no such previous grants have taken place.

That the Work does not infringe any existing copyright or other right

Since printing and issuing copies of a work to the public may be just as much a copyright infringement as copying, the publisher will be just as much at risk of any legal action as the author: this is therefore a fairly crucial warranty to seek. Ideally it should cover not only copyright infringement as such but also infringements of any other rights of third parties, which would include for example any breaches of the terms of any previous licence, or contract, or any breaches of confidentiality, or moral rights, or any trade mark infringement.

That it contains nothing defamatory (or libellous)

This is a key warranty, and possibly now the most important of all, if only because of the recent huge damages awarded for libel by some juries (although these are now beginning to come down – see chapter 7, p. 160). As with copyright infringement, the publisher will be equally at risk with the author for publishing any defamatory statement, and so indeed might anyone else involved in the publication, such as editors or even printers and distributors (although in some cases there may be a defence of innocent dissemination). Defamation (which includes libel) is therefore a very serious risk indeed and should be actively borne in mind at all stages by author and publisher alike. A (relatively) sober reading of chapter 7 might be a useful starting point. Above all, if either of them has any reason to suspect that a particular passage may be defamatory – the author when writing, or the editor when editing – it cannot be stressed too strongly that the safest policy is to *tell someone*. If there is any doubt, it may make sense to have some passages (or the whole Work) read for libel by a lawyer who knows about such things, and share the cost if appropriate. It is *infinitely* better to do this at an early stage than to run the risk of going ahead regardless and hoping no-one will notice. They (or their lawyers) always do. Defamatory statements, like viruses, can be dealt with if caught early enough, but once they are published, that is that: the damage is done.

Is it reasonable that the author should bear the risk? The author knows better than anyone else whether (and where) there might be defamatory passages and is in the best possible position to do something about them. If they are not disclosed at the outset then it seems fair for the author to bear the resulting legal risk. Some agents' agreements and Minimum Terms Agreements seek to limit the author's liability to passages 'unknown to the publishers' – this very significantly dilutes the value of the author's warranty, and rather begs the question: 'When?'. There might well be an argument for sharing the risk if a libel is disclosed during the course of writing, or at least between delivery and proofs – when it still might be said the publisher has a realistic opportunity to do something about it – but if a libel only comes to light after the Work has gone for press it may be thought that the author, not the publisher, should bear the risk.

It is, of course, possible to insure against the risk of libel (and other associated risks such as malicious falsehood), and many publishers now have comprehensive libel policies. It is also possible in some cases to add specific authors to the policy as co-insured. However, insurance premiums are increasingly expensive, and the level of cover is usually subject to a substantial excess and may not cover the largest awards. It seems likely that an author's warranty will be required for some time to come.

That it contains no obscene, blasphemous or otherwise unlawful material

Obscenity, like defamation, is a real risk in publishing and is not solely restricted to illustrated sex manuals: text can be obscene if it encourages drugs, or violence, for example, and the criminal penalties, including fines and imprisonment, can be severe (see chapter 7). Consider also the risk of publishing 'indecent' material, particularly photographs of children. Blasphemy is still an offence – so be careful what you say about Jesus Christ – and there are other possible offences such as seditious libels, incitement to racial hatred, or offences under the Official Secrets Acts which may well pose a serious legal threat to a published work. All these topics are dealt with fully in chapter 7.

That all statements are true and that no formula, recipe or instruction will harm the user

This is a fairly wide-ranging warranty, but is particularly common in contracts relating to STM and consumer books. The warranty is normally restricted to all statements 'purporting to be facts' but is still quite a wide guarantee; authors often insert a proviso 'to the best of their knowledge and belief'. This is a less all-embracing warranty, but may be more acceptable in some circumstances: it still gives the publisher some reassurance that the author will at least have checked. Similarly, there is usually a proviso that the warranty will only apply to recipes, formulae or instructions 'if followed accurately'.

The warranties given are normally accompanied by an indemnity, under which the author undertakes to indemnify the publishers against any legal actions or claims, including associated costs and expenses, caused by breach of any of the warranties given. Many contracts also provide for costs associated with claimed (as opposed to actual, or proved) breaches, which may equally involve significant costs and possibly out-of-court settlements. This may require some discussion between authors and publishers, since there may be cases where credible *prima facie* claims are made – but not proved – which the author may wish strenuously to resist but which the publisher (who has a publication to get out) will want to settle as quickly and cheaply as possible. It may also be a condition of some insurance policies – such as libel insurance – that the underwriter's views on whether to settle should prevail. Authors may feel that their publishers should defend them – and their honour – to the hilt in such circumstances, but sooner or later more commercial considerations may well prevail.

It is usually wise to make express provision for alterations to be made on the advice of the publisher's legal advisers.

Finally, it is important that any warranties and indemnities should last for as long as the legal risks may continue to exist – which may be long after the book has gone out of print or the agreement itself has terminated. A sentence or a clause to the effect that the warranties and indemnities 'shall survive the termination of this agreement' will achieve this.

THE PUBLISHER'S RESPONSIBILITY TO PUBLISH

If the author's main responsibility under the contract is to deliver the Work, the publisher's is to publish it (at their expense). A legal commitment to publish may arise even out of an informal, verbal contract (see *Malcolm v. OUP* above, p. 62) but it is better to have it in writing if possible. Most authors, for obvious reasons, will look for such a written commitment before signing a publishing contract, although there may be circumstances in which author and publisher agree that the work will be delivered but not considered for publication until some later date – such agreements are probably not publishing agreements at all, but merely options.

Where a firm undertaking to publish is given, it is normal to include a proviso that this shall be unless prevented by circumstances beyond the publisher's control (to allow for events such as war, fire, flood or terrorist attack). A contract for a tie-in publication linked to a specific event, such as a royal wedding, might also have a proviso giving the publisher the option not to publish if the event is called off – the payment clause, including the terms of any advances, will need to provide for this.

A crucial issue may be whether the publisher undertakes to publish within a particular time-scale, and if so when. Topicality may be a key issue not only for current affairs publications but also for many professional or scientific texts, where the area covered is constantly changing (the law is a good example). On the other hand, the publisher will want some reasonable flexibility to launch new works at optimum times, and also to allow for necessary changes to the publishing programme. Twelve or 18 months from delivery (and perhaps 'acceptance' – see above, p. 74) are both common undertakings, sometimes with a maximum period running from the date of the contract. Phrases not linked to any specific timetable, such as 'with reasonable promptitude' or (worse) 'within a reasonable period of acceptance' are not generally of very much effect, and it may be advisable to include a provision for the author to put the publisher on notice to publish after the author considers a 'reasonable period' has elapsed and terminate the contract and reclaim the rights if publication does not then take place within, say, 6 to 9 months.

PERMISSIONS, ILLUSTRATIONS AND INDEX

Most publishing contracts contain provisions covering the inclusion of necessary extra materials, such as quoted extracts or illustrations, which the author may have taken from elsewhere and copyright in which is likely to be owned by other people. It is absolutely essential to make sure that copyright permission to reproduce such material is obtained before publication, and preferably before the work is delivered, otherwise there may be a serious risk of copyright infringement (although defences such as Fair Dealing may sometimes be available for quoted extracts – see chapter 8).

It is equally important to ensure that the permission given actually covers all the formats, territories and languages in which the publisher is proposing (or at least realistically intends) to exploit the Work – the wording of any permission obtained should therefore follow as closely as possible the wording of the author's own grant of rights to the publisher (see above, p. 71). With some copyright owners, this may require some negotiation, so allow plenty of time. If the permission offered falls short of what is required – a picture agency may only be prepared to grant rights to reproduce a painting or a photograph in certain territories or in English-language editions, for example – then both author and publisher may need to reconsider whether that material can be used at all. It is not enough to write off to the copyright owners and then simply assume that permission will be given in due course: copyright owners are not obliged to license their material for use by others if they do not wish to. Bear in mind also that many permissions may extend only to one edition of the work – if a second edition is planned, it may be necessary to renew the permissions.

Responsibility for arranging and paying for permissions is almost always the author's, although this is entirely a matter for agreement, and in appropriate cases (such as major works) the publisher will often share the cost or sometimes take over the responsibility altogether.

As to indexes, many authors prefer to do their own, but good indexing is a professional skill in itself, and a tired author is not always the best indexer. Where the index is particularly important to the success of the work (as for example with a major work of reference) the contract should provide expressly for the kind of index required, when it should be supplied and who should do the work (and – if an outside indexer is required – who should pay their fee).

PRODUCTION, PROMOTION AND PROOFS

All matters relating to physical production, promotion, and sale of the work are normally reserved for the publisher's sole discretion and control, although in many cases a publisher will be willing to consult authors on matters of taste or style such as illustrations or jacket design. The key commercial issue of the price is usually for the publisher alone to decide, although the author may wish to be consulted on this as well as on the publication date itself, perhaps with a provision that the publisher's decision shall be final or that consent will not unreasonably be withheld.

Editorial changes to the work itself (beyond 'house-style' amendments already agreed, or specified in the contract) may not normally be made without the author's consent, particularly if they might amount to derogatory treatment and thus infringe the author's moral right of integrity (see chapter 3, p. 48). Publishers will usually provide proofs, but will want an undertaking from the author that they will be returned within a reasonable time (14 or 21 days are typical) and, if not (if the author is away, or ill, for example), that the publishers may pass them for press themselves.

Alterations to proofs above an agreed level (usually 10 to 15 per cent of the cost of composition) are usually charged to the author or deducted from royalties.

ROYALTIES AND ADVANCES

As we have seen, unless a contract is made under seal, or executed as a Deed, it must be supported by valuable 'consideration' (see above, p. 61). Although the publisher's undertaking to publish may in some circumstances count as adequate consideration the consideration most authors want to see is money. This may be in the form of a one-off fee (a frequent method of payment for commissioned work) but is more often expressed as a royalty on sales. This has the advantage for the publisher of minimising the upfront risk (if no sales are made, no royalties will be paid) and it has the potential advantage for the author of a direct financial link with any success the work might have: the better it sells, the greater the rewards the author will get (particularly if the royalty rate itself increases, via a sliding scale). There is often provision for a payment on account, in the form of an advance.

Needless to say, money can be a fertile source of author–publisher disputes (particularly where the contract is not as clear as it should be) but it is beyond the scope of a book like this to suggest financial terms; such commercial issues are matters for the parties to negotiate, in circumstances which may vary widely. From a purely legal point of view, there are perhaps only two golden rules:

- Be sure both sides fully understand all the terms being proposed (including the likely effect of discounts, and the meaning of phrases like 'net receipts').
- Be absolutely clear about what is finally agreed.

For good specialist commentaries see Charles Clark's *Publishing Agreements* or Lynette Owen's *Selling Rights*.

Issues which tend to crop up most frequently include the following:

Advances

Publishers are not legally obliged to give advances (unless they have contracted to do so, of course) but many do. They are normally regarded as payments on account of future royalty earnings, and are recoupable from the author's royalty account in due course; a large advance may therefore take some time to be earned back, before positive royalties start being paid – 50 per cent of the author's anticipated royalty earnings from the publisher's first printing is not untypical, although of course they vary widely depending on the type of publication, the status of the author and the presence or absence of a literary agent.

It is advisable to make it clear in the agreement whether outstanding advances already paid are to be repaid by the author if, for example, the work is never delivered (or is delivered but rejected) or in some cases as a prerequisite to reversion of rights. There will be greater pressure for outstanding sums to be repaid where termination is perceived to be the author's fault, and perhaps less if termination is the fault of the publisher: for example by allowing the work to go out of print or following some other breach of contract.

The editions covered

Make sure *all* likely editions are covered somewhere. The most common categories for volume sales are:

- *'Home' full-price hardback* – the publisher's own hardback. 'Home' may mean the UK and Ireland, or possibly now the EU and EEA (see p. 284). This is the 'base royalty' and is often calculated on a sliding scale.
- *Home cheap hardback* – a publisher's hardback at two-thirds or less of the full price: usually with a lower royalty.
- *Home trade paperback* – the publisher's own paperback: royalties are normally lower, but print-runs can be much higher. Again, sliding scales might apply.
- *Home mass-market paperback* – either issued by the publishers or licensed to a paperback house – smaller format, lower price, and even lower royalties – but even bigger print-runs. The author's consent may be required for this kind of sale, perhaps not unreasonably to be withheld.
- *Export editions* – export versions of all four home categories above – often sold at discounts of 50 per cent or more, and with correspondingly lower royalty rates.
- *Small reprints* – usually 1,000 to 1,500 or less (or 5,000 to 7,500 for paperbacks). Since small reprints are often uneconomic, the publisher often reserves the right to offer a lower royalty – often the lowest of the above rates. In order to prevent regular small reprinting, some contracts provide that the publisher may only do this once in any 12-month period, and not less than two years after publication.
- *Promotional and premium sales* – special editions, often under a different imprint, as part of someone else's promotion or special offer: this could mean cornflake packets, so the quantities may be high but royalties will be at low rates. The author may have strong views about this kind of sale: prior consent is advisable.
- *Book club sales* – normally regarded as 'volume' sales, although not usually in the publisher's imprint. Discounts given to book clubs can be very high

indeed, but they are generally felt to be a positive extension to the publisher's own market. Authors may well have views about book club editions, and consent (or at least prior consultation) is often written into the contract.

The author's moral right of integrity (see p. 48) should also be taken into account, since book clubs may wish not only to provide editions of the complete work, but also digest or condense it with a relatively free hand. It is therefore not uncommon for book club clauses to contain either an express consent to such treatment, or a partial waiver of the author's right of integrity (or at least an agreement to waive the right in the future) insofar as it becomes necessary in order for the publisher to exploit the book club rights effectively.

The basis of royalty calculation

It is essential to be clear in the contract how each given royalty percentage is calculated: are home hardback sales at 10 per cent (say) based on the UK published price, or are they 10 per cent of the net receipts (which normally means income actually received, that is net of any discount)? This can make a large difference to the sums the author will get if a significant proportion of the publisher's sales are likely to be at high discounts. Export sales are often at 60 per cent to 70 per cent discounts: bear this in mind if, say, the US market is going to be important. Equally important: is Europe home or export? Home sales may often also be at comparatively high discounts, if via major chains of bookshops: 50 per cent to 60 per cent is not unusual (although the average trade discount in the UK is probably closer to 35 per cent or 40 per cent). Mail-order sales are usually at no discount at all (so a net receipts calculation might make little difference).

Both publisher and author need to be clear about the likely markets and the probable basis of sales to each; it is infinitely better to sit down and talk about it, and eliminate any misunderstanding, at the outset, rather than wait for unpleasant surprises in the first royalty statement.

Free copies

Royalties are not usually paid on copies given away in the interests of promoting the work (such as review copies), or lost or damaged copies.

SUBSIDIARY RIGHTS

What are they?

Non-volume rights, such as TV or merchandising rights, are usually grouped together in a publishing contract under the generic heading of 'Subsidiary Rights'. A typical full list is given below. The division is not very precise, and many of the rights (such as book club rights) may appear confusingly under both volume and subsidiary rights: perhaps the most useful distinction to keep in mind is that, generally speaking:

- Volume rights license the publisher's own publishing.
- Subsidiary rights give the publisher the right to sub-license exploitation by others.

So, in the case of book club rights, the publisher might want both: the right to sell copies directly to a book club at a price per copy, and also the right to license a book club to prepare its own edition, usually for a royalty.

The grant of rights

As with the main grant of rights clause (see above, p. 71) the first and most important thing to check in a subsidiary rights clause is: does it actually grant the rights required? This may be crucial, because the main *grant* of rights clause may cover volume rights only, and may make no mention of subsidiary rights – so unless the particular rights the publisher wants are separately granted here, the publisher may not get them. The actual words 'the Author hereby grants' (the rights concerned) should ideally appear, preferably shortly followed by 'to the Publisher'. Simply listing some subsidiary rights, with some agreed percentages, may not be enough (although a limited grant of rights may be implied).

Ensure that the rights are granted in the correct terms – so that they cover the required territories, languages (where appropriate) and period of time, and (crucially) that they are expressly stated to be 'exclusive' if that is what author and publisher want. A grant of right will be regarded as *non*-exclusive unless it is expressly stated to be exclusive (and signed by the author).

Author's consent

Some grants of subsidiary rights may be conditional upon the publisher first securing the author's consent before exploitation can take place, or at least consulting him or her; this may apply to the whole list of rights, or be a specific requirement of certain rights only – book club, digest and condensation rights are frequent examples. To get round the publisher's need to do some deals quickly in the author's absence, some contracts require consent only 'wherever practicable'; in other cases, where the author is available but they can't agree, there may be a provision that the author's consent 'shall not unreasonably be withheld'. Ultimately, it is a question of bargaining position, and who wants to retain effective control – and who is best qualified to use it.

Waivers of moral rights

Contracts now often include a conditional waiver of the author's moral right of integrity (or an agreement to waive it in the future), insofar as it may be required in order to exploit the subsidiary rights. Book club sales often require this flexibility: so also do film and multimedia deals. See pp. 127 and 131, and on moral rights generally, see chapter 3.

The list of rights

Subsidiary rights most frequently dealt with include the following:

- *First serial rights*: the right to publish an extract or series of extracts in a newspaper or magazine before (or commencing before) publication – these can be extremely valuable, both to sales of the work and to the circulations of the periodicals concerned, and are often optioned.
- *Second and subsequent serial rights*: serial rights *after* publication has taken place – these are normally less valuable.
- *Anthology and quotation rights*: some quotations may count as fair dealing for the purposes of criticism and review, if accompanied by sufficient acknowledgement, and copyright permission need not therefore be sought (see chapter 8) – these rights cover all other substantial quotations and extracts.
- *Digest rights/digest book condensation rights*: these are, respectively, the right to publish an abridgement of the work in a single issue of a newspaper or periodical, and the right to publish an abridgement in separate volume form. They are sometimes grouped together under 'Condensation Rights', for both magazines and books.
- *One-shot periodical rights*: the right to publish the complete work in a single issue of a newspaper or periodical. These are also now regarded as part of volume rights, following *Jonathan Cape Ltd v. Consolidated Press Ltd* (1954) (see above, p. 73).
- *Licensed paperback rights*: for paperback editions sub-licensed to another publisher.
- *Hardcover and educational reprint rights*: the rights to publish straight hardback reprints (in someone else's library series, for example) and educational reprints, usually annotated.
- *Book club rights*: (see p. 115, and for dealings with book clubs, see p. 117).
- *US rights*: the USA may be a major market: these rights may be sold directly or via an agent. They will usually take the form of a straightforward licence to publish, for a royalty on the US price plus – usually – an advance, or will accompany a sale of bound stock or sheets (or a co-edition) and be dealt with under volume rights (see pp. 73–4). Permissions may need to be re-cleared for US editions (see p. 81).
- *Strip cartoon rights*: the right to make such visual adaptations may be highly valuable, particularly for childrens' books.
- *Translation rights*: these may be licensed separately, or accompany a co-

edition deal for bound copies in the foreign language concerned: in either case, the foreign publisher will be responsible for arranging a translation of a satisfactory standard, and will normally pay an advance and a royalty (see chapter 5, p. 118). Note that the territories covered should be made clear: a Portuguese translation may sell more copies in Brazil than in Portugal.

- *Dramatisation and documentary rights*: usually cover theatrical, radio and TV rights to the work in dramatised form.
- *Single-voice readings*: the right to read extracts directly from the work, either on radio or TV or as part of other public performances. *A Book at Bedtime* is a good example.
- *Film rights*: if Hollywood is likely to be interested, it is important to ensure that these rights are effectively exploited. The publisher may be best placed to do this, or the author or agent may wish to reserve these rights themselves (for exploitation of film rights, see chapter 5, p. 124).
- *Audio and video rights*: audio cassettes, often spoken by famous actors, are a growing market. Video rights are often dealt with separately from the film rights. These rights are often combined under the heading 'Mechanical Reproduction Rights' and may include CDs, tapes and those strange black vinyl things we used to buy called gramophone records. Given the speed with which formats are replaced nowadays, such clauses now usually extend the right not only to formats known at the time but also to those 'hereafter invented'.
- *Merchandising rights*: the right to exploit titles or characters from a successful work can be as profitable, if not more profitable, than the work itself. It is therefore worth making sure that these rights are included, particularly for childrens' books. They are often associated with film rights; indeed, merchandising rights achieved some kind of apotheosis in the film of *Jurassic Park* when the T-shirts and other merchandise actually featured in the film itself. On exploitation of merchandising rights, see chapter 5, pp. Titles, logos and characters with merchandising potential should also normally be registered as registered trade marks (see chapter 9).
- *Electronic publishing rights*: information, professional and database publishing via CD-ROM might be a key element of the market: there may also be potential for on-line services. In consumer, educational and reference publishing there may also be multimedia potential. Publishers initially tended to license such rights to others, and negotiate a deal with the author at the time: nowadays more publishers are exploiting such rights themselves or entering directly into joint ventures, for example with software or film companies. Arguably, therefore, these rights should often now be covered under volume rights as well, if they are to form part of the publisher's exploitation of the work. However, it probably does not make much difference, as long as they are covered somewhere.

The term 'Electronic Rights' has no special meaning, and in order to ensure that the rights you want are included it is advisable to define the term so as to include any particular rights required: multimedia is an obvious example. The split of proceeds with the author is normally left to be agreed at the time: author consent may therefore be crucial, as may regard for the author's moral rights, particularly of integrity and paternity (unless these have been waived). This form of exploitation is discussed more fully in the next chapter (pp. 127–33).

- *Reprographic reproduction rights*: photocopying is still a fertile source of copyright infringement in the UK, but collective licensing schemes run by bodies such as the Copyright Licensing Agency are now more widely available.
- *Non-commercial rights for the print-handicapped*: Braille, or tape (or computer) recorded copies for the Royal National Institute for the Blind and other registered handicapped users, are normally licensed free of charge by the publisher.

All other rights are reserved

Any rights not expressly set out in the agreement are normally taken to be retained by the author: there is often an express provision making this clear. This will include Public Lending Right, which under the Public Lending Right Act 1979 is given solely to the author (on PLR generally, see p. 54).

SALES STATEMENTS, ACCOUNTING AND VAT

Publishers' royalty statements have been the subject of grim humour for as long as anyone can remember, but most publishers now have computerised royalty systems to keep track of royalties and other rights revenue and most now pay their authors twice a year rather than the traditional annual payment. Educational and academic publishers still tend to pay annually, however, as do some professional imprints. Payment – when it comes – should normally be no longer than three months after the relevant accounting date (usually 30 June and/or 31 December).

Small credits, say £50.00 or less, are often carried over to the next accounting period. It is also common for the publisher to keep a reserve against returns – stock apparently 'sold' to bookshops, but then returned under normal sale or return terms later on. 10 per cent to 20 per cent is not unusual, and some reserves can be as high as 30 per cent. However, there is often provision, particularly in agents' contracts and Minimum Terms Agreements, that any significant subsidiary rights revenue should be paid out as agreed to the Author within 30 days of receipt, provided any advance has been earned back.

Royalty statements themselves should be as clear and informative (and accurate) as possible: if the contract does not specify the standard of information to be supplied, there is now a Publishers' Association/Society of Authors Model Royalty Statement for guidance.

With the best will in the world, however, computer errors can still occur (as anyone who has a bank account will know) so most contracts provide that the Author – or his or her appointed representative – may examine the Publisher's accounts in person during normal business hours. Who bears the costs of this normally depends on whether, and to what extent, errors are actually found.

Authors who are registered for VAT will be required to notify the Publishers and supply them with their VAT number: by agreement with Customs & Excise (who collect VAT) royalty statements can be treated as the author's tax invoices and VAT is added in the normal way.

COPYRIGHT

Where the Author assigns the full copyright to the Publisher, this should be set out in clear wording under the main grant of rights clause (see above, p. 71). But even where the Author retains the copyright, this should still be made clear here, and some special words are still advisable. As we have seen (above, p. 15) the Berne Convention forbids formal registration requirements of any kind, but it is still a requirement for copyright protection under the Universal Copyright Convention (UCC) that a copyright claim should be printed on all copies of the work, containing the following information:

- The letter C in a circle (©) now a worldwide copyright symbol.
- The name of the copyright owner.
- The year of first publication.

There is no stipulation in the Convention that the information should be printed in any particular order but it is customary to print it thus:

© Hugh Jones 1996

The word 'copyright' is sometimes also printed before the ©, although this is not strictly necessary.

UK works have carried the UCC symbol for many years, because prior to its joining the Berne Convention in 1989 the USA belonged to the UCC but not Berne: the printed notice above was therefore essential to secure copyright protection in the USA. Since 1989 this has no longer been necessary for US protection, but there are still some countries which belong only to the UCC and UK works should therefore keep the notice. It is also convenient to combine it with any assertion of the author's moral right of paternity (see p. 46), and a contractual undertaking to print such an assertion is now common. For the fullest protection of the right of paternity it is also advisable to include a term to the effect that such assertions will also be a condition of any sub-licences.

COPYRIGHT INFRINGEMENT

We will deal with this more fully in chapter 8: suffice it to say here that the publisher will necessarily bear the burden of protecting the work, once published, against pirates and other copyright infringers around the world, and where the author retains the copyright will therefore need clear authority from the author, as copyright owner, to do so. Exclusive licensees under the 1988 Act have the right to take legal action and join the copyright owner as a party to any action (on giving an indemnity against costs), but it is still advisable to confirm this in the contract. It also gives the author and publisher the opportunity to agree on the practical control of any such legal action (including the terms of any compromise or settlement), whether the author is required in any way to contribute to the costs, and if so whether the author will receive a corresponding share of any net damages.

AUTHOR'S COPIES

Most publishers will give authors at least six personal copies of their works, plus one or two copies of each sub-licensed edition (such as translations or US editions). Some are more generous than others. Additional copies, not for resale, are usually available at normal trade discounts (but like any trade customer, the author may need to haggle over these).

REVISION OF THE WORK

With some kinds of works, such as educational, professional and reference texts, keeping the work up to date once published is almost as important as publishing it in the first place. In such cases author contracts will usually contain a clause requiring the author to prepare new editions when they become necessary. It is prudent also to give the publisher the option of commissioning some other (competent) person to do the work of updating, should the author be unwilling or unable to do so (for example, through illness or death). The fees payable to such persons will then be deducted from the royalties payable to the author, or the author's estate – quite reasonably.

Who decides when new editions are required? This may be an important issue, and it is worth checking the wording of the contract to see what it says. Often the decision is for the publisher alone to make, or sometimes dependent upon mutual agreement – the author is unlikely to be in a position to insist. This perhaps is fair enough (it would be unreasonable to force a publisher to publish against its will and arguably unenforceable anyway) but if more regular new editions (or a more flexible system) are likely to be needed this should be agreed at the outset.

REMAINDERS

Remaindering is a sensitive issue, but most publishers know when a book has ceased to have any further sales potential and may want the power to remainder their remaining stock. Some agents' contracts forbid this within a specified period without the author's prior written consent: where this is not practicable it may be equally effective to ensure that, while the publisher retains the option to remainder, the author will at least have (say) 30 days' notice, and the right to purchase part or all of the remaining stock at the remainder price (which will probably be fairly low). Publishers should bear in mind that such a clause is fully enforceable, like any other clause of the contract, so if they fail to notify the author and remainder the book regardless they may face an action for damages for breach of contract. This was confirmed in one recent case, where a lecturer won damages against Cassell for breach of such a clause, on the grounds that she had been deprived of the (very real) chance to sell the books cheaply herself to her own students.

TERMINATION OF THE CONTRACT, AND REVERSION OF RIGHTS

Just as it is essential that rights granted should be granted for a specific period of time, so it is equally important that any grounds for early termination should be clearly set out. In the early clauses governing delivery and acceptance (see above, p. 74) the publisher is normally given grounds for termination of the contract if the work does not come in at all, or is unacceptable when it does – it is therefore in the author's interests to have similar grounds for termination if the *publisher* breaches any terms of the contract later on – for example, by not paying royalties on time, or allowing the work to go out of print.

All rights granted should revert to the author (in the case of an assignment of copyright, there may need to be specific provisions for formal re-assignment). Reversion is usually without prejudice to any sub-licences or other contracts properly entered into while the agreement was in force, or any outstanding claims or monies owing.

The most common grounds for termination and reversion are:

- Material breach by the publishers of any terms of the contract, and failure to remedy the breach within a specified period (1 to 3 months is normal).
- Insolvency of the publisher's business (or a substantial part of it) – including administration, receivership, winding-up and (in some cases) arrangements with creditors.
- Failure by the publishers to keep the work from going out of print (and failure to reprint after a given period of notice). It is important to agree what 'out of print' means – is this in the UK or in all editions worldwide?

OPTIONS

There is a school of thought that no option clause is enforceable. This is not strictly true – but a future option for no fixed consideration ('on terms to be agreed', for example) may be difficult to enforce. Generally speaking, the more specific the option, the easier it will be to enforce legally. A sweeping option over the author's next six works may be extremely difficult to enforce, and may well be in restraint of trade if it unduly restricts the author's future writing (see above, p. 75), but an option on the next one or two defined works (of fiction, say, or for children) and on specified terms (such as 'the same terms', or 'terms no less favourable') may well be enforceable and bind the author.

It makes sense to provide a clear timetable for the publishers to exercise the option, and provide for the author's freedom to go elsewhere if they do not (or if they cannot agree terms).

MORAL RIGHTS

This may be a suitable place to include an assertion of the author's moral right of paternity, as required under section 78 of the 1988 Act. The paternity right – the right to be credited as the author – is the only moral right which needs to be asserted under UK law before it can be enforced: on this generally, see chapter 3, pp. 46–7.

AGENCY

Where an author is represented by a literary agent, the agent's standard contract will usually contain a clause authorising the agent to receive all monies payable under the contract on behalf of the author. Since authors and agents do occasionally fall out, it should also specifically provide that payment to the agent would be a good and valid discharge of the debt – so that the publisher, having paid royalties to the agent in good faith, will not then get embroiled in arguments about payment of the agent's commission later on. It is not generally necessary or advisable to sign an 'irrevocable' appointment or authorisation: if an author wishes to revoke that particular payment arrangement, and be paid direct, he or she should be perfectly entitled to do so. There may then be a separate contractual dispute between author and agent about the agent's commission, but there is no reason why the publisher should become involved in that. There is a long-standing trade practice among literary agents that an agent will expect commission on *all* monies payable to the author under contracts which that agent negotiated – even long after the agent's appointment has been terminated. Such matters are entirely dependent on the author's contract with the agent: see chapter 5, pp. 140–1.

RESERVATION OF TITLE

Although this is implied, it is advisable to make it clear that no rights or licences or other interests are granted to the publisher other than those specifically set out and granted in the contract. A provision to this effect is often usefully included at the end of subsidiary rights clauses.

ASSIGNMENT OR NON-ASSIGNMENT

Many agents' contracts contain non-assignment clauses, which forbid any assignment of the benefit and burden of the contract to any third party without the author's consent: sometimes (and in some Minimum Terms Agreements) the objection is waived in the case of third parties who are at the same time acquiring the whole or a substantial part of the publisher's business. Non-assignment clauses may seriously restrict the future value of the rights granted, and the publisher's capacity to deal with them commercially, and should be carefully considered. The (significant) implications are discussed above, at p. 69.

ARBITRATION

Many publishing contracts contain provisions for arbitration in the event of any disputes. It is important to recognise that in general such clauses will survive the termination of the contract – so that both author and publisher will continue to be bound by an arbitration clause, even after the contract itself has come to an end. If one party unilaterally terminates the contract, the other party may (equally unilaterally) invoke the arbitration clause. Both parties should therefore consider how they would actually want any disputes to be resolved before agreeing to such a clause.

There are a number of arbitration methods. In some cases each party will appoint their own arbitrator, and agree to be bound by the decision of those two people, or (if they cannot agree either) a third arbitrator who they appoint (called their 'referee' or 'umpire'). Where the dispute can be reduced to written submissions, without any (or much) need for oral hearings, such arbitrations can be relatively quick and inexpensive. A full-scale arbitration under the Arbitration Acts 1950–79 (as amended) including hearings with lawyers on both sides, can however be just as expensive as a High Court action – indeed, more so, since the parties will have to pay for the arbitrators whereas judges are free. The UK arbitration statutes are being revised. It is expected that a replacement Act will be enacted during the course of 1996.

The Publishers Association offers a quick and inexpensive Informal Dispute Settlement scheme, but there is no industry-wide arbitration scheme for publishing as a whole; perhaps following UK implementation of the Duration Directive (see chapter 2, p. 37) this may shortly need to be reconsidered.

GOVERNING LAW AND JURISDICTION

It is essential to make it clear which country's laws will govern the interpretation and enforcement of the contract. For most UK publishing contracts it will be advisable for this to be English law: note that Scots law is a separate legal system and may require separate advice.

Bear in mind that a contract offered by a foreign publisher is likely to specify their law as the applicable law – in the case of a US co-edition, for example, this may mean that the relevant state law (such as Delaware, or New York) will govern the contract, and any disputes arising under it.

If no applicable law is specified in the contract itself, there are statutory rules which UK courts will apply. As a general rule, they will apply the law with which the contract is most closely connected: in the context of publishing contracts this will usually mean the law of the party who is primarily to perform the contract. In the case of contracts entered into since 1991, if the contract is entered into in the course of a trade or profession, it is presumed that it is

> most closely connected with the country where the party who is to effect the performance which is characteristic of the contract has, at the time of conclusion of the contract, [its] . . . principal place of business

(or, if the contract is to be effected through a secondary place of business, *that* place of business). If the contract is for a UK based publisher to (say) supply sheet stock to New York, UK law will prevail. If it is for the New York based publisher to perform, New York State law will apply.

It is important to note that whose law applies is a different issue to whose courts have jurisdiction to hear the case. UK courts regularly hear cases involving issues of New York or other foreign laws. A good contract should always therefore provide for whose courts will have jurisdiction, and in most cases preferably UK (or English) courts. In the absence of any express provision, there are complex rules governing the right of UK courts to assume jurisdiction over a dispute. These vary, depending among other things on whether the defendant is based inside or outside the EU.

STAMP DUTY

An assignment of copyright and an irrevocable grant of an exclusive licence, are both normally liable to UK stamp duty at the standard rate, if the value of the transaction is for £60,000 (currently) or more – if the value is below that level, it is necessary to include at the end of the contract a clause in approved form saying so.

Stamp duty is not however normally payable on revocable, or non-exclusive, grants or licences, or where the value cannot be ascertained at the time the contract was signed (as may often be the case with uncertain future royalties). In cases of doubt, specialist advice should be sought.

Other contracts

5

ACADEMIC/PROFESSIONAL/STM AUTHORS

CONTRACTS FOR SPECIALISTS

Some authors (lucky things) write for a living: many authors earn their living primarily doing other things, but can sometimes be encouraged (or provoked) into writing on topics connected with their work or their research. Increasingly now their writing will be published in electronic form as well as (or instead of) the traditional hard copy formats. They are often experts in their fields, with established (often international) reputations, and their names as authors, or as members of an editorial team, will sell all kinds of publications and services to what are often highly profitable specialist markets. Even if they are not all yet acknowledged experts, they are all specialists. The works they create tend to have distinctive features, and these need to be reflected in the publishing contracts which they sign. We will highlight these features in this section: bear in mind, however, that most of the general legal principles set out in chapter 4 will still apply as well.

For convenience, we will use the abbreviation 'specialist works' throughout this section to refer to all academic, professional or STM works, and we will call their authors 'specialist authors'.

COPYRIGHT: TEAMS AND INSTITUTIONS

Specialist works are often highly detailed and complex, and may require contributions from several different authors: indeed, a major work may need hundreds of contributors all over the world and an international editorial board. More straightforwardly, two colleagues may co-author a text, or jointly write up some research. At both ends of the scale, it is equally important:

- to ensure that *all* those involved in the project are under contract;

- to be clear who is doing what;
- to agree who owns the copyright (and other rights) in all the work(s) which result;
- to make sure that the publication envisaged is fully licensed by all those owners.

To make absolutely sure, a publisher investing in a major project may wish to take a full assignment of copyright from all the contributors involved (including editors): such assignments will give the publisher complete control of the material, but they must be in writing and signed by or on behalf of each contributor (see above, p. 72). The contributors may in some cases be allowed to re-use their material elsewhere, but it is advisable to confirm the details of this at the same time. In other cases a sole and exclusive publishing licence may be sufficient, (provided it is wide enough to cover all forms of exploitation envisaged), but it is still essential to make sure that all the relevant copyrights and other rights are covered by the licence(s) given, so that no rights will be infringed.

Copyright

Depending on the publication, a number of different copyright works might be created, including a range of literary, artistic and other works: for the full list, see chapter 2, (pp. 27–8). As well as the obvious ones, such as text and illustrations, do not forget copyright in any overall compilation, and also – if it is available electronically – copyright in any computer software. All these copyrights will probably be owned by the people who created the works, but with specialist writing or research teams there may be joint authors to consider (p. 29) – if there is a risk they might fall out, it may be advisable to legislate for this in the contract since as joint authors neither will have the right to publish (or license) the work without the consent of the other. Also, it may well be that some of the employee authors will have created the works in the course of their employment, in which case their employer (which may be their university, or company) might own copyright in the works they create, not them (pp. 32–3). They might also, of course, have been persuaded to assign their copyright to the institution or company concerned, and some institutions such as universities are increasingly requiring this.

Other rights

With collaborative works, there may be issues of confidentiality to consider – if draft research findings (say) are circulated confidentially, it may be a breach of a duty of confidence to publish them without consent (see p. 5). Such a duty might be owed to a fellow researcher, or to an institute or other employer.

Also, for material created after 1 August 1989, do not overlook authors' moral rights, which are likely to be more than usually significant for specialist writing, where academic or professional reputations are at stake. Moral rights may not apply to certain 'collective works' such as dictionaries and encyclopaedias (see pp. 47 and 52), but if they do there will be at least three moral rights to consider:

- the right for each author to be identified (this right must be specifically asserted);
- their right to object to derogatory treatment of their work (especially if editorial changes are planned);
- the right to prevent false attribution.

(For moral rights generally, see pp. 44–54.) These rights may not apply to any acts done with the author's (or in some cases, the copyright owner's) consent, and will also not apply where the rights have been waived. For smaller contributions, or for major works, complete waivers may be appropriate – for others, it may be necessary to rely on partial waivers or contractual consents.

WARRANTIES

For specialist works, these may need revising to take account of joint authorship, or limiting to the author's particular *contributions* to the work, rather than the work as a whole – clearly a specialist author cannot be expected to make warranties about other people's work. However, the personal warranty against plagiarism which amounts to copyright infringement may be particularly important in an academic work, and the warranty against libel may prove useful to protect the publisher against academic vendettas carried on in the footnotes.

The warranties should ideally also include negligent mis-statement (although negligence will be hard to prove (see p. 250)) and should cover statements of fact, and the reliability and safety of formulae or instructions. It may also be advisable to require the author to provide for safety warnings, to put users on notice of any hazards arising out of dangerous experiments or procedures, and refer to any appropriate safety precautions or standards or codes of practice.

Some specialist authors may only feel able to warrant that statements of fact are true 'to the best of their knowledge' – the publisher may be willing to accept this risk, particularly if adequate insurance is in place. On warranties generally, see pp. 76–80.

QUOTATIONS, ILLUSTRATIONS AND PERMISSIONS

These are likely to be important in all specialist works, particularly source books or anthologies. Some quotations may freely be used, if they count as fair dealing for the purposes of criticism or review (see chapter 8, pp. 200–1), but otherwise permission to reproduce all quoted extracts and illustrations must be obtained from the copyright owners. Most publishers will place responsibility for this – including paying any permissions fees – on the author, but for a major project where permissions are likely to be a significant item, the publishers may be willing (in fact, may prefer) to arrange this themselves.

Where the author is responsible for permissions, it may be advisable to specify an agreed financial limit. It is also advisable for the publisher to have copies of any permissions correspondence, for future reference.

CORRECTIONS

In specialist works, last-minute corrections may be essential to take account of recent research or knowledge, or legal or technical changes. The work may be unsaleable without them, if it becomes dangerously unreliable or out of date. It is advisable for the publisher to be alerted well in advance if there is a risk of significant corrections. It is also important to agree who will pay for them, otherwise the authors may find themselves paying substantial sums for dealing with changes which the book needs, but which were totally outside their control.

ROYALTIES AND FEES

One-off fees may be more appropriate for a multi-author work, or where the copyright is assigned: many specialist authors are happy to write for money upfront (or at least on delivery and acceptance), especially where there is some academic or professional kudos involved as well. The timing of the fee payment may be crucial – most contributors will prefer to be paid when they have delivered their own work, and not wait until the last (and slowest) contribution comes in, still less until publication. Advance payments may get round this problem. There should also be provision for fee payments if for some reason the project collapses and the work is never published.

Consider, also, any reprints or further exploitation of the work, and whether further fees or royalties may be appropriate then, if the contribution is a significant proportion of the whole work (or the part of it to be exploited). If the material later proves suitable for electronic delivery, or multimedia exploitation, the contract will need to allow room for a suitable new payment structure for such use in due course. Ideally, this should allow for exploitation by the publishers themselves, as well as any exploitation sub-licensed to others (see further, on this, pp. 84–8).

Another factor to consider in contracts for specialist works is the need to phase out royalty payments in a realistic manner where an original author or editor retires or dies. In order to keep the work up-to-date, and maintain its reputation against rivals, it will be necessary for co-authors to take over, or for new editors to be brought in, and to be paid at realistic rates. As they prune old text and contribute new original material of their own, each edition or update for which they are responsible will contain a smaller and smaller proportion of the original author's copyright material, so it is reasonable that the royalty rates payable to the author or author's estate should decline also. Many specialist contracts now provide for the original author's royalties to continue for one, or perhaps two, further editions but then to cease; an alternative method is to agree a gradually declining percentage, over perhaps three or four editions.

REVISIONS

A publisher who has taken full assignments of copyright will normally have complete freedom to revise and update a work, although in many cases the publisher will still prefer to give the author first option to make any revisions. The fact that the publisher owns the copyright will normally mean that the author's moral right of integrity will also not apply to any changes the publisher authorises unless the author is identified, and then not if there is a sufficient disclaimer. In the case of a publishing licence, however, this will probably not be the case, and provision should be made in the contract for revised editions. In any event, many specialist authors will want to retain at least a first option to make any required revisions themselves.

COMPETING WORKS

Non-competition clauses may have particular significance for specialist authors whose reputations often depend on their writing. They must not be drafted so widely as to amount to an unreasonable restraint of trade (see p. 269) and specialist authors must not be so prevented from writing in their own field that they cannot develop their work properly or earn a living. If such clauses are to be enforceable, it is advisable to be as clear as possible about the level of competition restricted: a blanket ban on a whole subject is unlikely to be upheld, but directly competing works at the same level in the same market may well be prevented. To avoid any doubt, it may help to list some or all of the activities which *may* be undertaken, such as journal articles, conference papers or anthologies.

REMAINDERS

As we saw in the last chapter (p. 91) the courts are willing to enforce an author's contractual right to be consulted before any remaindering. Where the contract contains such a right, damages may be payable to an academic author (for example) who could have sold the remaining copies to students had he or she known the remaindering was about to take place.

GENERAL EDITORS

DON'T FORGET THE EDITOR

As we saw in the last section, major projects often require whole teams of contributors, and the General Editor – there usually is one – will probably be a contributor too. He or she will probably need a quite different type of contract from that of the typical contributor, however, because there are two quite different legal matters to sort out:

- the Editor's practical duties and responsibilities in relation to the team and the project as a whole;
- the Editor's rights (including copyright) in the material produced, and any associated warranties or liabilities.

COMMISSIONING AND DELIVERY

It is essential that the publisher and the Editor should agree on the scope of the Editor's role, and set this out as clearly as possible in their contract. Does the Editor commission the work – and the contributors – from scratch, or is the publisher doing this? If the Editor does it, it will be advisable for the agreement to settle:

- the overall scope of the work, including length and schedule;
- the management of contributors, and responsibility for ensuring each of them is put under contract with the publisher;
- any responsibility the Editor has for negotiating fees or other payments and budgets for these;
- who is responsible for clearing and paying for permissions;
- the Editor's duty to review and edit each contribution, and powers of acceptance, amendment or rejection;
- who decides on any extra text (is this entirely at the Editor's discretion, or only as necessary in the publisher's opinion?)

The schedule itself is (of course) usually crucial – note that time will not normally be regarded as being of the essence unless the Editor's contract (and those of contributors) expressly makes it so.

COPYRIGHT AND MORAL RIGHTS

The Editor is likely to own copyright in:

- his or her own contributions as a contributor;
- any other original material he or she creates (such as introductions, forewords and so forth);
- the overall scheme and plan of the work as a whole, as a compilation.

If the Editor does the work, and creates the works in the scope of employment (by a university or research institute, for example) it may well be that the employer will own the copyright – in which case any publishing contract should be with them (but preferably including the Editor in his or her personal capacity too). The publisher may wish to secure a full assignment of all the relevant copyrights – in which case this should be in writing and signed by or on behalf of the assignor – or a sole and exclusive licence in terms wide enough to cover all forms and media envisaged.

The Editor is likely to have the same statutory moral rights as individual contributors over his or her work. Unless one or other of the exceptions applies (see chapter 3, pp. 47 and 52) these are likely to include the right to be credited as the Editor (this right must be specifically asserted), the right to object to derogatory treatment, and the right to prevent false attribution. These rights may not be assigned but they may be waived. On waiver, and moral rights generally, see chapter 3.

If the Editor is responsible for procuring assignments of copyright and waivers of moral rights from contributors, the contract should make this clear, although it will probably be more appropriate for the publisher to negotiate for these.

WARRANTIES

The publisher will want the usual warranties (see pp. 76–80), covering at least the Editor's own contributions, and (crucially) any amendments, alterations or additions which are made to contributor's text or other material. It is important that there should be no gaps in libel cover (for example) – libels can be introduced just as much by editorial additions (or deletions) as by original text.

CORRECTIONS

Does the Editor get an extra correction allowance, or is there one overall percentage? Ideally, the Editor will share with the publisher the responsibility for keeping corrections under control.

BUDGET, FEES AND EXPENSES

All fees and other expenses payable to the Editor, or on his or her behalf, should be settled at the outset. These may include royalty payments (and any advances) or fees, and also any honorarium. In particular a budget for expenses such as travel expenses should be agreed, and any overheads such as secretarial support.

It may be advisable to clarify in the agreement whether the Editor has any responsibility at all for negotiating fees with contributors (or even paying them) and if not to confirm that the publisher will do this, and hold the Editor harmless against any liability for such payments.

REVISIONS AND NEW EDITIONS

It is desirable to agree who initiates these, and what happens if publisher and Editor cannot agree. If the Editor is unwilling or unable to edit a revision or new edition, the publisher will need the right to bring in someone else and pay them for the work they do out of any royalties or fees which might otherwise have been paid to the Editor, or the Editor's estate.

Remember that any moral right of integrity (to object to derogatory treatment) the Editor might have, and which has not been waived, will last for as long as the work remains in copyright, as will the Editor's right of paternity (to be credited as the editor). In the event of a dispute, the converse right – to prevent false attribution – might also be important, and may stop the publisher putting out a new edition under the Editor's name if it contains substantial amounts of material which the Editor did not write or of which the Editor disapproves. This right lasts for 20 years after the Editor's death.

CONTRIBUTORS (COMMISSIONED TEXT)

WRITING TO ORDER

Commissioned writing has distinctive features which any contract will need to reflect, but it is otherwise substantially the same as any other original writing. Contrary to what many people think, the copyright position is now fundamentally the same as well. Much of what was said in chapter 4 about author–publisher agreements will thus apply here too, as will the comments about specialist authors at the beginning of this chapter.

DELIVERY AND ACCEPTANCE

Where a project depends on many contributions, the schedule and delivery requirements for each one are likely to be much less flexible. Time may well be of the essence (if so, this must be expressly stated), and if on the due date the contributor shows no fairly immediate prospect of delivering, the Editor and the publisher will probably want the option of cancelling the contract and re-commissioning the work from someone else, rather than jeopardise the whole project by waiting.

There should be provision for what happens if the contribution is delivered but is unacceptable. Most General Editors will want considerable freedom in such circumstances to require alterations, or reject the contribution altogether – this should be agreed in advance, and set out in the contract. It is common in contributors' contracts for the work – if it comes in at all – to be accepted for one edition only. This is probably no worse than the position most authors are in, and if different teams seem to make more sense on future editions there will be no inconvenient long-term commitments to get in the way. If a contributor is dropped, there should of course be appropriate arrangements for reversion or re-assignment of his or her rights.

EDITORIAL CHANGES AND MORAL RIGHTS

It is important to agree in the contract whether and how far the Editor can make the editorial changes which the Editor may consider necessary, since these may well involve quite heavy revisions in the interests of uniformity or overall style. Although for some projects it may be appropriate to have a proviso that no substantial alterations may be made without the contributor's prior written approval, it is probably more usual for the Editor to be given a completely free hand.

In these circumstances it is essential either to secure a full waiver of the contributor's moral rights, or at least to include a clear consent to such alterations in the contract (since moral rights will not apply to any acts which are done with the author's consent). Otherwise there will be a danger that significant editorial changes to the contribution may amount to derogatory treatment, and thus infringe the contributor's moral rights (unless one of the 'collective work' exceptions applies – on all this generally, see chapter 3, pp. 47 and 52).

The contributor's moral right of paternity – to be credited as the author – will not apply unless the contributor specifically asserts it.

COPYRIGHT

Generally speaking, the fact that text is commissioned makes no difference to copyright ownership in it (which is normally vested in the author). There were some limited provisions relating to commissioned artistic works prior to 1989 (see pp. 31–2 below) but these have never extended to literary works. So the author of commissioned text will almost certainly own the copyright, unless:

- there are joint authors;
- the author is an employee, and wrote the work in the course of that employment.

These exceptions, and copyright generally, are dealt with fully in chapter 2, at pp. 29 and 32.

Whoever owns the copyright, the publisher will want to secure a sufficient grant of exclusive publishing rights to cover all likely exploitation of the work, and probably – in the case of commissioned text – a full assignment of the copyright. If a full copyright assignment is required it must be in writing and signed by or on behalf of the copyright owner in order to be effective.

Not all contributors will be willing to assign copyright in their work, so a publisher embarking on a major project would be well advised to raise the question with each contributor at an early stage and not, for example, leave exchange of formal commissioning letters until right at the end, when it may be too late to re-commission someone else. Without a signed written assignment, the publisher will not acquire the copyright, and indeed if there is no agreement at all the best that the publisher will get is an implied non-exclusive publishing licence, probably for one edition only.

If a contributor is unwilling to assign his or her copyright, the publisher will need to decide whether that particular contributor is crucial to the project, and if so whether a sole and exclusive licence will suffice. In that case, it will be highly desirable for the publisher to obtain an undertaking that the contributor will not assign the copyright elsewhere without giving the assignee written notice of the publisher's exclusive licence.

WARRANTIES

The usual warranties will be needed (see above, p. 76) but relating of course only to that contributor's particular contribution(s). The warranties that the work is original, and contains nothing defamatory, are particularly important. In the case of scientific or technical material, the warranties may also need to cover safety warnings, and reference to appropriate codes and standards.

ILLUSTRATIONS AND PERMISSIONS

In the case of contributors writing text to order, so to speak, it is important to be clear about any other, non-text, material which may also be required and which the contributor might wrongly assume is being commissioned by the publisher from somewhere else. This would include not only quoted text, illustrations and photographs, but also charts, graphs, diagrams and maps. If these are not created by the contributor, and they are still in copyright, then permission to reproduce them will be needed from the copyright owners, and the contract will need to specify who is responsible for getting those permissions and who pays for them.

PROOFS

It is not uncommon for the contract to give the Editor the right to correct and pass proofs on the contributor's behalf if the schedule requires this.

FEES

It is customary for a one-off fee payment to cover all uses of the work, and all future exploitation, but it is advisable to check this. If the contract refers to existing formats and media only, or is not clear on the point, it may be necessary to agree additional fees later on for any new forms of exploitation which subsequently appear (see p. 98). Recent arrivals such as multimedia are a good example.

CONTRIBUTORS (ILLUSTRATIONS AND PHOTOGRAPHS)

ILLUSTRATED WORKS

The illustrations in some works can be more valuable than the words – indeed some publications (children's books, for example) might consist almost entirely of pictures. In such cases the illustrator will for contractual purposes become the primary author (and much of chapter 4 will apply) – in others, the publisher will probably need two separate contracts, with author and illustrator, reflecting the contribution the illustrator has made and granting the publisher the necessary rights in what the illustrator has produced.

DELIVERY AND ACCEPTANCE

Since so many decisions about illustrations are matters of suitability and taste, most delivery schedules allow for submission and approval of roughs, as well as finished artwork. If time is of the essence (if the illustrations are to form part of an encyclopaedia or medical text book on a tight schedule for instance) then this must be expressly stated in the contract.

It also makes sense to provide for the possibility that the illustrations when finally delivered will not be felt to be suitable after all, either by the author or editor (if he or she has a say in the matter) or by the publisher. A termination fee (known as a 'kill fee') is usually agreed in advance to cover such an eventuality. If rights are to revert to the illustrator, this should be made clear as well.

COPYRIGHT

Ownership

Illustrations of most kinds, including photographs and computer graphics, are defined as artistic works for copyright purposes, and are dealt with fully in chapter 2. As a general rule, for all artistic works created after 1 August 1989, the copyright is owned by the artist or photographer, unless one of the limited exceptions applies (such as employee works – see below). This is true whether the works are commissioned or not: there are no special provisions for commissioned works in the 1988 Act.

However, for certain kinds of commissioned artistic works created before the 1988 Act came into force, copyright may have been owned by the Commissioner. This applied to three kinds of artistic works only:

- commissioned photographs;
- commissioned portraits (painted or drawn);
- commissioned engravings.

The person commissioning such works made prior to 1 August 1989 would own the copyright, provided the work was actually made in response to that commission, and was paid for (or payment was at least agreed).

These exceptions do not apply to works created *after* 1989, but the general exception relating to employee works might still do so. It is important to remember, therefore, that an employed artist or illustrator (employed 'as part of the business', rather than a freelancer), and who creates artistic works *as part of* that employment, will probably not own copyright in those works – the employer will. Even where the artist does initially own the copyright, many employers later request an assignment of the copyright to them, so it is as well to check carefully with all employed contributors what the current copyright position regarding their work actually is.

Rights granted

Whoever owns the copyright, the publisher will want control of all the necessary publishing rights in order to exploit the work (or works) fully. It is not unusual for the publisher to ask the artist or illustrator for a full assignment of their copyright; if this is agreed it must be in writing, and signed by or on behalf of the artist. Where a licence only is granted, the publisher will want to make sure that this is a sole and exclusive licence, and is granted in terms wide enough to cover all the languages, territories, forms and media in which the works are likely to be exploited, and for the same period of time; ideally the grant of rights covering the illustrations should at least match that covering the text, so there are no gaps.

With illustrations (particularly characters) bear in mind any merchandising potential including sale of photographs as posters, animated cartoon, film and TV rights, and any possible video and multimedia exploitation. Are these characters or illustrations likely to have potential for interactive products such as CD-I and video games? If so, the parties should agree who will control the relevant rights: where the publisher is not clearly acquiring all rights, the rights which are included should be expressly listed.

Bear in mind also the desirability of registering characters and logos with merchandising potential as registered trade marks – and consider who should be the proprietor of the marks. For more on trade marks, see chapter 9.

OWNERSHIP OF ARTWORK

Do not forget that ownership of copyright in something is quite different from ownership of the physical material on which it is recorded. An illustrator may assign copyright in illustrations but still own the original artwork – which may of course have a substantial value of its own, for resale or exhibition purposes. When completed artwork or photographs are delivered, therefore, the publisher should remember that they are probably someone else's (valuable) property (unless of course the publisher already owned them, or has purchased them separately) and take reasonable care of them. It is also probably useful for publishers and illustrators to agree on a reasonable level of mutual access, so that the publisher can have access to the material for publicity or promotion purposes, even after it has been returned, and the artist can include the work if required in exhibitions. Particularly valuable artwork, or negatives, may need to be specially insured while under the publisher's control: if so, it will be necessary to agree a valuation, and decide who is paying the premium or whether this is to be shared.

MORAL RIGHTS

Although the four statutory moral rights included in the 1988 Act are often referred to as moral rights of authors, the word 'author' is used in its widest sense – they apply equally to artists and photographers. So, unless one of the exceptions applies (see below), a publisher needs to remember that illustrators will probably have:

- a right of paternity (to be credited as the artist/illustrator/photographer);
- a right of integrity (to object to derogatory treatment of the work);
- a right to prevent false attribution (not to be wrongly credited with other artists' work).

There is also a right of privacy in films and photographs commissioned for domestic purposes, which photographers and their publishers will need to bear in mind (see warranties below).

Moral rights and their implications are explained in greater detail in chapter 3. The first two moral rights will probably be of most immediate concern here; bear in mind that the right of paternity needs to be specifically 'asserted' before it can be enforced – this is usually most conveniently achieved by printed notice on the title pages. There may therefore be two (or more) separate copyright claims and assertions of paternity rights on the title pages, depending on how many authors and illustrators there are. Moral rights can be waived, however – so if the contributors have assigned their copyrights to the publisher and waived their moral rights the only name to appear may be the publisher's.

The right of integrity is fully discussed at pp. 48–52. As with written text, if editorial alterations are likely to be required, it is advisable to provide for this specifically in the contract, so as not to run any risk of infringing the illustrator's moral rights: under the 1988 Act the right of integrity is not infringed by anything done with the author's (or copyright owner's) consent. What are (or are not) reasonable amendments will vary; the right of paternity will not be infringed unless changes so drastic are made that they would prejudice the honour and reputation of the artist but reputations vary – a world-famous artist or photographer might have good grounds for objecting to even relatively minor alterations, or retouching or cropping, whereas with the work of a less well known freelancer editorial changes might have a less damaging effect. If in doubt, err on the safe side, and agree any appropriate level of changes in the contract.

The moral rights of paternity and integrity may not apply to commissioned artistic works made for the purpose of:

- reporting current events;
- publication in a newspaper, magazine or similar periodical;
- publication in an encyclopaedia, dictionary, year book or other collective work of reference.

WARRANTIES

The publisher will be looking for the usual warranties, such as those covering originality of the work (see above, p. 71); in the case of illustrations and photographs the warranty against obscenity might be particularly important, and should perhaps be coupled with a warranty against indecency (for the dangers of publishing indecent photographs, particularly of children, see chapter 7, pp. 181–2). Do not forget the importance of guarding against defamation, however, especially where recognisable likenesses of identifiable human beings are included: it may be advisable to ask an artist or photographer for an undertaking that they will secure a form of release, or written consent, from any such identifiable people.

FEES AND EXPENSES

If the agreed fee does not clearly cover exploitation in all forms and media, it may be necessary to agree additional fees for some kinds of exploitation which occur later on, such as merchandising or multimedia exploitation. It is also desirable to agree in advance how any extra payments are to be split between the author and illustrator if (as is likely) the words and illustrations are exploited together.

Expenses should also be clarified – for a major commissioned work the publisher may be willing to meet (allowed) expenses, but in general artists and illustrators are expected to meet the costs of materials and roughs and photographers are expected to pay for their own developing, printing and enlarging, and also for the hire of any studios, props or other equipment, as well as assistants and staff. If separate budgets need to be fixed for these items, this should be clearly agreed.

TRANSLATORS

TRANSLATORS AND TRANSLATIONS

A significant proportion of the works we want – or need – to read have to be translated from other languages, and this supports a substantial international trade in translation rights – for physics and accountancy textbooks as much as great literature. We shall look at translation rights contracts later, at pp. 118–20: in this section we will look first at the equally important contract with the translator (whose skill – or lack of it – can make or break a work).

COPYRIGHT AND TRANSLATIONS

Under UK law, if you translate someone's work into another language you are making an adaptation of that work. Since adaptation is one of the restricted acts which only copyright owners can do, or authorise (see chapter 8) you will need the copyright owner's permission, otherwise you will be in danger of infringing their copyright (for this reason, a translator might need some assurance that the publisher actually has the relevant translation rights, and may seek a warranty to cover this risk – see below).

At the same time, creating a translation (even an unauthorised one) creates a new original copyright work, and as with most copyright works – apart from employee works – the copyright in that is owned by the person who created it: in this case, the translator. A publisher commissioning a translation will not own the copyright simply by virtue of having commissioned the work – if the publisher wants to own the copyright, it will have to be assigned by the translator in a written, signed document. Publishers often do seek a full assignment of copyright, particularly for reference or STM works where there is a high risk of piracy – alternatively, they will need an exclusive licence in terms at least as wide as the translation rights deal.

Whether or not the translator retains the copyright, there will need to be two separate copyright claims on the title pages, one relating to the original work, the other covering the translation.

MORAL RIGHTS

Even if copyright has been assigned, it is important to remember that the translator may still have statutory moral rights – and so, indeed, may the original author. We will look at the two key rights below: see generally, on all this, chapter 3.

The right of paternity

This right – to be credited as the author – needs to be asserted before it can be enforced under UK law, and this limitation applies to the original (foreign) author's right as much as to the English translator's (even though the foreign author may not have needed to make any assertion in his or her own country). However, it is probably advisable to err on the safe side and credit both author and translator fully: most publishers will want to do this anyway.

The right does not apply to translations created in the course of employment, where the employer owns the copyright and has authorised the acts (or, presumably, omissions) complained of.

The right of integrity

Although a bad translation can do serious harm to an author's reputation, section 80 of the 1988 Act expressly excludes translations from the definition of a 'treatment' – so, by definition, even the most appalling translation cannot be a derogatory treatment of the original work under UK law (because it is not a treatment at all).

It *is* possible, however, to subject the translation itself to derogatory treatment, by making additions, deletions, alterations or adaptations which are bad enough to amount to 'distortion or mutilation', or are otherwise prejudicial to the honour or reputation of the translator. There are as yet no decided UK cases on this, and it may be that it will prove difficult in practice to satisfy a court that a publisher's alterations in this context are sufficiently bad to amount to derogatory treatment. Translators who have assigned their copyright will also have the difficulty that anything done with the consent of the copyright owner will not infringe the right of integrity unless the translator is identified, and then not if there is a sufficient disclaimer – there are also exceptions for works written for publication in newspapers, magazines or other periodicals, or in collective works such as encyclopaedias, dictionaries or year books (for a full list of exceptions, see chapter 3, p. 52).

DELIVERY AND ACCEPTANCE

One of the key undertakings a translator will be asked to make is to render a 'faithful and accurate' translation, not only in reasonably good and accurate English but also true to the style, spirit and character of the original work. This is usually accompanied by a specific undertaking to translate the whole work, and not to make any alterations, additions or omissions without the publisher's (and probably the original author's) consent.

Since the publisher is often required under the translation rights contract to submit the translation, or specimen sections of it, to the original foreign publisher for approval, there is usually a requirement to this effect in the translator's contract too. Given the difficulties of checking work in another language, the material may only be given a fairly cursory structural check, but the original author may be entitled under the contract (or under a more informal agreement resulting from the licensing correspondence) to examine the work and it is therefore advisable to allow a reasonable period of time for approval. Needless to say, it is also advisable to provide for what happens if amendments are required, and who pays for them, and also what happens if the translation for some reason is rejected altogether – specifically, do the rights in that particular translation revert to the translator (see below), and is he or she paid a proportion of the agreed fee, or merely allowed to keep any advances? All this should be spelt out as clearly as possible.

WARRANTIES

The publisher will want a warranty that the translator will not introduce any objectionable new material, particularly nothing that is defamatory, obscene or indecent or otherwise illegal, and nothing that infringes the copyright or other rights of anyone else. In return, the translator may often seek a counter-warranty and indemnity from the publisher that the original work being translated does not itself carry any such legal risks, since these would put the translator at risk too.

Since the work is not the publisher's own, any such warranties are unlikely to go beyond those given by the original publisher of the work, and the best warranty the publisher of the translation may feel able to give is 'to the best of the publisher's knowledge and belief'.

FEES

Fees – normally at a rate per thousand words – are more common than royalties, but translators are increasingly being regarded as secondary authors and in some cases a royalty may be more appropriate. Payment of fees is usually preferred on delivery – for obvious reasons – although the publisher may wish to hold some instalments of the payment back until final approval or even publication. Some payments might be made to the translator on signature of the contract, some on delivery and acceptance, and some on publication.

TERMINATION

Normal termination provisions will usually apply – on rejection, breach, or insolvency, for example (see p. 91) – but it is important to make clear what rights, if any, will revert to the translator in these circumstances. Since the publisher is likely to have exclusive translation rights for that work in a relevant language, then as long as those rights are still in force the publisher is not going to want the translator to publish or exploit the original translation or any part of it without its consent (particularly if it was rejected and the publisher has had to go to the trouble and expense of commissioning a new one).

SUBSIDIARY RIGHTS CONTRACTS

RIGHTS DEALS

As we saw in the last chapter, it may be important for a publisher to have the right not only to produce and publish the work itself, but also to sub-license others in different areas to do so too. There may be a market for a book club edition, or a Russian translation, or a film or TV version, in which case the relevant subsidiary rights will need to be licensed (see pp. 84–8). Indeed, the revenue from rights deals may well mean the difference between overall profit and loss for a publisher, and may even exceed that derived from the publisher's own editions. Some authors and agents will prefer to retain and exploit subsidiary rights – or some of them – themselves; in other cases a publisher with an experienced rights manager will probably prefer to control such exploitation itself (in which case the publisher must make sure it *has* the rights in the first place – see p. 84). Whoever ends up doing it would be well advised first to consult Lynette Owen's indispensable guide to *Selling Rights* (second edition, 1994, Blueprint).

In the rest of this section we will concentrate on the legal issues arising out of agreements for some of the key subsidiary rights.

PAPERBACK RIGHTS

In these days of 'vertical publishing', it is increasingly common for one publisher to undertake both hardback and paperback editions (although mass-market paperback rights may still be licensed to a separate paperback house). Not all publishers are in a position to undertake both, however, and sub-licensing paperback rights is still therefore a major business, at Frankfurt and elsewhere. In the case of authors with proven sales records, such as Jeffrey Archer, there may be a full-scale auction of the paperback rights, with considerable sums changing hands by way of advance.

Grant of rights

As with the original publisher's main grant of rights from the author (which must be checked: see p. 71), it is essential that the rights then granted by the original publisher to others – and their limitations – are clearly spelt out. The roles are of course reversed for such sub-licensing: the original publisher, having up till now been the author's (and others') licensee of the head rights, now becomes a licensor of individual subsidiary rights to others. The original publisher will usually now become 'the Grantor', and 'the Publisher' will now be the paperback publisher acquiring the rights.

The Publisher will almost certainly want exclusive rights to produce and publish the work in all paperback formats: if this is not possible, the Publisher will at least want to know which other paperback editions already exist, or are planned. Has the Grantor already published its own trade, or educational, paperback, or might it want to in the future? Is any book club edition (paperback or otherwise) licensed, or being planned? If any competing paperbacks exist (or might), a licence for 'all paperback editions' will not be possible and it will be advisable to specify as clearly as possible exactly which paperback rights are being granted. It may be necessary to refer to markets (such as mass-market) or to specific formats (such as A or B format). In the case of book club paperbacks, the publisher may wish to avoid possible conflict by seeking an undertaking from the Grantor that it will not license any such book club editions without the publisher's prior consent.

Although it is unlikely that a paperback publisher would acquire translation rights, the grant of rights should also specify the language(s) covered – English-language only, or in other (or all) languages – and the territories included – specific territories (such as the USA) or lists of territories (such as the former Commonwealth, which should be clearly set out, preferably in a Schedule) or the whole world. Any 'open' territories should also be carefully considered, bearing in mind the free movement of goods provisions of the EU, within Europe (see p. 284).

Duration and timing

Paperback licences are normally granted for a limited term rather than for the full term of copyright; it is therefore essential to specify what the term is going to be. Eight years is the most common period: in some cases, such as an encyclopaedia or dictionary, paperback rights are granted edition by edition. There is usually provision for renewal of the licence thereafter, on terms to be agreed.

It is also advisable to agree well in advance – and as clearly as possible – what the *timing* of the licensed paperback edition is going to be. Since the appearance of a cheaper paperback is bound to affect sales of the hardback, and other existing editions, it is normal to provide a breathing space of at least six months or a year before the paperback may be published: earliest and latest dates are often specified. There may also be external events to consider, such as film or TV tie-ins which may be a reason to allow for early release of the paperback with a tie-in cover.

Timing may be particularly crucial in the case of US paperback editions, whose larger home markets and print-runs may lead to highly competitive prices in a number of open markets around the world. Beware in particular of leaving Europe (specifically the EU and EEA) as an 'open' territory if you wish to retain UK exclusivity (see p. 284) and equally the problems of parallel importation into territories such as Australia: it may be worth the original publisher considering a simultaneous (or earlier) export edition of its own in order not to lose some open markets completely.

Finally, timing of an English language paperback may be highly relevant to markets which are already (or may be) served by a foreign-language translation: a Dutch or Japanese translation (for example) could be killed stone dead by the untimely appearance of an English paperback in either territory, since in both places English is widely spoken and read.

Warranties

Any warranties given by the grantor should ideally match those it has itself received from the author, although the new publisher will usually require a warranty that the work has not previously been published in a particular format in the territory concerned. If any new or additional warranties are required the grantor should carefully consider whether it is willing (or able) to bear the risk.

Alterations and permissions

Given that the author (probably) has a moral right of integrity, it is now even more important to keep amendments to the work itself under control; to be on the safe side, no abridgements, expansions or alterations to the work should be allowed without at least the Grantor's consent, and the author's consent (or waiver) may also be necessary in order to avoid any claim of derogatory treatment (see p. 48). Exceptions are sometimes allowed for alterations made on the advice of the paperback publisher's lawyers, on giving due notice to the Grantor (the Grantor – and its own lawyers – will then need to consider whether its own editions are at risk).

The Grantor may supply originals of artwork or prints, or other supplementary material, but it is vital to check that any original copyright permissions granted for this do actually extend to paperback publication in the territories covered: it may well be necessary to renew many (or even all) of the permissions, if they do not include the re-use of the material in sub-licensed editions.

Copyright and credits

The Grantor will want to ensure that its original copyright claim, including its name and the date of first publication, are included in all subsequent paperback editions (for UCC copyright notices, see p. 89). This is also an opportunity to ensure that the author's name appears in its customary form with due prominence, and (if appropriate) to include an assertion of the author's moral right of paternity, to be identified as the author (for the wording of assertions, see p. 46).

Royalties and accounts

The normal considerations will apply (see chapter 4, p. 82) although royalties under paperback licences are usually paid twice a year. A percentage of this (normally 50 per cent or more) will of course go to the author. It is common for a paperback publisher to wish to make some reserve against returns, and there may be a small reprint clause.

Termination and reversion

Apart from the normal termination provisions – for breach, or insolvency, for example – the Grantor will want the right to terminate the licence if the publisher allows the paperback edition to go out of print or fails to put it back on the market within, say, 9 or 12 months of formal notice to do so. Conversely, when the licence expires, or comes to an end for other reasons, the publisher will probably want a reasonable sell-off period to clear remaining stocks.

BOOK CLUB RIGHTS

Britain, like the USA, has a vigorous, healthy book club market, the larger clubs claiming well over a million members. The two largest book club groups, Book Club Associates (BCA) and Readers Union, each contain a large number of individual clubs, and there are also many other independent clubs: some of them are general book clubs such as BCA's Literary Guild, and others specialise in particular areas, such as the Mystery and Thriller Guild (BCA) and the Gardener's Book Society (Readers Union). All of them operate primarily by mail order. Members are regularly recruited via national press advertising, often being induced to join with loss-leading 'premium' offers of the 'four books for £1' variety, with in most cases a modest annual purchasing obligation thereafter.

Although the larger clubs will demand substantial discounts, there can be significant economies of scale on both sides: not only to the club's members, in reduced prices, but also to the licensing publisher, in increased print-runs and lower unit costs.

Such a large, distinct market, dominated by one or two major players, has obvious competition-law implications (see chapter 12) and indeed BCA and Leisure Circle were the subject of a Monopolies and Mergers Commission report in January 1988. The clubs have, however, by and large managed so far to remain within UK competition law by agreeing a measure of self-regulation. Prior to the demise of the Net Book Agreement, this was under Regulations and a Concordat supervised under the auspices of the Publishers Association: the current basis of regulation is unclear.

REGULATIONS FOR THE CONDUCT OF BOOK CLUBS

The latest (1985) Regulations applied only within the UK and only to titles the trade editions of which were published net (that is, within the Net Book Agreement). Sixteen UK book clubs were on the September 1995 Register, all of which had signed the Regulations, and agreed to be bound by them.

At the time of writing it seems likely that the present Regulations will be superseded, or replaced, although they may still provide useful guidelines to what the competition authorities are likely to accept.

Key regulations include the following:

- Book clubs must keep registers of members (going back at least 12 months) and must supply books only to those members, or to potential members applying to join.

- Clubs must have a minimum period of membership of not less than 6 months, and in most cases within the first year members must purchase not less than three club choices (excluding premiums). In fact, most clubs have a 1-year membership minimum, and require four 'positive options' in that period.
- Clubs must send details of forthcoming offers to the Publishers Association at least 4 months in advance, so that they may be published in the trade press.
- No title may be offered as a 'premium' until at least 6 months after trade publication, and no surplus stock may be remaindered without the publisher's consent.
- Club offers must always be in the club's own imprint, or using their crest or legend, unless:
  - (a) there is an insufficient supply, in which case up to 20 per cent of the total order may be filled by trade editions; or
  - (b) there is no exclusive licence, when the publisher may supply the club with up to 5,000 trade copies, or 50 per cent of the total trade print number, whichever is lower.
- Clubs must not indulge in unfair comparative advertising (for more on this see chapter 11): the only permitted comparisons are straightforward comparisons of price, and there must be no suggestion that the publisher's and book club editions are physically identical if they are not.

CONCORDAT BETWEEN BOOK CLUBS

In addition to the 1985 Regulations, a Concordat signed between the leading book clubs in 1983, and updated in 1988, encourages competition 'on an equitable basis'. It was not dependent in any way on the Net Book Agreement and at the time of writing remains fully in force. It facilitates reasonable access to titles by competing clubs (particularly smaller clubs), and provides for example that:

- No club will seek exclusive rights for more than 3 years or for an edition of less than 3,500 copies.
- No general club will attempt to deny titles of specialist interest to smaller clubs.
- No single club will attempt to obtain exclusive rights over complete categories of titles (such as atlases, dictionaries or year books).

LICENSING BOOK CLUB RIGHTS

Selling bound copies

Despite the considerable degree of self-regulation which surrounds book clubs in the UK, and the occasional attentions of the Office of Fair Trading, the larger clubs still undoubtably occupy a pre-eminent position and can command discounts from licensing publishers of well over 60 per cent – often as high as 75 per cent or even over 80 per cent. However, even these figures can make publishing sense, and publishers are not always negotiating at a disadvantage. The following licensing points should be borne in mind:

1 The Publishers Association recommends that relevant publishers should deal only with registered clubs, and the licence of book club rights should therefore specify that the club is so registered, or at least intends to comply with the book club regulations (see above).
2 If the club is to have an exclusive licence, it must order at least 3,500 copies.
3 No exclusive licence may last for longer than 3 years (although an initial exclusive licence may be extendable by a further non-exclusive licence).
4 Copies supplied as club editions must always be in the club's imprint, or carry its logo, unless either of the two exceptions contained in the Regulations (above, p. 115) applies.
5 Timing may very well be crucial: in which case time should be clearly stated to be of the essence. Publishers will normally be required to specify their own publication date. Any penalties for late delivery should be spelt out, and it should also be made clear at what point – if at all – the club has the right to cancel the order altogether.
6 The normal warranties and indemnities will apply (no copyright infringement, or defamation, for example) and the publisher must therefore make sure it has the necessary book club rights itself, and has re-cleared any permissions which do not already cover book club editions.
7 The book club is normally restricted from offering a title as a premium within a specified period, or from remaindering stock without consent: these may in fact take the form of mutual undertakings, since the club will also want some reassurance from the publisher that it will not have to compete with the publisher's own remainder stock during the period of the licence. The club may similarly seek an undertaking, if it is buying hardbacks, that the publisher will not publish a paperback within (say) one year.
8 The licence should normally provide for termination if the club exhausts its stock within the licence period and does not re-order.

Licensed reprints

As an alternative to buying bound copies, a club may prefer to take a reprint licence and manufacture its own stock (for use as a regular premium, for example). Such licences are again usually for fairly short fixed terms, and if exclusive may not be for longer than three years (see above, p. 116). There will be similar provisions to those listed above. Clubs usually pay an advance and the royalty is normally based on the club price.

TRANSLATION RIGHTS

Not all works have the potential to sell in translation, but many UK works do – non-fiction as well as fiction. For most UK publishers and agents, selling translation rights can therefore be a major source of revenue, and a significant way of extending the market for an author's work – for a definitive treatment, see Owen, *Selling Rights*. It can also be an effective way of combating unauthorised translations (including those given compulsory licences under some local copyright laws) and piracy of the English edition, in the territory concerned.

Not surprisingly, most publishers and agents who regularly sell translation rights will have one or more standard-form contracts, either for a straightforward sale of rights, or for a co-edition deal. We will deal here with sales of translation rights: co-edition deals are dealt with later at pp. 133.

Rights granted

Before translation rights are granted to others, it is highly advisable to check that the person who wants to grant them – usually the publisher, or the agent on the author's behalf – owns or controls them in the first place. You cannot legally give what you do not have. Publishers in particular often assume that they control foreign language translation rights when in fact their publishing licence from the author covers English-language volume rights only. If this happens, any accidental omissions can usually be remedied by a quick phone call to the author or agent and a simple exchange of letters, but this is not always possible. The author or agent may quite well have plans of their own, and indeed may already have sold the relevant rights to someone else. If in doubt, check.

Once the rights are secured, they will normally be sub-licensed to individual foreign publishers for separate languages and territories. Most local publishers will want exclusive rights in their territory; this is usually acceptable, provided that (within Europe) it does not fall foul of EU competition law (see pp. 278 and 284), and provided that the territory and formats covered are clearly defined, and also the length of time the licence lasts. Does a Portuguese translation licence cover the whole world (so that it may therefore sell in Brazil, and former colonies like Macau), or just Portugal itself? Does it cover hardbacks only, or paperback and book club editions, and even perhaps other forms of exploitation in that language such as merchandising or serial rights? Most importantly, how long does the licence last? Five to eight years is fairly common, depending on the work, and the local publisher's plans; licences are normally renewable thereafter. In the case of major reference works and non-fiction works which are likely to be revised, a grant of rights may extend to one edition only, rather than a fixed term of years. All rights not expressly granted should be reserved to the Proprietor.

Publisher's responsibility to publish

Once the rights are granted, the Proprietor will want to ensure that an accurate translation appears reasonably promptly. The local publisher is normally required to undertake that it will commission a faithful and accurate translation by a competent translator (from the original language, based on the latest edition, and with no unauthorised alterations, omissions or additions – see above, p. 110) and will publish it at its own risk and expense within a specified number of months. If publication does not take place within the given time-scale, the licence will normally terminate and the rights revert, so it is advisable to allow reasonable time for the translation itself (especially if approval is required) as well as local production. The Proprietor will normally wish to be informed of the actual publication date. To assist with production (and accuracy) the Proprietor may supply duplicate film, or otherwise may wish to see samples of any illustrations to be reproduced directly from the original edition in order to assess their quality.

Warranties

The local publisher will normally seek the standard warranties from the Proprietor: that the work is not, for example, an infringement of someone else's copyright and has not previously been published in that territory before – any warranties outside the Proprietor's own control should ideally match, and not exceed, those originally given by the author (see chapter 4, p. 76). The publisher may want the right (on notifying the Proprietors) to remove passages which on local legal advice may be actionable in the territory concerned.

Commissions and illustrations

Copyright permissions for extracts and illustrations may need to be re-sought for foreign language editions; it is important to agree who is going to undertake this (and who will pay any new fees). For a major work, it may be a complex and time consuming task, and the Proprietor may prefer to arrange it, and charge the publisher the cost, plus an administration fee. If the local publisher is going to do it, it may be advisable for the Proprietor to ask for written proof that it has been done.

Illustrations may present unique problems for foreign translations of children's books: pictures that are perfect for one country may not be acceptable in another (for example, on grounds of racial mix, or on moral, social or religious grounds). Some pictures may need to be omitted or replaced; in some cases, a complete set of fresh illustrations better adapted to the local market may need to be commissioned, in which case they will need to be costed in.

Copyright notice

As the making of a translation creates a new copyright work (see above, p. 109) there will normally be two separate copyright lines – one for the original author, or whoever now owns copyright in the original work, and one for the translator, or whoever owns copyright in the translation. The Proprietor will also probably require details to be included of the Proprietor's original edition, and when and where it was first published, so that it is clear the translation is an authorised arrangement.

In some territories, there may be local registration or other legal formalities before copyrights can be protected; it is important that the local publisher should be obliged to make the necessary arrangements, and also undertake to comply with any local copyright regulations.

Advance and royalties

Sometimes a lump sum fee is agreed for a limited print-run, but royalties on the local selling price are probably more common. An advance is normally required, with part at least of the payment due immediately on signature of the agreement; there is often a provision that if the agreement is not signed, and the first tranche of the advance paid, within a given period (such as 60 days), the licence will terminate and the rights revert to the Proprietor.

The usual detailed accounting information should be required (see above, p. 88), and it is also wise to agree the currency in which royalties are to be paid; not all local currencies are fully convertible, and payments in blocked currencies which cannot be sent outside the country concerned are of limited use to foreign rights owners (although they may be better than nothing).

Updates/new editions

The publisher will normally want an option on any new or revised editions, on the understanding that all changes notified will be incorporated.

Termination and reversion of rights

The normal provisions for termination of the licence will apply, for example for insolvency or breach (see above, p. 91) but special attention may need to be paid to the terms on which rights may revert if a translation goes out of print. Does 'out of print' mean only in the local publisher's home territory, or in all territories (so that a Spanish edition, say, might still be 'in print' if it is available in South America)? There may also be a need for a provision that the licence will terminate and rights will revert if sales of the translation fall below a certain minimum level in any single accounting period (or perhaps any two periods in succession).

MERCHANDISING RIGHTS

Some publications – particularly children's books – may contain names, characters, designs or illustrations which are popular enough in their own right to be exploited not only via the medium of books but also on T-shirts, stationery, mugs and other merchandise (hence the label 'merchandising rights'). Film and TV exposure usually helps. The characters of Beatrix Potter were early examples of successful merchandising, widely licensed now for a range of merchandise, such as children's crockery and other nursery goods; other examples are Jill Barklem's *Brambly Hedge* series, *Ninja Turtles*, and *Jurassic Park* (where the merchandise even featured in the film). If handled properly, such exploitation, across a wide range of goods, can add very considerably to the earning potential of the original work (and in some cases – such as *Batman* – exceed it).

Where a work has merchandising potential, the author or agent may grant the merchandising rights to the publisher, together with other publishing rights, or they may retain them for separate exploitation. Exploitation may be bit by bit, product by product, in which case the publisher or agent may end up dealing with multiple licences for a whole range of goods; alternatively (and increasingly nowadays) the rights might be licensed in one go to a specialist merchandising company who will then take on the task of seeking out, and sub-licensing, suitable manufacturers and products. Whoever handles the rights, there are a number of key points to bear in mind, two of the most important of which are:

- protection of rights;
- quality control.

Grant of rights

You can't grant merchandising rights if you don't own them or control them yourself. So the first and most essential thing to do is check the contract. If you are a publisher, check your author contract to see that it contains a specific grant of rights, or a clearly inclusive grant of rights such as 'all subsidiary rights' or 'any other rights'. If an author or agent, make sure that merchandising rights have not already been granted elsewhere. And if you want to use original illustrations as well as names of characters, make sure that the illustrator, or other rights owner, has granted you merchandising rights in them too (otherwise – if agreement cannot be reached – you may need to re-commission new illustrations).

Assuming – subject to all the above – that you do have the relevant rights, you will need to consider the terms on which you are going to sub-license them (or some of them) to others.

In particular:

- Will the rights granted be exclusive or non-exclusive? (This may depend on your view of the market, and the status of the particular licensee.)

- Will the licence cover the world, or a specific territory or territories? (Merchandising rights are often licensed country by country.)
- How long will the licence last? (Three or 5-year terms are common, usually renewable, and often with a sell-off period at the end.)

Product specifications and approval

Unless an overall licence is being granted, the products on which the names or images may be exploited by that licensee must be clearly specified and described in as much detail as possible (for example, T-shirts or breakfast crockery). They are usually set out in an appendix. Any products that the licensor wishes to exploit itself (such as videos, or electronic publishing and games) should be expressly reserved.

The licensee should have a clear obligation to seek out (actively) potential sub-licensees and in some cases distributors and propose the most suitable ones for particular products to the licensor; once selected, the licensee should be responsible for their regular supervision and control. All sub-licences should be in a form approved by the licensor, and should not exceed the term of the original licence. If there is not already an agreed plan, it is advisable in the interests of quality control to set out a regular procedure for submission and approval of product proposals, within set timetables. It should be clear that the products selected should in no way reflect adversely on the image, reputation or goodwill of the licensor, and the licensor should at all times retain a right of rejection or veto. This quality control should not only apply to initial prototypes or mock-ups and packaging, but also continue after the products have been launched, with regular samples submitted for approval, either at random, or on demand. The licensor needs to be satisfied at all times that the products are suitable in themselves, and manufactured to a high enough standard. They must also be safe; the licensee must take legal responsibility for any product liability, for example for defective goods, or for breach of any safety standards (and insure where necessary). Needless to say, once approved, there should be no changes without consent.

Promotion and marketing

The licence will normally specify merchandise to be on the market within a given timetable. There is often a launch deadline, within a given number of months or by a particular deadline (for example to tie in with a film or TV series). Thereafter, the licensee should undertake to continue advertising, marketing and distributing the licensed products within the Territory. All packaging and promotional material should conform to samples – the licensor may also wish to specify the choice of media used. It is customary for the licensee to undertake to sell only to reputable wholesalers or retail outlets, and the licensor may exclude certain kinds of sales (for example premium sales, or door to door) and retain the right to order the suspension of sales to any particular outlet of which it disapproves.

There will usually be agreed sales targets: quarterly targets are common. If targets are not met (sometimes two or more in succession) the licence will normally terminate, and the rights revert to the licensor.

Copyright and trade marks

The names, characters or illustrations being merchandised will probably be copyright works and quite possibly registered trade marks too (for more on trade marks, see chapter 9). It is essential in any merchandising licence that all these copyrights and trade marks should be expressly acknowledged and recognised by the licensee and on the products themselves. A copyright claim in agreed form, with the name of the copyright owner (see p. 89) should normally appear on all relevant products and packaging, and a trade mark notice, in the UK usually ® or ™, next to all words, phrases or logos which are registered trade marks. If the merchandising licence is for an overseas territory, it may be necessary to make the licensee responsible for registering any copyrights or trade marks locally – this should be done in the licensor's name, not the licensee's. The licensee may, however, need to be recorded as a licensee at the Trade Marks Registry and the parties may need to supply details of the licensing agreement.

In addition, of course, it is very likely that the product itself will constitute a new copyright work, in which case it will be desirable in order to avoid any conflict for the new copyright to be acquired from the manufacturer or designer and assigned back to the licensor; it will normally be the licensee's responsibility to see that this is done.

Infringements and insurance

It is customary to require the licensee to exercise vigilance on the licensor's or proprietor's behalf, against any unauthorised copying or use and notify any infringements at once so that any necessary legal action may be taken. The licensor will normally indemnify the licensee against any legal risks and costs arising from permitted use, provided any claims are notified at once, and the licensee will normally give a corresponding indemnity to the licensor for any activities outside the terms of the agreement. The licensee is normally well advised to arrange general liability insurance of its own, although mutual insurance, to spread the risk, is sometimes agreed.

Moral rights

Bear in mind that an illustrator might not only own copyright in original illustrations but also now have personal moral rights in them, particularly a right of paternity – to be credited as the illustrator – and a right of integrity – to object to derogatory treatment (see chapter 3). If the illustrator agrees, these rights may be waived, either unconditionally or insofar as necessary to exploit the particular merchandising rights concerned.

Royalties and commissions

There may be an initial one-off fee for permission to test the market over, say, a 1-year trial. Thereafter fees or royalties entirely depend on the popularity and marketability of the character, design or name being licensed: the range is normally between 5 per cent and 15 per cent of the invoice price, but higher commissions – up to 45 per cent, are not unknown for major licensees with a proven track record. Any percentage commission should cease with the end of the licence agreement.

Quarterly sales figures and accounts are usual – the normal requirements to keep accurate accounts, and inspection for errors, should apply. Payments should be made for all sales in the period, irrespective of whether the licensee has yet been paid.

Non-assignment, and key men

A merchandising licence is normally non-transferable and non-assignable, without the licensor's prior consent in writing. There is also often a stipulation (called a 'Key Man' clause) that the licence will end, and the rights revert, if any key individual within the licensee's organisation departs, or at least giving the licensor the option to terminate.

Termination

Termination is usually on the normal terms, for example, for breach or insolvency; merchandising licences may also terminate if a Key Man leaves the licensee, or there is any other unacceptable change in the control or management of the licensee.

On termination, the licensee should arrange the termination of any sub-licences, with due notice, and arrange for any samples, artwork or other materials to be returned and any unsold stock to be delivered up (usually at cost) or certified as destroyed. Needless to say, any outstanding payments should be paid forthwith.

FILM AND TV RIGHTS

Making a feature film or TV series is an immensely complex – and expensive – business, and negotiating rights with film and TV companies is not a recommended pastime for the faint hearted. For the right literary 'property', however, it can be a highly lucrative form of exploitation, not only in fees and royalties from the film itself but also in increased exposure and sales of the book.

This can happen years after publication: the 1980s TV serialisation of Evelyn Waugh's *Brideshead Revisited,* first published in 1945, and the more recent filming of Edith Wharton's turn of the century novels, were both good examples. Film and TV rights often therefore need long-term management, and since the media involved are so different control of them is often retained by the author's agent rather than granted to the publisher of the book.

It is not possible in a book of this length to give more than a brief bird's-eye view of film rights: for more detailed guidance on this complex topic, see Rhonda Baker's user-friendly guide, *Media Law* (Blueprint, 1995).

Underlying rights

A film or TV producer or production company wishing to make a film based on a book which is still in copyright will need to clear the 'underlying' literary rights at the outset (and, equally, any artistic, musical, dramatic and other rights which may be involved). Initially, as a rule, clearing the rights does not involve actually acquiring them outright; at this stage the film is still an idea only and may never be made, so they may never be needed. What happens first almost invariably is that the producer will seek to secure an option.

Options

The advantage of an option, rather than an outright purchase of rights, is that it enables the film producer to reserve the underlying rights for a (comparatively) modest upfront fee whilst spending anything up to 2 years preparing a script, finding investors, putting together the necessary film finance, and finding a director, leading actors and suitable locations. It also limits the copyright owner's risk, by avoiding a full grant of rights until it is certain that the film will actually be made and that the producer is able to pay for the rights.

Unless the subject is very topical, options are normally granted initially for a year or 18 months, for a non-returnable fee which is usually not more than 10 per cent of the total intended purchase price (for low budget films, it may be lower). The option is usually extendable for one or two further 6- or 12-month periods, in case developing a satisfactory script and putting together the finance proves harder than expected (it often does). During the option period, the producer will need the right to make certain uses of the literary work concerned, specifically to copy extracts and make an adaptation in the form of a screenplay to show potential investors, or even to make a pilot if TV rights are being acquired.

The exact rights (and media) over which the option is granted should be set out clearly: the usual way of doing this is to cross-refer to the intended final Acquisition document (see below) and attach it as an appendix to the option.

If the project falls through, and the option is not exercised within the option period, the rights owner should ideally have the right to buy back any new copyrights created in (for example) the screenplay or any other adaptations of the work – although a producer who does not own the underlying rights, and whose option has expired, will not be able to do much with scripts or other material without infringing existing rights.

Acquisition and assignment

If and when the option is exercised, the Acquisition agreement may then be signed, under which the balance of the purchase price is paid, and in which the necessary film rights are finally granted. This may be via an assignment of the copyright, but now often takes the form of a sole and exclusive licence of (specified) film rights, usually for the full term of copyright, although the period of exclusivity may be limited to 10 or 15 years, for example for made-for-TV films. 'Quitclaims' are often required at the same time, under which the relevant (usually English-language) publishers confirm that they have no conflicting interest in the film rights.

   It is essential to set out clearly what rights are included (and which are not), and particularly whether TV rights are included. The definition of 'film' in the 1988 Act would normally include TV programmes, so it is important to be clear about this: if it is not the intention to grant TV rights, a narrower definition of films should be used, such as 'theatrical feature films'. Most producers will want both the film and TV rights, for obvious reasons – a TV channel will not surprisingly usually seek to acquire unlimited film and TV rights, but even if the film is being made primarily for theatrical (that is, cinema) exploitation, the producer will still usually wish to show it on television. If despite this, TV rights are not available the producer may require a 'hold back' clause, restricting the proprietor's own exploitation of TV rights for an agreed number of years.

   The rights granted will normally include most or all of the following:

- the right to make one or more films (including TV) plus re-makes, prequels, and sequels;
- the right to show the work in public;
- the right to broadcast the work (including excerpts or trailers, and including TV, satellite and cable);
- the right to make adaptations of the work (such as dramatisations and screenplays);
- the right to issue copies to the public (including video rental);
- 'publicity rights': to create written synopses (usually of up to 5,000 or 10,000 words), and broadcast and publish extracts;
- the right to compose music to accompany the work, and the right to make sound recordings;
- the right to use the author's name, likeness and biographical details for promotional purposes;
- the right to publish a 'book of the film' (often withheld by the rights owner);
- associated merchandising rights.

If the film is not made within a specified number of years (for example, 5) the Acquisition agreement should provide that the rights revert to the owner, perhaps upon payment of an agreed sum. This is often calculated by reference to the sum originally paid by the producer and also possibly the further amounts the producer has spent in developing the project. During that period it is advisable for the rights owner to specify that the film rights should not be assigned without its consent, at least not without a full novation (see p. 70).

There will normally be warranties and indemnities on both sides: the producer will want the usual warranties covering the original work (see p. 76), and the owner will often seek a specific indemnity covering any liability arising out of changes made in the film.

Producers and production companies will normally insist on a full waiver of the author's moral rights – at least insofar as they relate to film exploitation form. The right of paternity is not likely to be infringed, since specific on-screen credits are usually agreed in the Acquisition agreement, but the author's right of integrity (to object to derogatory treatment) may become an issue unless the author is willing to consent generally to 'treatments', as defined in the 1988 Act, being made: 'any addition to, deletion from or alteration to or adaptation of the work' would include most changes a film director would need to make.

Payment of fees or royalties depends on the status of the author, and the nature of the adaptation. Usually, the purchase price will be a fixed sum, possibly with a further sum on top calculated by reference to a percentage of the film's budget, up to a cap. Most rights owners will also be entitled to a share of the 'net profits'. It is, however, essential to define 'profits' clearly – after deducting the cost of production, financing, distribution and deferments, there may not be very much 'profit' left at all. On top of this, there should be repeat fees, and additional revenue from any re-makes, prequels and sequels. TV payments are normally payable a month after the first broadcast or transmission.

Video rentals may generate significant revenue in due course, which may entitle the rights owner to additional specific payments or simply contribute to 'profits'. Bear in mind that under the EU Directive on rental and lending rights, likely to be brought into force in the UK during the course of 1996, authors and screenwriters will have an unwaivable right to 'equitable remuneration' from any such rental exploitation.

ELECTRONIC AND MULTIMEDIA RIGHTS

Although reports of The Death Of The Book are probably exaggerated (books about computers abound), publishing is now a part of a rapidly developing digital environment in which information published in electronic form can be accessed worldwide more or less instantaneously using telephone or cable and satellite links. This opens up new opportunities for exploitation and licensing of data (and sound and visual images), but it also poses threats. Subscriber-based on-line databases such as the legal database LEXIS can monitor and control the copyright data which licensed subscribers receive, and the use they make of it, but worldwide open information networks such as the Internet, accessible to anyone with a PC and a modem, have no such controls (yet). Between these two extremes there are 'closed' systems or networks such as CompuServe – these may offer subscribers Internet access as part of the package, but they also offer a wide range of other services, some free and some chargeable. Not surprisingly, there are already cases of copyright infringement via bulletin boards on the Internet and on closed subscription networks, together with libel and (depressingly) incitement to racial hatred, and it cannot be long before some method of international control for such networks is required, and a secure means of encrypting copyright data (for further examples of the legal risks of the Internet see pp. 161, 166, 174, 179 and 190).

For electronic information sold via more traditional routes, such as CD-ROM, there is at least some opportunity to license users – even (where the end user is unknown) via 'shrinkwrap' licences. This is customary in the commercial software industry. However, for an 'entertainment/leisure' product such as a book or game, the more informal practices of the video games and record industries might apply. These are to limit the scope of the licence associated with the software by a notice on the CD-ROM (such as no unauthorised rental, broadcast, public performance, diffusion or cable transmission – home use only). It is perhaps questionable whether the rights holder could effectively restrict use of the CD-ROM only to the original buyer. However, if such products are regarded as similar to printed books the inability in practice to restrict transfer or resale might be thought academic.

Where CD-ROM products differ from printed works is in the ease with which information can be copied (and manipulated) once it is made available electronically – this presents challenges to copyright owners worldwide. The need for clear licensing control is particularly great where copyright text is 'bundled' with other material, such as illustrations, films, music and sound recordings, to make entirely new multimedia products; where a right owner's text, however valuable, is reduced to one contribution among many the task of protecting its integrity (and the author's moral rights), controlling the use made of it, and ensuring a fair reward for (all of) that use, becomes correspondingly harder. These clear risks come with any availability of the text in digital form. However, to put this concern in context, the very wide availability of OCRs and scanners even now means that printed publications are already exposed to similar control problems. So, turning one's back on new technology altogether will not avoid control and licensing issues created by new media. The legal means do exist to control exploitation in the digital domain.

Acquiring electronic rights

In order to licence electronic rights (however that phrase may be defined) you first need to own them, or acquire them. From the publisher's point of view, this means acquiring a specific grant of the necessary rights from the copyright owner, usually the author. However, most publishing contracts more than 20 or so years old make no mention of electronic rights, and even more recent agreements may be somewhat vague on the two key issues of:

1 what rights exactly are granted; and
2 what will be paid for them.

(Often the second of these is left 'to be agreed', although arguably this reduces the 'grant' to a mere option.)

The golden rule is: *never assume*. A publishing contract decades old, which granted 'all rights', or 'publishing rights' (even 'including all subsidiary rights') at a time when the relevant type of digital exploitation could not possibly have been in the minds of the parties, cannot safely be assumed to grant those specific digital exploitation rights now. A more recent phrase such as 'electronic rights' might be sufficient to cover straightforward exploitation of the verbatim text in digital form, via CD-ROM or (perhaps) on-line, but it might not be specific enough to grant, for example, the right to make an interactive multimedia product based on or derived from the text. With the current rapid development of technology, it cannot be stressed strongly enough that a specific platform for electronic exploitation must be supported by an equally specific grant of rights – especially if (as is often the case) substantial investment is proposed. If it isn't clearly provided for in the contract already, it is highly advisable to secure an additional, specific, grant of rights from the rights owner(s) (there may be more than one – in the case of multimedia exploitation of a children's book, for example, a fresh grant of rights may well be required from the illustrator as well as the author. A simple exchange of letters will normally suffice.)

The initial grant of rights: author–publisher licensing

In the early days of electronic licensing, publishers were often advised to 'acquire broadly, and license narrowly': this seemed to make sense from their point of view, but has increasingly been resisted by authors and agents. Some publishers (especially reference and periodical publishers) may be in a sufficiently strong bargaining position with their authors and contributors to be able to insist on a full buy-out of electronic rights, but in other cases the author will want some evidence that the publisher actually intends to *exploit* those rights, and has the skill and capacity to do so. If all the publisher is doing is acquiring rights pre-emptively, just in case they may be needed later on, authors – particularly those with agents – may feel it unwise to do more than grant a first option, reserving the rights generally until a firm proposal can be made which refers to a defined platform and product and offers specific payment terms. A publisher who controls all other publishing rights in a work, however, will at least want some reassurance by way of undertaking that the author or agent is not going to exploit the work electronically elsewhere without prior consultation.

If electronic rights are granted, it is advisable to specify as far as possible what rights exactly this rather vague phrase includes. There will be particular types of exploitation which the publisher may wish to see expressly included, or which an author equally may wish to withhold. In this context it is important to distinguish and deal separately with the 'Products' which can be based on, include or be derived from the text being licensed, and the 'Distribution Media' for those Products. For example:

Product categories

- original text in digital form;
- information databases and multimedia products, which include the text;
- Entertainment/leisure software (such as a video game) derived form the text or its characters;
- recordings of performances/readings of the text;
- film based on text.

Distribution media

- PC CD-ROM/PC floppy forms of magnetic/optical storage for home Mac/ other use;
- broadcast/public performance/cable transmission;
- open/closed network distribution rights;
- on-line access;
- payment for use.

These Distribution Media options may vary in relation to each of the various Product categories being licensed. Also, of course, the appropriate royalty structure and percentages may vary.

The key to maximising commercial potential is to divide rights by reference to actual market sectors. It is essential to avoid giving away rights to an operator in one sector which may limit the exploitation and marketing of the text in another sector. For example, the exclusive licensing of text for use in an encyclopaedia or database may inadvertently pass rights to video game or multimedia products if not properly phrased. In such cases these rights may remain unexploited and commercial opportunities missed. Equally when defining the scope of 'distribution media' many problems can be avoided by tying the licence and any exclusivity down to the 'distribution media' and particular product categories or even only the licensed product itself. Again this means driving licensing practices by reference to market sectors and not the technology that delivers to them. So, to take an example, the text could be exclusively licensed to a database compiler for text – only compilations of literary works about wine and/or vineyards for publication only on PC CD-ROM. This leaves the rights holder free to license a multimedia company or video games producer later on to satisfy different market sectors on the same PC CD-ROM distribution medium.

The following points should generally be borne in mind:

- Is the licence exclusive or non-exclusive?
- Are the rights limited to electronic use of the (unaltered) verbatim text (arguably, simple storage and retrieval should be part of volume rights anyway)? Does this include on-line delivery?
- May the work only be used complete, or may it be condensed or abridged, manipulated or altered?
- May it be used in a compilation with other works? Does this include an interactive/multimedia version?
- Is the licence limited to delivery platforms currently in existence (for example CD-ROM or CD-I) or is the intention to include 'any other devices hereafter invented'?
- Is the licence for all languages (human and machine) and all territories? (Bear in mind that the Internet knows no frontiers.)
- What payment methods are available (fees, payments per use, royalties based on net receipts, or dealer price?) and what proportion will the author/ contributor get?
- Does the licence last for the full term of copyright, or only for a limited term of years? Do (or should) the rights revert to the author if they are not being exploited (or if a product is launched, but then allowed to go 'out of promotion')?

Major publishers planning (or investing in) ambitious multimedia works may prefer to commission authors, illustrators and other contributors specifically for those projects, and take full assignments of copyright from them in their work – or at least sole and exclusive licences for all such exploitation for the full term of copyright. In other cases, where a full buy-out does not seem appropriate, authors and agents may prefer to grant electronic rights for limited periods at a time (perhaps for as little as 5 years) with provision for the rights to revert if a publisher or other licensee concerned has not exploited them within a given period. Following the EU Rental and Lending Directive, it will also be important to deal with authors' rights to 'equitable remuneration' on the rental of films based on their work. It is still uncertain whether it will be possible to buy this out for all countries and in all circumstances.

The author's moral rights – particularly of paternity and integrity (see pp. 44–54) should also not be forgotten, where they apply (for exceptions, see pp. 47 and 52). Unless moral rights are going to be completely waived, it will be necessary to make sure that authors who have asserted their paternity rights are credited adequately, and also that the works are not subjected to derogatory treatment, and – ideally – are not subjected to any significant 'treatment' at all, without the author's consent. As with film and book club rights it is possible with rights in new media for authors to waive moral rights conditionally – in other words only insofar as necessary in order to exploit the text in accordance with the licence.

Electronic licensing and joint ventures

Owners or licensees of electronic rights – such as publishers – may seek to exploit those rights in a number of different ways. Some will have the experience and resources to develop electronic products themselves in-house – but this may be difficult initially for a traditional publisher. Some will acquire electronic publishing expertise by bolt-ons or buy-ins of existing teams from outside, but again this can be expensive. Most will rely on straightforward licensing or sub-licensing to service providers already in the market, or – where more active collaboration is required – joint ventures. As electronic publishing develops, many will use a mixture of all these strategies. As with all such licensing, however many legal constraints are imposed, at the end of the day it is largely a question of who has (or is perceived to have) the relevant expertise, and who you trust.

Key issues which should be covered in any such licence include the following:

- Is the licence exclusive or non-exclusive (for example where only part of the work is to be used) and can the rights be sub-licensed to others? Some licensees and producers may need exclusivity in order to enter the market effectively: bear in mind any possible conflict with existing film or TV rights.
- Define the languages (computer as well as human) and the territories (where appropriate) in which exploitation may take place.
- Define the permitted platforms (for example CD-ROM) if necessary; in some cases it may be advisable to licence only a specific format or product.
- Agree on (and cost in) any necessary backup facilities, helplines or other support overheads: who will provide for these, and how will any costs be shared, or deducted? Will the author(s) need to be involved in regular revisions or updates, and on what terms?
- If necessary, specify permitted kinds of *use*, any restrictions on authorised or permitted *users* and in appropriate cases consider a *site* licence, restricting use to particular geographical sites (such as offices or university campuses).
- May the work be altered or adapted in any way, and may it – or parts of it – be 'bundled' with other works? Think seriously about the integrity of the work (including the author's moral rights): will you retain a right of consultation (or even veto) over any changes? With a new product in a new medium, quality control may be crucial – don't leave approval until it's too late. Agree if necessary a staged consultation/approval procedure as the product develops, and retain the right to withdraw approval and terminate the licence as and when necessary.
- How long will the licence last for (3 to 5 years is common)? Is there a launch deadline or specified release date? Consider the circumstances in which you might wish to terminate the licence early and regain the rights: breach of key terms (such as non-payment, or unauthorised use), unsatisfactory sales

performance or failure to meet agreed targets, and the usual termination and reversion provisions, for example, on insolvency.

- Be clear about ownership of all relevant copyrights, and any other relevant intellectual property rights such as any trade marks. In the case of a joint venture, the joint venture company may need to acquire the rights. Do not forget to renew any necessary copyright permissions (and agree who will do this – and pay any fees).
- Provide adequately for any moral rights of all relevant authors, and any required waivers (see pp. 47/8, and 85). If possible ensure that any sub-licences are also made subject to the author's moral rights. Agree specific credits, not only to the authors but to the licensing publisher, and ensure that this covers advertising and packaging as well as the product itself. Be particularly careful about any permitted use of brand names, logos or trade marks.
- Agree clearly what is to happen about money – who gets what and when. For a compilation or multimedia work, this may involve agreeing on the comparative 'value' of each work included: bear in mind the text occupies far less space on a CD than pictures, yet may be far more valuable in selling the product. Allow for the value of any digital amendments which individual rights owners may need to make, but equally bear in mind the high upfront development costs a software house may incur. Agree a payment system appropriate for the product and medium concerned – this may be a familiar royalty structure, or payments-per-use, or a proportion of agreed profits (as in the film and TV industries). In each case be clear about the method of calculation to be used. In an unfamiliar environment, it may be wise to provide for a review of financial terms after 3 to 5 years, and perhaps minimum revenue in a given period.

SAME LANGUAGE RIGHTS: CO-EDITIONS AND JOINT VENTURES

As we have seen, even in the English language, there may be forms and media of exploitation which publishers, authors or agents cannot develop alone; there may also be key English language markets (such as the USA) where the market may require local promotion and distribution and may best be serviced by a local publisher with daily hands-on contact and goodwill. In many such cases, a straightforward licensing deal may be sufficient, but in others a more collaborative co-edition agreement may be preferred. For newer or more complex products, a formal division of functions, responsibilities and profits (or losses) may be necessary, usually best set out in a co-publication or joint venture agreement.

Co-editions

Unlike a standard licence, where the proprietor simply grants a publisher a licence to print its own local edition in return (usually) for a royalty on sales, a co-edition normally features a combined printing operation in which the local publisher will buy copies (or sheets) in its own imprint at an agreed price per copy. This requires a more upfront payment from the local publisher, but usually gives a realistic price and provides economies of scale to the proprietor, who can print more copies and thereby reduce the unit cost. It also gives the proprietor more control over the production process which is often an important factor, for example for illustrated or children's books using four-colour printing.

Whoever's standard terms are used – a US co-publisher will often propose its own version – the following points should be covered:

Rights granted and territories

Local publishers will normally want exclusive rights in their home territory but that territory will usually need careful definition, and also any 'open markets' in which either publisher's edition may sell, particularly Europe. The European Union's rules on free movement of goods (see p. 284) mean that an open market edition lawfully on sale in any EU or EEA member state cannot be prevented from entering the UK, despite licensing terms to the contrary – so that making the UK an 'exclusive' territory may in effect be unenforceable if, say, Belgium or Germany are open.

The forms and media in which territorial rights may be exploited also need careful definition: are volume rights only granted, or may the local publisher sell electronic versions, or exploit subsidiary rights such as film, TV, serial and book club rights? Can the rights be sub-licensed or assigned? (Not normally without consent, but if so this must be stated.) It is advisable for the proprietor to reserve all rights not expressly granted.

Term of licence

A US co-publisher may expect to be granted a licence for the full duration of copyright, although this may sometimes be resisted if inappropriate; a 5- or 7-year licence is more usual, otherwise, or perhaps a restriction to the number of copies supplied, with termination to take place when copies are exhausted. For major works, it is often preferable to limit licences to the life of a single edition. It is customary to provide for the term to be extended, if required, by mutual agreement, together with an option to take further copies of a reprint or new edition.

Delivery and timing

If time is of the essence, say so – equally any mutually agreed publication dates. The proprietor will be expected to undertake shipment of the publisher's copies by a certain date – often in agreed stages – but this may need to be conditional upon the publisher's timely supply of film for any permitted local amendments:

both sets of dates should be clearly set out. Final delivery details will also need to be specified: which shipping agent, who will supply documentation, whether advance copies by air are required, and time limits for any complaints.

The price

Payment should be in an agreed currency, if necessary at an agreed exchange rate (perhaps providing for a 5 per cent or other fluctuation either way, any excess to be borne equally). The price is often held for a limited period only. Payment is often staged, for example with one-third payable on signature, one-third on delivery, and one-third 30 or 60 days later. Is there an advance? Is the price royalty – inclusive or royalty – exclusive? Does it include freight and insurance, and are the terms CIF or FOB? (See appendix A.)

Even though the price may be a royalty-inclusive price per copy, it may still make sense to specify annual accounting, and the usual provisions for audit, if only to monitor any subsidiary rights exploitation and be forewarned of any need to re-order or reprint.

Local alterations

Where the proprietor is producing copies, the publisher will usually be required to provide film of any permitted amendments or alterations (in good time within the schedule). Consider carefully any substantial amendments proposed, and bear in mind the author's moral right of integrity (see p. 48), and the similar rights of illustrators and other contributors: ideally, no amendments should be permitted without consent.

Permissions

It is crucial to check that any copyright permissions apply to *all* the territories and media to be exploited: some may need to be re-cleared if the original clearance was restricted to publication in the original language, for a limited market, and/or under the original publisher's imprint. For a major reference or illustrated work permissions can be very expensive indeed, so it is best to agree as early as possible who will undertake the task of securing necessary permissions, and also who will pay, or how costs will be shared.

Copyright notice and credits

The proprietor will need to ensure that its own copyright credit appears (see p. 89), and any assertion of the author's right of paternity. It is also advisable to require the publisher to take all necessary and reasonable steps to protect the copyrights (and any trade marks) locally, including local registration where required.

Warranties and indemnities

Make sure that any warranties match those already given by the author, or (if not) that they can reasonably be given. Often this may be a matter for the insurers on either side – it may not be possible for a UK publisher, for example, to warrant with any certainty that nothing in a book will infringe US law (although a warranty about UK law may be perfectly reasonable). It is normal to limit warranties to the licensor's own national law.

Termination

As with all licences, any co-edition agreement should provide clearly for termination under specified conditions: normally breach, insolvency or change of control, or allowing the work to go out of print (with no reprint order in hand with the proprietor). It may be advisable to provide for arbitration in the event of any dispute – particularly if the applicable law is not English law.

Joint ventures

For more ambitious or elaborate projects (such as a large series of illustrated books or a major multimedia product), one publisher may not have all the skills – or finance – necessary. It may make sense in such circumstances to enter into a formal joint venture agreement with another publisher or with a film or TV company or software house – there may often be several parties involved. Joint venture agreements may be entered into at the outset, with all participants sitting down well in advance to plan the contributions – and profit shares – each will make, or sometimes relatively late in a project's development, for example to bring in extra finance, or distribution skills. As a general rule however, the earlier such agreements can be reached the better.

There are a number of key points to watch:

Define the product

It may be a single book or CD-ROM, or a series or on-line service, or a multimedia product involving several partners: however many partners are involved, agree as soon as possible on your mutual aims, on the form and the scope of the enterprise, and define any product(s) as clearly as you can, including delivery media. A detailed specification for the product attached as a schedule might be advisable. Include any agreed details such as a General Editor or particular contributors, or intended price or format.

Decide who does what

Agree what each of you brings to the party – be it text, illustrations, other copyright material, software, or simply finance, and how the various publishing functions will be split up – how any research will be tackled, who will undertake design and production, who will be responsible for clearing permissions and underlying rights, who will do the promotion, marketing and distribution, and who will account for the proceeds, and distribute any profits (or losses).

Timing

If there are specific launch targets, write them in. Agree in particular when the joint venture agreement starts to run, and if it has a fixed term, when it will terminate.

Budget

Budget – and re-budget – carefully, bearing in mind that for a new project in an unfamiliar medium cashflow may be crucial. Agree on allowable costs – what each party may claim back from the project before any profits are shared out. Include any administrative overheads if necessary (such as subsidiary rights management), and distribution costs such as freight and insurance. Needless to say, agree clearly how any profits will be shared out – and what will happen in the event of losses.

Ownership of rights

Assuming all necessary permissions have been granted and underlying rights secured, it is important to specify clearly who owns which copyrights and also how any new copyrights which are created – for example in a new compilation or database – are owned: it may be necessary for a joint venture company to acquire the rights. Do not forget other key rights, such as trade marks in any names or logos: will these be registered, and who will be the proprietor and licensed users?

Termination

Don't forget to provide a get-out route if it all goes horribly wrong, and allow for individual opt outs if necessary. Agree initial terms, grounds for early termination and suitable notice periods, with arbitration provisions if necessary. Most importantly, agree who will own which rights post-termination in the joint venture product itself, including work in progress, roughs and artwork. Agree the applicable law which will govern any disputes which cannot be settled by arbitration and which country's courts will have jurisdiction (see pp. 93–4).

CONTRACTS WITH BOOK PACKAGERS

Book packagers are a relatively recent phenomenon: they commission and produce books, particularly those which require larger than average print-runs –

such as illustrated books – and then sell them ready-packaged (off the peg, so to speak) to a variety of different publishers around the world. They therefore take over the publisher's normal roles of research and development, commissioning, contracting with authors, illustrators and other contributors, design and production, and deliver completed bound copies to the publishers at an agreed price so that all that the publishers then have to do is promote and distribute them in the normal way. It suits the publishers by saving their editorial and production overheads while still giving a competitive price, and it enables the packager to profit from the economies of scale which combined international co-edition print-runs can bring.

Packagers normally prefer to contract with publishers using the Book Packagers Association (BPA) Standard Agreement, or something based on it, so in this section we will use the latest (April 1995) version of that document as a starting point. The basic agreement is currently set out in Charles Clark's *Publishing Agreements*, but the Agreement is frequently revised: the latest version is obtainable from the BPA, whose address is in appendix B. Some publishers may of course prefer to use their own standard agreements.

SALE AND PURCHASE

The Agreement is normally structured as a sale and purchase of a given number of bound copies at a specified price. The Work itself is defined in detail in a separate Appendix. The price – the key issue – may be payable in several staged instalments, the first payment usually being due on signature and the last on delivery of the books, or shortly thereafter. It is normally, but by no means always, royalty-inclusive (so the book packager, and not the publisher, pays the author), and normally also includes the costs of bulk packing, insurance and shipping to the publisher's warehouse (or nominated port). An over- or under-delivery of 5 per cent either way is a standard tolerance, and a run-on price is usually agreed: it may also be advisable to provide for currency fluctuations – or unforeseen price increases (such as paper prices) – if the price is to be held for any significant period of time. It is increasingly advisable to provide for payment of interest if the publisher does not make payments on the due date.

The BPA Agreement now has a full retention of title clause in the event of non-payment (for an explanation of these, see p. 239).

RIGHTS AND TERRITORY

Since book packaging is an international business, the book packager will almost certainly have needed to require exclusive worldwide publishing rights from the author, illustrator(s) and any other contributors, probably for the full period of copyright – in some cases, the copyrights themselves may have been assigned. It is important to check that all the necessary rights (and permissions such as those from picture libraries) have in fact been acquired, before licences to individual publishers can be granted – not only for particular territories, but also for all relevant media and formats.

Which rights are then licensed on to individual publishers will depend of course on the form of exploitation envisaged and the territory concerned in each case; the book packager, having acquired the necessary bundle of rights, will act in many ways like an agent. In the BPA Standard Agreement the right granted is a somewhat limited exclusive licence to publish, distribute and sell the work in hardback volume form in the English language in the specified Territory (set out in an Appendix) – it might equally be a grant of paperback rights, or worldwide volume rights in the French language, or even merchandising or electronic and multimedia rights. Permissions may need to be renewed or extended; the Agreement should specify who is responsible for this.

TERM OF LICENCE

The term may be for the full period of copyright, or (as in the BPA Standard Agreement) for a fixed term of years, renewable by mutual agreement. Publishers embarking on major exploitation will want the longest term they can get, but for most a 5- to 8-year renewable licence will probably suffice.

SUBSIDIARY RIGHTS

If the main grant of rights clause is limited to volume rights, it is essential that any subsidiary rights which are also to be granted should be spelt out clearly. The fact that the extra rights are actually granted should be as clear as the percentage payments, and also what the rights actually entitle the publisher to do: is the publisher merely entitled to sub-licence other people to do things (as with serial rights) or is the publisher also given the right to exploit the work *itself* in given media (such as electronic media)? There is often much needless confusion about this – if the intention in fact is to grant (say) a full range of electronic publishing rights, this should be made clear in the main grant of rights clause and not added on as an afterthought under subsidiary rights.

WARRANTIES AND INDEMNITIES

The book packager will normally be expected to make the usual warranties (see p. 76), in particular that it actually owns or controls all the rights now granted, that those rights have not previously been granted (even partially) elsewhere, plus the usual warranties about libel, obscenity, infringement of other copyrights, and any other illegality. The packager may only feel able to make some of the warranties relating to the content of the book itself 'to the best of the book packager's knowledge and belief': this may need to be discussed if it fails to give the publisher the cover it needs.

IMPERFECT COPIES

With a packaging operation, where publishers do not themselves control the production process, the quality of the (whole) shipment delivered is often a cause for anxiety. The latest BPA Agreement makes detailed provision for notification of any imperfect copies due to faulty materials or workmanship or damage in transit within specified time limits (time is usually of the essence in notifying of such claims, if only to preserve the relevant insurance cover). The book packager may reserve the option of crediting the agreement value of the defective copies, or reprinting or re-jacketing them as required; it may also seek to exclude any additional liability for loss of profits or consequential loss. Since stock checks are time consuming and expensive, there may be a provision that the publisher shall bear the cost if defects to fewer than a specified percentage of copies are found.

MORAL RIGHTS

The moral rights of authors and illustrators should not be forgotten, particularly their right to be credited, and their right to object to any derogatory treatment of the material supplied. The right to be credited may need to be specifically asserted, if it has not already been. If the rights have not been waived, it may be necessary to stipulate in the agreement that any further sub-licences will expressly be made subject to the author's moral rights.

TERMINATION

Normal termination provisions will apply – including termination for breach (for example, failure to publish by the agreed date, or failure to pay the price), for assignment without consent, for unauthorised remaindering or allowing the work to go out of print (in the home market, or in all editions worldwide?), and for insolvency and bankruptcy. The rights granted will normally then revert to the book packager. It is customary to allow the publisher a limited sell off period (6 months is common) in order to clear remaining stock.

AGREEMENTS BETWEEN AUTHORS AND AGENTS

We looked in some detail in chapter 4 at literary agents' own standard publishing contracts, in the context of the author – publisher agreement. In the final section of this chapter we will take a quick look at the legal relationship between agents and authors themselves.

Most established literary agencies now enter into some kind of written agreement with authors who they take on, usually in the form of an extended letter. It is possible in some circumstances for an agent to acquire actual or implied authority to represent someone else (called their 'principal') *without* entering into a written agreement, but this is not generally recommended as a long-term business practice, and it is always advisable to record such agreements in writing as soon as possible – if only to confirm the extent of the agent's authority, and (the source of most disputes) what payment or commission they will be entitled to receive.

Where there is an agreement, the terms of that agreement will govern the relationship; there is however probably also an overriding obligation on all agents to perform their duties in good faith and with reasonable care and skill. Contracts with all commercial agents within the EU are now regulated by the Commercial Agents Directive, implemented in the UK in the shape of the Commercial Agents (Council Directive) Regulations 1993. Some of the key criteria include the following:

- there should be no conflicts of interest;
- the agent's powers or duties should not be delegated without consent;
- agents should not make secret profits or undeclared commissions;
- agents have a right to be indemnified by their principals when acting within their authority;
- all agents have a right to reasonable remuneration.

The entitlement to reasonable remuneration normally comes to an end straight away when the agency is terminated, unless the contract provides otherwise. However, although this makes sense for most commercial agencies, it does not allow for agents (such as literary agents) who – apart from a share of any advance – are paid substantially by means of a commission on long-term future earnings. Most literary agency agreements therefore expressly provide that the agent's agreed commission will be paid on *all* future earnings, from all sources, which derive from agreements which that agent actually negotiated (or, in some cases, signed while the agency was in force, even if the agent was not directly involved). If the author accepts this, it means that many agents will continue to be paid commission on their former author's titles long after the agency arrangement itself has been terminated. For this reason, most agents' standard publishing agreements include a clause 'irrevocably' appointing them as the author's authorised recipient for all monies payable on that particular title. Some authors may not be willing to make an irrevocable appointment – there is no legal reason why agency appointments should not be revoked at any time if the author wishes later to be paid direct, or via some other agent – but there will then be a separate contractual issue between the author and the agent about outstanding commission. There is however no reason why the publisher should become involved in this: it is entirely a matter between author and agent.

For authors wishing to enter into an agreement with an agent, the Association of Authors' Agents maintains a professional code of conduct. Some general guidance, and comparison of commission rates, may be found in various annual publications such as the *Writers Handbook* and the *Writers and Artists' Yearbook*.

Delivery, editing and production

III

Delivery, editing and production 6

DELIVERY: ACCEPTANCE OR REJECTION

DELIVERY

The emotional trauma and sheer physical effort of delivering a completed copyright work has often been likened to childbirth (usually by men). It is probably true that few authors – apart from the most experienced – realise quite what they are letting themselves in for when they sign their publishing contracts; first time authors in particular may underestimate what is required (although a good agent or editor should spot this). In addition, even the best organised authors may be overtaken by unexpected events, especially if they have any kind of family or social life and a full-time job to hold down too. As a result:

- the work may be delivered late;
- bits of it – or the whole thing – may not be of the standard expected.

A good publishing contract will foresee both these eventualities and make provision for them (see chapter 4, pp. 74–5).

Non-delivery or late delivery

Time will not be regarded as being of the essence unless the contract expressly says that it is (it often does, for example, if the work is a contribution to a major reference project on a tight schedule, or linked into some external event such as a royal wedding). Where time *is* of the essence, non-delivery by the specified date will normally be an automatic ground for termination of the contract, although in many cases – particularly where the author is not to blame – a publisher may retain the option to keep the contract alive a while longer if there seems a reasonable prospect that the work will come in soon and there is in fact a little leeway in the schedule.

Where time is *not* stated to be of the essence, late delivery may still constitute adequate performance of the author's contractual obligation to deliver (indeed, an author may deliver 20 years late and still perform the contract, if the publisher is prepared to wait that long). All other things being equal, 2 or 3 months either way would almost certainly be regarded as reasonably acceptable performance, and a publisher might find it difficult to terminate the contract on grounds of non-delivery alone if the author had a reasonable excuse for being late and was ready and willing to deliver in, say, 3 months time. Beyond that, however, it is probably advisable to confirm any revised schedule in a formal exchange of letters, varying the delivery terms of the original contract: otherwise the author will be at increasing risk of termination for breach of contract, particularly where the publisher makes it clear (preferably in writing) that continued lateness will not be acceptable. It is important, however, to look at all the surrounding circumstances, and bear in mind any informal meetings or telephone conversations, or any previous dealings between the parties, as well as actual correspondence; a publisher may impliedly extend a delivery deadline by conduct as well as by a formal letter.

Acceptance

If and when the work does finally come in, the publisher will want to check as soon as possible whether it conforms to the publishing contract – whether it is, in fact, the thing contracted for. Any specified formats and delivery requirements – such as delivery on disk – should also be complied with. Under general contract law principles, there is probably only a limited window of opportunity here for the publisher either to reject the work on clear grounds as being unacceptable – not a sufficient performance of the contract by the author – or else expressly or impliedly accept it. Putting the work into production (or even editing, or marking up for house style) might well constitute implied acceptance, so that even if unacceptable defects were discovered later it might then be difficult for the publisher to reject the work as a whole. Accepting delivery of a work should therefore not merely be a process of passive collection, but should involve at some point a positive inspection and approval of what is delivered. For most works, the person to do this will be the commissioning publisher or in-house editor: for major works the approval of a General Editor or Section Editor may be required. Whoever it is should be aware of the contractual significance of what they are doing – once a work is substantially accepted, then the publisher is to all intents and purposes probably stuck with it.

As to what is or is not 'acceptable', this will be entirely governed by the publishing contract, whether written or informal. Where no written contract exists, or where the contract does not refer to any specification or acceptance criteria (it is surprising how many do not) then any reasonably competent work of approximately the right length in the subject area concerned would probably be sufficient to perform the contract. Most good publishing contracts, however, contain at least some acceptance criteria, ranging from a full detailed specification set out in an Appendix – probably the clearest method – to generalised phrases such as 'of a standard which might reasonably be expected' or sometimes just the single, and wonderfully simple, word 'acceptable' (which, unless further defined, probably does not mean very much, but can give the publisher very wide discretion, particularly if 'in the Publisher's sole opinion').

Rejection

What happens if the work – or a substantial part of it – is not acceptable to the publisher? The general rule in law is that the contract will prevail; if the publisher has a wide discretion under the contract, or if what the author delivers cannot reasonably be regarded as fulfilling his or her obligations under the contract, then the publisher may well have the right to reject it and terminate the contract in accordance with any relevant termination provisions. An author commissioned to write a 300-page textbook who delivers instead a 50-page pamphlet (this has been known) is clearly not delivering the work contracted for. Similarly, a work commissioned for inclusion in a post-graduate series which turns out to have no references or footnotes and to be written at a much lower level would be a fairly obvious candidate for rejection, provided that the requirement to write at post-graduate level had been clearly agreed. But what if the publisher simply does not like the work, or is disappointed by it?

If it complies with the contract, but just isn't as good as hoped for, then the publisher will probably not have the right to reject the work for that reason alone, unless the contract gives the publisher virtually complete discretion. In most cases, the publisher's only remedy will be to persuade the author to improve it (see below), and if that still does not produce the desired result, make the most of what was clearly a commissioning mistake.

Rejection, if it happens, should be in accordance with any procedures set out in the contract: the publisher may have the option either to reject at once, or to put the author on notice to make specified alterations or improvements to bring the work up to contract standard within a given timetable, and then to reject if this is not done. Where improvements are feasible, some contracts give the publisher a further option of commissioning a competent editor to make the necessary improvements and deduct the cost from the author's royalties or other earnings in due course (this would now be subject to the author's moral rights, on which see further below).

Disputes

There are often disputes surrounding rejection of a work and termination of the contract may not always turn out to be as straightforward as the publisher might hope. Where the contract gives the publisher absolute discretion, and the work as delivered is obviously not in accordance with the contract terms, there should be little cause for dispute, but in other cases – particularly where alterations are involved – there may be considerable disagreement. If such disputes cannot be resolved amicably between the parties, many contracts provide arbitration clauses as a means of avoiding full scale litigation. Arbitration clauses normally survive termination of the contract, and can usually be invoked unilaterally by either party, but formal arbitration is not always any quicker or cheaper than pursuing a claim in the High Court (see p. 93). It is still, therefore, comparatively rare in publishing disputes; most are settled one way or another between the parties.

In the event of rejection and termination it is important to confirm:

- what happens to the rights granted under the contract; and
- what happens to any advances, or other payments made.

In most cases the author will quite reasonably want his or her rights back, and most contracts provide for all rights granted to revert under such circumstances – so that the author can still exploit the work, even if this will now have to be elsewhere. If the author assigned full copyright to the publisher (or someone else) under the contract, this may have to be formally re-assigned; to be effective, this should be in writing, and signed by or on behalf of the current copyright owner (see p. 64).

Advances, though always a fertile area for dispute, are either a matter for the contract or entirely at the publisher's discretion: where the publisher has paid an advance (or advances) the publisher will normally be entitled to ask for these to be repaid if the work is rejected unless they are clearly stated to be non-returnable.

SUMMARY CHECKLIST: DELIVERY

- Is time of the essence?
- Has the delivery schedule been revised (even impliedly)?
- Is the work delivered the work which was contracted for?
- Does it comply with any 'acceptance' criteria in the contract?
- Are there any grounds for rejection?
- Is there any rejection or disputes procedure?
- What happens to the rights, and any advances?

EDITING AND ALTERATIONS

Once a work is accepted, it may be sent straight off for production as it is but in the great majority of cases the publisher will want to edit it first. This mysterious process is regarded by many authors as equivalent to being thrown to the lions, and horror stories abound of uncontrolled, demented editors mutilating what were previously perfectly publishable works. In reality, of course, editing varies widely from publisher to publisher, some doing little more than marking up to conform with agreed house style, and others adopting a more interventionist role. From a legal point of view, the position is fairly clear: subject to any agreement to the contrary, a publisher who contracts to publish an author's work is obliged to publish that work substantially as delivered by the author, and is not entitled to adapt or (improve) it without the author's consent. This is particularly so, now that authors have a moral right of integrity and other moral rights in the UK under the 1988 Act. We will consider the implications of the right of integrity below.

AGREEMENT BY CONTRACT

As a general rule, authors will not be entitled in law to prevent editorial changes to which they have freely consented. Even their moral rights (see below) will not apply to anything done with their consent. Consent may be express (and set out, for example, in a contract) or implied – perhaps by conduct, or a previous course of dealing – but implied consent may be harder to prove. Most publishers will therefore seek the author's express consent in advance to the level of editorial changes they think they might need to make by including a specific clause to that effect in the publishing agreement. What changes may or may not be permitted will therefore become a question of interpreting the relevant wording of the contract.

Contracts, as we saw in chapter 4, vary widely but most publishing agreements try to give the publisher some leeway at least to make necessary and reasonable alterations in accordance with any agreed specifications, and the relevant house style. Where a detailed house style book is available this should ideally be made available to the author well before the time the contract is signed and expressly referred to in the contract itself: you cannot generally incorporate express terms into a contract which have not been disclosed and agreed by the time the contract is signed.

In addition, many contracts give the publisher the right to make alterations on the advice of its legal advisers, for example to remove passages which might be libellous or obscene, or which might otherwise be in breach of the author's warranties (see pp. 76–80). Libel is a particular risk (see p. 160), and it may be advisable to have any suspect passages read for libel by a lawyer who specialises in this kind of work and knows what to look for; many publishers retain lawyers to do regular libel reading for them, since a legal opinion may often be required at short notice.

Any alterations beyond the level clearly provided for in the contract, or otherwise agreed by the author, are highly dangerous, and where they cause damage to the author or his or her reputation may entitle the author to bring an action for breach of contract, infringement of moral rights, or – in severe cases – for defamation. Editors who feel an author's work could be 'improved' should therefore keep any urge to rewrite it firmly under control.

NECESSARY CHANGES

A publisher might be entitled in an emergency to make last-minute deletions, or minor consequential amendments, in order to avoid publishing infringing or illegal material (such as defamatory or obscene matter) and the moral right of integrity in particular does not apply to anything done to avoid the commission of an offence or comply with a statutory duty. However, in the absence of a clear contractual right to make the changes concerned, changes the publisher considers 'necessary' may not always be entirely safe: if time allows it is always advisable to consult the author, and ideally get the author to make the changes personally. Obtaining the author's participation, or at least express agreement, will give the greatest possible protection against future claims by the author, for example, of breach of contract, or defamation. In addition, anything done with the author's consent cannot infringe his or her moral rights.

IMPLIED CONSENT

An author's consent to alterations may be implied in some circumstances – by the author's conduct (in accepting previous changes, for example), or in some cases by the nature of the publication or the list itself: where an author submits a contribution to a periodical or a major work known to be edited to a certain standard, or submits a work to a series or list of titles with a distinctive house style of its own, then it is quite likely that he or she will be deemed to have consented to a reasonable level of editorial changes consistent with those standards or styles. Where the changes made go a significant way beyond what might reasonably be expected, however, an author may well have a cause of action, for example for breach of contract or infringement of moral rights (see below).

MORAL RIGHTS

As we saw in chapter 3, authors now have statutory moral rights in the UK. In the context of editorial alterations, the two moral rights most likely to be in issue are:

- the right of integrity – the right to object to derogatory treatment of the work; and
- the right to prevent false attribution – the right not to be wrongly described as the author of something in fact written by someone else.

The right of integrity

We considered this key moral right fully at pp. 48–52; to recap briefly, section 80 of the 1988 Act gives the author of relevant copyright works (including both literary and artistic works) the right not to have those works subjected to 'derogatory treatment' – additions or deletions, alterations or adaptations which are so serious that they amount to distortion or mutilation of the work, or are otherwise prejudicial to the author's honour or reputation. The right lasts for as long as the work remains in copyright. Infringement of the right is actionable by the author as a breach of statutory duty, and the author may be entitled not only to appropriate damages but also to the grant of an injunction.

Potentially, therefore, this is a powerful right which editors embarking upon in-house alterations should bear constantly in mind. It is, however, hedged about with limitations and restrictions under the 1988 Act, and may not apply in every case. It will *not* apply in the following circumstances:

- where the changes made do not meet the strict definition of 'derogatory treatment' given above – for a discussion of this, see pp. 48–51;
- where the author has consented to the changes made (for example, by signing a publishing contract which provides for them);
- where the author has waived his or her moral right of integrity, or moral rights generally;
- in the case of employee works (see chapter 2 pp. 32–3), where the employer owns the copyright, authorises the treatment concerned and provides a sufficient disclaimer;
- where the work was written for publication in a 'collective work' such as an encyclopaedia, dictionary or year book;
- where the work was written for publication in a newspaper, magazine or similar periodical;
- to works made for the purpose of reporting current events;
- to computer programs or computer-generated works;
- to anything done to avoid the commission of an offence or in order to comply with a statutory duty.

- Finally, there is also a specific exemption to cover changes made by the BBC to avoid offending against good taste or decency, inciting crime or disorder, or offending public feeling; this may affect script writers and playwrights writing for the BBC, but does not apply to any other publishers or broadcasters.

The right to prevent false attribution

Under section 84 of the 1988 Act, authors (indeed any persons) have the right not to have material written by others falsely attributed to them (see pp. 53–4). Adding to the existing law of defamation, this is a new statutory right designed to protect authors' reputations from harmful association with work which they did not write, and over which they had not control, but which the publisher may try to pass off as theirs. Since it is a right protecting personal reputations, rather than the integrity of copyright works themselves, it lasts not for the full period of copyright but only for 20 years after the person's death. As with other moral rights, infringement of the right is actionable as a breach of statutory duty.

The right of paternity

Do not forget that the author is also likely to have a right of paternity – the right to be credited as the author in a clear and reasonably prominent way on each published copy of the work. There are a number of exceptions to this right such as employee and collective works (for a full list, see p. 47), and the right also crucially depends on being asserted by the author. Where it applies, many contracts therefore provide for a printed assertion of the right to appear on the reverse title page – usually together with the UCC copyright notice (see p. 89). Most publishers will have no difficulty about crediting their authors prominently on the works themselves, but it is important to remember that this is now a statutory right. It is also equally likely to apply to authors of copyright material other than text, such as artists, illustrators and photographers.

SUMMARY CHECKLIST: EDITING

- Are alterations really necessary?
- Has the author consented to alterations (for example, in the contract)?
- Do author's moral rights apply to this type of work?
- Has the author waived his or her moral rights?
- If not, can the author make any alterations personally, or at least be consulted?
- Is there any danger that the author's moral right of integrity may be infringed?
- Might there be a risk of false attribution?
- Has the right of paternity been complied with, and has it been asserted?

PERMISSIONS

Most published works contain extracts or quotations from other copyright works, and often reproductions of complete works such as illustrations, maps or photographs. If these works are still in copyright – older illustrations, for example, may by now be in the public domain – it will be an infringement of the owner's copyright to reproduce any substantial part of those works without permission. A court may award the copyright owner damages or an account of profits, delivery up or destruction of infringing stock, and in appropriate cases an injunction preventing publication (see chapter 8). It is therefore crucially important to check the copyright status of all such material as soon as possible and ensure that permission to reproduce it is obtained from the copyright owner well before the work goes into production – and preferably before or soon after delivery. Most publishing contracts require the author to arrange (and pay) for all such permissions and indeed a warranty and indemnity against any copyright infringement which may take place, but this of course does not help the author, and is not always sufficient to remove legal risk from the publisher, who is very likely to be joined as a co-defendant in any legal action. It will also not cover any copyright permissions necessary for material not included in the author's work itself, for example, an illustration or photograph selected by the publisher for the jacket. Editors should therefore check as soon as possible:

- whether permissions have already been obtained by the author (preferably in writing);
- if not, which existing copyright works have been reproduced, at least in substantial part (if the author does not have a reliable list, the editor should compile one);
- whether they are still in copyright, or have fallen into the public domain (for duration of copyright, see p. 46). As a general rule, a literary or artistic work is still likely to be in copyright if the author died less than 70 years ago;
- whether they may be copied without permission under the fair dealing provisions of the 1988 Act: for example limited extracts reproduced for the purpose of criticism or review, and accompanied by a sufficient acknowledgement (see p. 201);

This may remove the risk of copyright infringement from a number of extracts, but in all other cases permission should be sought from the copyright owner straight away.

Who should arrange (and pay for) permissions is a matter for the author and publisher to agree, if they have not already agreed it in the contract. For large-scale works, such as dictionaries and encyclopaedias, or for multimedia works, clearing permissions might be a major undertaking, so whoever does it needs to allow plenty of time. It is worth remembering the following points:

- Owning copyright means being able to prevent others from copying your work, so the copyright owner may say 'no'. It is highly dangerous to write off a batch of letters and just assume that permission will be granted in due course – it may not be.
- The copyright owner may demand a permissions fee, particularly if a print or transparency is supplied as well. Museums and galleries are raising increasing amounts of revenue from this source, even for works which are themselves long since out of copyright (since the authorised reproduction which is supplied is of course a new copyright work). These fees can mount up very quickly: it may therefore be necessary to reconsider some of the more expensive ones if production budgets are tight. Give yourself time to consider all this, and if necessary select something else.
- If permission *is* given, check that the licence covers all formats, languages and territories in which the work is likely to be exploited (if permission is

only granted for the UK, for example, including that extract or illustration in a French edition would not be licensed).

- Bear in mind that some permissions may only be given for one edition at a time – for example, of a dictionary. If subsequent editions are planned, these permissions will need to be renewed.

What happens if you cannot find out who – if anyone – owns the copyright? In the case of extracts from a book, the obvious place to start is the publisher of the most recent published edition: even though copyright in the literary work may vest in the author, the publisher will normally handle permissions requests. If, however, the publisher is no longer in business, and the author cannot be traced personally (for example, via the Society of Authors, PLR Registrar, or simply via the telephone directory) then you will have to accept the risk that if the work is still in copyright publishing a substantial part of it without express permission may well be infringing someone's copyright. If the owner subsequently appears (possibly after publication) then he or she may have a legitimate claim of copyright infringement. There is no absolutely secure protection against such a possibility, but evidence that the copyright owner was difficult to trace, and that you had made serious efforts in that direction – not merely sent off a single letter – would probably be taken into account by any court. So also would the fact that you had credited the copyright owner, via a suitable acknowledgement. Any sums you had set aside by way of royalty or fee, against the possibility the copyright owner may one day turn up, would also be convincing evidence of good faith. The only entirely safe course of action, however, is not to copy the material at all.

PRODUCTION AND PROOFS

Although it is a solidly established trade practice that publishers will supply the author with proofs of the work for correction before it is sent for press, there is no general legal obligation on them to do this, and in some cases there may simply not be time. However, most publishing contracts provide for proofs, which therefore gives the author a contractual entitlement to see and approve them, on the terms set out in the contract. These normally provide for proofs to be returned within a reasonably prompt schedule – 14 or 21 days is common. In many cases the publisher will retain the right to pass the proofs for press if the author does not return them on time, or cannot check them personally or arrange for someone else to (or simply cannot be contacted). Most contracts also make it clear that the supply of proofs is an opportunity to correct errors, not an open invitation to revise and rewrite sections over which the author may have had second thoughts (and which can be expensive). It is therefore common for an upper limit to be set on any author's corrections: 10 or 15 per cent of the cost of composition is fairly standard (although what the cost of 'composition' actually is where the author has supplied the work on disk might need to be separately agreed: 10 per cent of the cost of editorial revisions alone might not pay for very many corrections). Whatever the percentage, it is important to consider when signing the contract whether this is appropriate for the work concerned – in the case of a scientific, technical or professional text, for example, unforeseen new standards or legislation, or new research findings, may make corrections at proof stage essential if the work is not to be seriously inaccurate and misleading, and the contract should allow sufficient flexibility for this.

If an index is necessary, the contract should say so, and specify whether the author is to do this or whether it is the publisher's responsibility. In many cases, the contract will give the author the option either of doing the index personally, or arranging for it to be done, or authorise the publisher to make the necessary arrangements – usually with a professional freelance indexer – and deduct the cost from the author's royalties in due course. A good index, especially for a major work, can be expensive, so it is advisable to obtain an estimate of cost in advance (and agree any standard of quality required, so that, whoever pays, the work does end up with a satisfactory and reliable index).

Most other aspects of design, production, promotion and marketing are normally reserved to the publisher's sole discretion, and most publishing contracts reflect this. The price at which the work is sold, and the discounts and other terms of trade which would apply, are also normally entirely under the publisher's control. However, some Minimum Terms Agreements or agents' contracts provide for the author to be consulted on subjective matters of taste and style, such as design, or the jacket.

Publish and be damned IV

Defamation and other risks   7

DEFAMATION

LIES, DAMNED LIES, AND DEFAMATION

Every publication which contains statements of fact or opinion runs the risk that some of them may be untrue, or unjustified. However hard authors and editors try, a certain number of inaccuracies will always slip through the net and get published. Some will not matter very much, or will simply look unfortunate. Some, more serious, mis-statements may raise allegations of negligence, and we will look at negligent mis-statement below (p. 177). There is a particular category of untruth, however, which publishers would be well advised to avoid at all costs, and that is any untrue statement which might be taken to impugn a person's reputation. In essence, this is what defamation is.

It is not necessarily illegal to publish untruths about someone, although there is still a law of criminal libel (see below, p. 175). English law still has considerable sympathy with the concept of free speech and a free press (although the Editor of *Private Eye* may occasionally disagree), but at the same time it also seeks to protect honest citizens from the publication of false allegations which may harm their reputation. It is not always easy to balance these opposing needs. There usually comes a point, however, where a critical or disparaging comment becomes a recognisably more serious allegation of fact, or of unsupported opinion: at that point, if it or the facts on which it is based are untrue, the law may intervene and decide that it becomes defamatory.

It may also become expensive, because ever since the Libel Act of 1792 it has been settled law in the UK that damages for defamation are not a matter for judges to settle, but are primarily for a *jury* to decide. As the Court of Appeal said in a recent leading case: 'the question whether someone's reputation has or has not been falsely discredited ought to be tried by other ordinary men and women and . . . it is the jury who are the people of England'. This still remains a fundamental principle of English law. Juries, however, can be unpredictable.

Whatever they think the actual damage to the plaintiff's reputation was, a jury may also decide to punish a defendant for behaviour of which it disapproves, particularly if the defendant has repeated the libel or failed to take opportunities to apologise. They might not care for your defence, or think much of your witnesses. At a time when reports of six-figure advances and cheque-book journalism appear regularly in the media, they may have great sympathy for a lone individual fighting to clear his or her name against what they see as a wealthy publisher or newspaper, and may award very substantial damages. For a publisher seeking to defend a defamation action, therefore, it means that the financial risks of losing a case – quite apart from the costs – are impossible to calculate with any certainty in advance.

Awards of damages by English juries at one point reached levels in excess of £1 million – the record is still held by an award of £1.5 million to Lord Aldington for allegations of war crimes contained in a book by Count Tolstoy. Publishers might have been forgiven for sympathising with Ian Hislop, Editor of *Private Eye*, who remarked after yet another spectacular award: 'If that's justice, I'm a banana.' Out-of-court settlements were often reached later at a more reasonable level, particularly where the alternative was bankruptcy, and the Court of Appeal has had the power since 1991 to substitute an award of its own if it considers the original award excessive, but the financial risks for a defendant accused of defamation are still very great. Following a Court of Appeal decision in December 1995, however, in which the court reduced an award of damages to Elton John against the publishers of the *Sunday Mirror* from £350,000 to £75,000, it is now open to judges to give much clearer guidelines to libel juries on what may or may not be appropriate damages, and most now do. These guidelines may take account, among other things, of the maximum sums normally available for personal injury awards, such as loss of a limb (then £52,000), loss of sight (£90,000) and severe brain damage (£125,000). In the opinion of the court:

> It was rightly offensive to public opinion that a defamation plaintiff should recover damages for injury to reputation greater, perhaps by a significant factor, than if that same plaintiff had been rendered a helpless cripple or an insensate vegetable.

It is unlikely now that there will be many further seven-figure libel awards, but even at the new, more realistic, levels the financial risks can still be considerable.

WHAT IS DEFAMATION?

Any statement in a book or journal or newspaper, or any other published matter (an advertisement, for example), runs the risk of being defamatory if it contains an untrue allegation or imputation which disparages the reputation of another. *All* those elements must be present, before a statement can be defamatory:

- It must have been published (or in the case of slander, spoken) to a third party.
- It must be untrue (truth – if you can prove it – is normally a complete defence).
- It must either include an allegation of fact, or of opinion which is not factually based.
- It must be understood – directly or indirectly – to refer to the person complaining about it.
- It must be 'capable of bearing a defamatory meaning' – a judge must be satisfied in law that the words used are *capable* of disparaging that person's reputation.
- It must actually defame – a jury must agree on the facts that the reputation actually *was* disparaged.

We shall look at each of these categories in turn. But first, a distinguishing note about libel and slander.

LIBEL AND SLANDER

Broadly speaking, libel is defamation in written or permanent form (such as a book or newspaper): slander uses the more transitory medium of face to face words and gestures. Traditionally, printed libel was felt to have a more serious long-term effect on a person's reputation than words spoken during an argument or at a public meeting – spoken words might be forgotten, but words you had printed would still be there the next morning.

As a result, there was – and still is – an important practical distinction between libel and slander: in an action for libel, damage is regarded as self-evident, and does not have to be proved; in order to succeed in an action for slander, however, plaintiffs must normally provide evidence that they have incurred a specific quantifiable loss. The only exceptions are:

- accusations of a crime punishable by imprisonment;
- allegations of contagious disease;
- imputations on a person's ability to carry on an office, business or profession, or on the reputation or credit of a trader;
- imputations of adultery or unchastity in women.

In recent years, technology has rendered this distinction between libel and slander increasingly out of date. The printed word is no longer the only permanent medium capable of inflicting damage, and words spoken on radio and TV, and via cable services and satellite broadcasts, are all now specifically treated as libels (since the Broadcasting Act 1990). Accessible or retrievable messages delivered via a computer network – such as the Internet – may also now be regarded as libels 'permanent' enough for damage to be assumed. This is also true of E-mail as well as bulletin boards.

'DEFAMATORY MEANING'

Before an action for defamation can proceed, the trial judge must decide whether the words complained of are capable of bearing a 'defamatory meaning'. Because it is possible to defame a person's reputation in a number of different ways, there is no single test for defamation, but several. Judges have sought to remedy each category in a succession of cases since the 17th century. Generally speaking, a statement will be defamatory of a person today if it tends to do any of the following:

Disparages them in their office, profession, calling, trade or business

You may defame someone not only in their personal or social capacity, but also at work, for example by alleging immorality or hypocrisy of a politician or a clergyman, professional misconduct or incompetence of a lawyer or doctor, plagiarism of an author, or fraud, false accounting or general lack of creditworthiness of an agent or publisher.

Exposes them to hatred, contempt or ridicule

It was defamatory of a man in 1680 to allege that his wife beat him, and possibly still is: anything which exposes someone to ridicule is actionable, particularly if they have a professional or social position to protect (even repeating a story they originally told as a joke against themselves). It is certainly defamatory to publish a statement causing someone to be despised – for example by falsely accusing them of child-abuse, or even perhaps cowardice. It might not be defamatory, however, to accuse someone merely of politically incorrect behaviour.

Causes them to be shunned or avoided

Even if an allegation inspires only sympathy, rather than contempt, it may still be defamatory if it has the same effect of causing people to avoid you, or excluding you from the society in which you normally move. Imputations of insanity or serious disease (such as leprosy) often had this effect in the past, even though they implied no blame or discredit: in the 1930s it was still defamatory of a woman to say that she had been raped. It would be less likely to amount to defamation today, when rape victims – on the whole – are not shunned but actively supported; however, it might well be defamatory today to say of someone that they are HIV positive or have AIDS.

Lowers them in the estimation of right-thinking members of society generally

A statement may still defame you, even if it does not fall under any of the other categories, if most normal, decent people would think the worse of you as a result. It would almost certainly be defamatory, for example, to say that you have a criminal record, but it may also defame you to say that you regularly drink and drive.

SOCIAL CONTEXT

In deciding whether a particular set of words is capable of being defamatory or not, a judge will have to bear in mind two things: current social standards and what the 'ordinary reader', applying those standards, would think. These standards may change, of course (and do), and what right-thinking members of society may have thought in our grandparents day may not strike us as defamatory at all.

Social standards

It was defamatory to say of a man during the First World War that he was German, or a Communist in the 1920s, and the word 'appeasement' was capable of being defamatory in the 1930s. However, it was not regarded as defamatory to say of someone in the 1920s that they had worked during a strike, even though they were active trade unionists, since ordinary, decent members of society then were clearly not expected to strike, or even belong to trade unions. The standard is of society *generally*, not of any particular group. So, to say of a person that they have given information to the police is not necessarily defamatory, since right-thinking members of society generally – even today – are expected to do their civic duty and assist the police, despite the fact that it may make you unpopular with your neighbours, or fellow members of the choral society, or even lead to death threats from the IRA.

The 'ordinary reader'

The objective test for defamation is not what the writer intended or had in mind in writing the words complained of, but what an ordinary reader would have thought when he or she read them. This hypothetical ordinary reader is not merely a reasonable person of normal intelligence but also moves about in society, probably reads newspapers and watches TV, has a reasonable sense of humour and is fairly up to date with common linguistic usages, including current slang. As the House of Lords said in one case: 'The ordinary man does not live in an ivory tower . . . He can and does read between the lines in the light of his general knowledge and experience of worldly affairs.'

Thus, in the classic 1930 case of *Tolley v. Fry*, the depiction of a champion amateur golfer apparently advertising a Fry's chocolate bar was defamatory, since the ordinary reader would assume that he would have been paid for such sponsorship and had therefore prostituted his amateur status. The advertisement itself did not say that, but that is what the ordinary reader would have thought.

The ordinary reader is not, however, unduly suspicious or cynical. In a more recent case it was held not to be defamatory to say that officers of the City of London Fraud Squad were inquiring into the affairs of a company: although some cynics might have thought so, the ordinary reader would not necessarily conclude that the company was guilty, simply because an inquiry was under way. Similarly, it is not defamatory in itself to say that a person is 'helping the police with their inquiries'.

HIDDEN MEANINGS AND INNUENDOES

Words are normally to be construed in their 'natural and ordinary meaning' – might reasonable people understand those words in a defamatory sense? To call someone a thief or a murderer is fairly plainly defamatory. Remember, however, that the ordinary reader is also capable of reading between the lines. Words not so plainly defamatory in themselves may still carry a defamatory *innuendo*, when read in context, or when used against certain people. To say of someone that they frequently visit a particular place is not in itself defamatory, but it might be if the place concerned houses a notorious brothel or is known to be a haunt of prostitutes: Cleveland Street in London in the last century, or perhaps today Shepherd Market. Similarly, to describe a person as voting Liberal Democrat is not (yet) defamatory, but it could be if the person concerned is a well-known Labour supporter, because it would imply the person was a hypocrite, or even a liar.

Even if the specific facts which you are describing are true, it is still dangerously easy to go beyond those specific facts and draw a more general *inference* which might *not* be true, and would therefore be defamatory. To say of a publishing company that they were once found to have committed a trading standards offence in their advertising would not be defamatory, if it was true, but it might become defamation if you then go on to imply from that that they are the sort of publisher that regularly defrauds the public with misleading advertising. A tour operator might on one occasion have sent tourists to a non-existent hotel, but if you publish an inference that they *habitually* do so they might well have an action against you for defamation.

IDENTIFICATION

Once you have established that a statement is defamatory, you must still prove that you personally are identifiable as the target before you can succeed in a defamation action. The words must not only be defamatory, and be published, but they must also be published 'of the plaintiff': that is, the finger must point at you. Put another way, the words complained of must be capable of being understood by reasonable people to refer to you, so that those who know you would think that you were the person meant.

It is not necessary that you should actually be named. If you are well known as the head of a particular publishing house, or the leader of a religious cult, or even the headteacher of a school, then you may be sufficiently identifiable to have an action for defamation – on the grounds that you were known to be responsible at the time, or must at least have known what was going on. 'A wealthy benefactor of the Liberal party' secured damages on one occasion on the grounds that there were so few wealthy benefactors of the Liberal Party that everyone knew the words referred to him. Authors and publishers should therefore take great care over 'fictionalised' accounts of real-life situations or events. However much the names are changed, if it would be quite clear to any reasonable person which actual people, or companies, are being described those concerned might well have an action for defamation. Were Robert Maxwell to be still alive, statements made in a novel about a 'fictitious' overweight, bullying newspaper magnate called The Captain could very easily be defamatory of him: everyone would know who was really meant.

It would not be defamatory, however, to make generalised statements about *all* members of a broad group or class, such as members of the Garrick Club or the Groucho Club: the statement must be taken to refer to you personally, or to an identifiable group of you. To say that 'all lawyers are thieves' is not defamatory (however shocking), but it may be defamatory to criticise a particular group of lawyers, or particular members of a jury: each of them would then have an action.

Authors, and their publishers, should therefore be particularly careful how they select names of fictitious characters, particularly if they are planning to put those characters in compromising positions. A humorous article in which a fictitious character called Artemus Jones appeared on the continent 'with a woman who is not his wife' was held to be defamatory in 1910, when a real Artemus Jones turned up with several witnesses, all of whom claimed they thought the article referred to him. It would be similarly dangerous to publish unflattering references to any fictitious, but named, character, for example a fat actress: a real actress who happened to have the same name and who was a little plump may be able to prove that her friends (and potential theatrical employers) thought the references were to her. Selecting names of wicked aristocrats, dissolute women, or any other fictitious rogues or crooks, should therefore be undertaken with great care. In cases of complete coincidence, where some care has been taken to avoid real names, (for example by checking professional or theatrical directories) there is now a defence of unintentional defamation (see below, p. 173) but this has so far proved to be of limited use. There may also be the possibility of making an 'offer of amends' – a defence due to be expanded under the Defamation Bill currently before Parliament. The general rule however is: if you think there is any risk you may be identifying a real person, do everything you reasonably can to check that no-one of that name and description already exists, and if still in doubt, pick another name.

Finally, bear in mind the risk of *juxtaposition* of unconnected pieces of text or photographs, a risk particularly run by periodical and newspaper publishers. The most extreme recent example of this was Jason Donovan's successful libel action against *The Face* magazine, when his face was superimposed on to a photograph of someone else wearing a T-shirt which read 'Queer as Fuck'. It can be done quite innocently and accidentally, however: it is possible to defame someone simply by printing their photograph, or some other reference to them, next to quite unconnected text which is critical or unflattering of other people – a picture of a reputable literary agent next to an article on corruption or tax evasion, or of a happily married author next to a piece about prostitution or pornography. The fact that you did not intend any defamatory reference will not necessarily give you a defence, if the friends of those people would assume the piece referred to them. Those responsible for final page make-up should therefore be made well aware of the risks.

PUBLICATION

Finally, and perhaps most obviously, a statement in order to be defamatory must be *published* to a third party, other than the person being defamed. Most publications or information services put on to the market by most publishers will, by definition, satisfy that requirement, although simple communication to a third party might well constitute publication for defamation purposes. Two points in particular should be noted:

Liability for publication

All those involved in a publication are *prima facie* liable for defamatory statements contained in it. This includes not only the original author of the words concerned, but everyone else who has taken part in publishing them. This could potentially include the editor, or sub-editor, publishing director, publisher or proprietor, although the current Defamation Bill proposes that those 'primarily responsible' should be limited to the author, the editor and the publisher. Responsibility could also extend to the printer, distributor, bookseller or even newspaper vendor – those at the production and distribution end of the chain would probably now have a defence of unintentional defamation or innocent dissemination (see below, p. 173) if they could prove that they had no reason to suspect the defamation existed and took all reasonable precautions. If the UK follows the most recent US cases, it is likely that an electronic service provider might be responsible for the contents of bulletin boards if they are monitored or subjected to editorial or publishing controls of any kind.

Unless the author is in the rare position of being able to provide an effective indemnity against defamation for everyone else involved in the entire publishing chain, the only way of spreading the risk is through comprehensive libel insurance.

Repeating a libel

Every republication of a libel is a new libel. It is not a defence to say that you are simply a commentator or reporter repeating a statement made by someone else: defamatory statements do not somehow come into the 'public domain' once published or uttered, so that the subject thereafter becomes fair game: a libel is a libel, and the more often it is repeated – even as a 'rumour' or as an attributed quote – the more damage it can do and the more libel writs it may provoke. Different newspapers repeating the same story can *all* therefore be sued (and often are), and a remainder merchant or bookshop re-publishing an old title as a remainder might well find that they are repeating an old libel.

DEFENCES

Once a claimant has proved that the words complained of were defamatory, that they refer to him or her, and that they were published by the particular publisher concerned (note that claimants do *not* need to prove that the words were false), then the burden of proof shifts to the publisher: they must then prove (if they can) that there is a valid defence. English law provides a number of possible defences to an action for defamation. We will look at all of them in turn, but the main defences are:

- truth, or justification;
- fair comment;
- absolute or qualified privilege;
- unintentional defamation.

Justification

With one very limited statutory exception (below, p. 168) it is an absolute defence to a charge of defamation to prove that the statement you published was true. It is not necessary to prove that every word of the statement is true, provided that it is *substantially* true. Minor errors of detail, which do not form the main substance, or essence, of the libel, will not prevent a defence of justification from succeeding. So if you state that a person robbed a bank in Manchester, having travelled there from Leeds, you will still be able to plead justification if the Manchester robbery was true, even though it turns out they were never in Leeds at all. The same would be true if they robbed not a bank but a jewellers. The whole substance of the libel consists in the allegation of robbery, not the peripheral detail of the kind of establishment, or how they got there.

What is the position, however, if the fact which turns out to be untrue is not some minor detail of time or place, but is also defamatory itself? What if you wrongly said that the person travelled to Manchester in a getaway car which was stolen in Leeds? It used to be the position that every defamatory statement of fact had to be separately justified, but since the Defamation Act 1952 this is no longer the case. Section 5 of the 1952 Act now provides that a defence of justification will still succeed 'if the words not proved to be true do not materially injure the plaintiff's reputation, having regard to the truth of the remaining charges'. In other words, in our example, if the extra accusation of car theft does not significantly lower the plaintiff's reputation – any further than your main charge of bank robbery has already lowered it – then your defence of justification will still succeed, even though the bit about the car theft may have been untrue. No-one thinks any less of a bank robber for stealing a getaway car (even in Leeds).

Remember, however, that if you go beyond individual facts and make a much more serious general inference or innuendo which is *not* true, a defence of justification may not protect you. All material facts must be substantially true, *including* innuendoes. If it turns out that the person did steal the car, but *didn't* steal it in order to rob banks, you may be in some difficulties.

It is no defence to claim afterwards that you were merely repeating rumours which genuinely existed, although it might constitute a defence if you make it clear at the time of the statement that what you are saying is only a rumour. As a general rule, the truth you must prove is the truth of the main allegation itself – not the fact that it was being rumoured. It is therefore important, if you are going to plead justification as a defence, to have reliable witnesses who will be prepared to testify in person as to the main fact on your behalf at a trial. If they are likely to become unreliable or disappear altogether, it may be in your interests to secure an affidavit from them, or at least ensure that they have kept a written note, or some other record such as a tape recording, but such evidence will not always be admissible.

The one exception to the general rule that truth is an absolute defence is the statutory provision relating to 'spent' convictions under the Rehabilitation of Offenders Act 1974.

It is considered socially useful that relatively minor offences should be erased from the public memory after a certain period of time – the periods vary from 3 to 10 years, depending on how serious the original offence was. After such convictions have become 'spent', evidence relating to them will not generally be admissible but such evidence *will* be available in defamation actions to support a plea of justification, provided the original publication was not made with malice. We will deal more fully with 'malice' below, but for practical purposes here this is a very restricted exception.

Fair comment

Although the United Kingdom has no written constitution and we have no general 'right' of free speech as such, English courts have long recognised a limited right of fair *comment*, by accepting it as a valid defence to a charge of defamation. This does not protect every form of comment, but it does provide a real defence for honest opinions, based on real facts and honestly expressed, on matters of public interest. There are three criteria for fair comment:

1 The facts on which it is based must be true.
2 It must express a genuine opinion, held in good faith (without malice).
3 It must be on a matter of public interest.

Fair comment must be based on true fact

The statement must clearly be recognisable as personal comment, but it must be comment *on* something. It is not fair comment simply to express random opinions on other people. So, to say of a well-known entrepreneur that they are not fit to be a director of a British company, without any supporting facts, would not normally be regarded as fair comment. If, however, you said that the person was unfit to be a director because they had just been convicted of specific crimes (and that was true), then your comment is likely to be justifiable as fair comment.

It is very important to separate comment from statements of fact. Fair comment will be based on true facts, but it is still recognisably *comment*. If it consists merely of fresh, unsupported allegations of (*un*true) fact, or is mixed up with such statements, it may not be defensible as 'fair comment' at all. Something that is clearly intended to be healthy, vigorous comment may still be found to be defamatory if it contains strong inferences of (untrue) fact. A book reviewer might run such a risk, if he or she significantly misdescribes the book being reviewed, for example in basing criticism on its irresponsible approach to some topic such as adultery or child abuse when in fact the book does not adopt that approach, or even deal with those topics at all. If you impute to an author that they have written something which they have not in fact written, you are making an allegation of fact, not making a fair comment – and that allegation of fact might well be defamatory.

Reviewers and columnists are as much at risk from this as anyone else, even though they may think their copy is self-evidently fair comment. So too are biographers, and even those who write Letters to the Editor, if they include new facts which are untrue. In a recent (1991) case, a Russian emigré wrote a newspaper article not only suggesting 'that Communism is as alien to the religious and national aspirations of the Russian people as those of any other nation' but also criticising the BBC World Service for recruiting so few of its Russian Service from 'those who associate themselves ethnically, spiritually, or religiously with Russian people'. Another emigré, a Russian Jew who had been persecuted in Russia and now worked for another radio station in London, took exception to this and wrote a letter to the Editor in response, denouncing the article as racist and anti-semitic. Unfortunately, he also went further than this and described it as having included demands that 'the BBC's Russian Service should switch from professional testing to a blood test', and that, whatever the qualifications 'of ethnically alien' Russian staff might be, they should be dismissed. In fact, the article had not advocated blood tests, or dismissals, and the apparent quotation 'of ethnically alien' had not appeared in the original article. The author of the article sued for libel, and won. Although the writer of the letter pleaded fair comment, the House of Lords found that he had misrepresented the original article in what were new defamatory allegations of fact:

> The writer of a letter to a newspaper has a duty to take reasonable care to make clear that he is writing comment, and not making misrepresentations about the subject matter on which he is commenting.

If any passage of text which includes both fact and opinion is giving concern, therefore, it is a good idea to run the following tests:

- Are *all* the facts stated (and quotations) true and accurate – and can we prove it?
- Is any 'comment' *based* on facts, and are they also true?
- If the comment contains new, ancillary, statements of fact, are they true as well?

If the answer to any of the above questions is 'no', a defence of fair comment may not succeed, and there may be a risk of defamation.

Fair comment and honest opinion

'Fair comment' may be profoundly biased and deeply *un*fair as long as it is an honest opinion. To succeed in a defence of fair comment, the defence need only establish that the statement was objectively capable of representing an honest opinion, or in other words that any person, however subjectively unreasonable, might honestly have held those views. The opinion need not be 'fair' in the colloquial sense of reasonable, balanced or even-handed. Commentators and critics are expected to express vigorous, often highly subjective, opinions. However, your defence may still fail if the plaintiff can show that you were not in that particular case being *subjectively* honest, and for example did not honestly hold those views yourself, or were motivated by some improper ulterior motive, such as malice.

'Malice', for these purposes, is any improper motive, including not only personal spite and ill-will but also any desire to cause injury, directly or indirectly – usually to the person who is defamed, but also including his or her family, or company, for example. Seeking a personal benefit without any desire to harm others can also be malice. Evidence that someone has gone ahead with publication of a statement, knowing it to be false, is *prima facie* proof of malice. A refusal to apologise, or offer any amends, once it has become clear that the statement is false or misleading, may also in some circumstances be regarded as malice. Similarly, a failure to give the other side a reasonable opportunity to state their own case, or comment on criticisms prior to publication, may be seen as malicious, especially if the allegations are likely to cause damage. Product reviews in trade journals may particularly be at risk from this. A good example was the recent (1994) *Yachting World* case. *Yachting World*'s Technical Editor conducted a performance test in 1992 of a controversial new catamaran, called Blue Nova, designed and built by Walker Wingsail Systems. The boat had already sailed the Atlantic and picked up a Technical Innovation award by the time of the test. The reviewer conducted his own sea tests using his own instruments but gave the boat a highly critical review in the February 1993 (Boat Show) issue, criticising various claims which the designers had allegedly been making for its speed and handling, and also querying the value of orders already claimed to be on the makers' books. His review made it clear he thought the boat's performance was disappointing and well below the company's claims ('During our test Planesail's performance barely exceeded that of a similar-sized monohull, let alone an equivalent multi-hull – a far cry from the claims that have been made by Walker Wingsail') and a supporting commentary in the Editorial even suggested the Technical Innovation award had not been deserved. The makers sued the reviewer, the Editor, and the magazine for libel. In defence *Yachting World* pleaded justification and fair comment. They argued that, although they believed the makers' claims, in the brochure and elsewhere, were exaggerated, they had never alleged dishonesty or fraud as such. The boat's makers argued not only that the reviewer's test was inadequate, and therefore unfair, but also that anyone reading the article would take it to mean that they had seriously and deliberately – or at least recklessly – misled people about the boat. Neither the reviewer, nor anyone else from the magazine, had interviewed the makers about the discrepancies, or given them any opportunity to comment even though (it was argued) the magazine must have realised the effect which publishing this review would have. The makers argued that to go ahead with publication on this basis was in itself evidence of malice.

The jury clearly agreed with the makers, and awarded them almost £1.48 million in libel damages including £1 million to the company. The publishers appealed, and the case settled at a sum which was roughly half of the jury's award, but the decision may still have considerable significance for trade reviewers. Where a review is likely to cause serious damage to a company, particularly if it seems also to question the company's integrity, it may become correspondingly harder to succeed with a defence of 'fair comment'.

Fair comment and public interest

Finally, fair comment must be comment on a matter of public interest. Nowadays, public interest is fairly widely defined to include any matters in which the public might have a legitimate interest, including (up to a point) the private lives of politicians or public officials. It covers, by definition, all published works available to the public at large, such as books, plays, newspapers, theatrical or musical performances, exhibited paintings, or photographs. It would probably *not* include the private lives of authors, but it may well include their public activities and equally the public conduct of anyone else – taxi drivers, publicans, doctors, teachers or company directors. The question is for the judge to decide, but few matters are now considered not to be of any public interest.

Privilege

English law regards some occasions as being self-evidently of public interest, and therefore protects statements made on those occasions from any actions for defamation. Such statements are said to be 'privileged'. The law will protect them, however untruthful they may turn out to be, in order to give the greatest possible freedom of speech to those who are regarded in the public interest as having a social or professional duty to speak freely.

Privilege comes in two kinds – absolute privilege, and a lesser form of conditional privilege known as qualified privilege.

Absolute privilege

As the name implies, statements carrying absolute privilege are completely protected from defamation actions, even though they may have been made maliciously or with reckless unconcern for the truth. Statements made by MPs or peers in Parliament are absolutely privileged, as are statements made in court, or during quasi-judicial proceedings, for example before tribunals, inquests or courts martial. Statements made by government ministers, senior civil servants or officers of the armed forces in the course of their official duty are absolutely privileged. So too are official Parliamentary or government reports such as Reports of Select Committees or White Papers.

However, second-hand reports of such statements, for example in newspapers, are *not* generally protected by absolute privilege, although they may be given qualified privilege. There are two exceptions to this rule:

1 *Hansard*. The official daily report of proceedings in Parliament is absolutely privileged.
2 *Contemporaneous court reports*. Reports of judicial proceedings in newspapers and on radio and TV are also protected by absolute privilege, provided they are 'fair and accurate', and published 'contemporaneously', that is in the next reasonably available issue or broadcast.

Qualified privilege

Although only a conditional form of protection, qualified privilege still gives considerable protection to many statements made on matters of public interest, or in the context of a social or professional duty, provided that they are made without malice. Subject to that proviso, it will protect much objective newspaper reporting, but only on matters of real public interest – which is for the court, and not the newspaper, to decide. The 'Public' whose interests might be served by publication can be a comparatively small section of the community, but publication must be *in* the public interest, not merely of interest to some of them.

Statements to and from those with a common interest may also be protected by qualified privilege – for example, between doctor and patient, or solicitor and client, company shareholders, employers (sharing references), or even members of a club. They must, however, be on an actual topic of shared interest, and be made without any hint of malice.

The 1952 Defamation Act specifically grants qualified privilege for fair and accurate newspaper reports of certain international organisations and courts, Commonwealth Parliaments, courts and inquiries, copies or extracts from UK public registers and court notices. It also provides a further category of qualified privilege for the following (fair and accurate) reports, but 'subject to explanation and contradiction', which involves offering a reasonable right of reply to those considering themselves to be defamed:

- Reports of associations promoting:
  (a) art, science, religion or learning;
  (b) any trade, industry, business or profession;
  (c) any game, sport or pastime;
- Reports of lawful public meetings (on any matter of public concern).
- Proceedings of local authorities (and local authority inquiries), meetings of magistrates, committees of inquiry, or any other bodies constituted under Act of Parliament.
- General Meetings of public companies or associations.
- Any notice (or 'other matter') issued by a government department, officer of state, local authority or chief constable.

Unintentional defamation

Unintentional, or 'innocent', defamation is a statutory defence under section 4 of the Defamation Act 1952. It is designed to offer a simple, straightforward, defence where the defamation complained of was purely accidental – where, for example, no defamation at all was intended, or where there was no intention to refer to the plaintiff. Such a defence might have proved useful in the case of the 'fictitious' character, Artemus Jones, off on a fling with a woman 'not his wife' (above p. 165), who turned out to be a real person, or in a case such as that of Harold Newstead, 30-year-old Camberwell man, reported (truthfully) by the *Daily Express* in the 1930s as having been imprisoned for bigamy; it turned out that there were *two* Harold Newsteads, both 30 and living in Camberwell, and the other one sued for libel (and won). The 1952 Act now provides a defence for such accidental libels, provided that an offer of amends has been made promptly (and accepted), or an offer is still on the table and the publisher can prove they acted 'innocently' (that is without intent or knowledge, and having exercised all reasonable care). This proviso is important – it would probably have defeated a defence on the facts of the Newstead case, since the paper did not exercise 'all reasonable care', but in other cases it does now provide an opportunity for a publisher responsible for a purely innocent, accidental defamation to put the matter right with a timely offer of amends.

The Defamation Bill currently before Parliament promises to provide a more straightforward 'offer of amends' defence, and also an extension of the 'innocent dissemination' defence to any parties who can show that they were not 'primarily responsible' for the statement concerned, such as those involved only in printing, production, distribution, or marketing, or (for electronic publications) processing, retrieving or copying, provided they did not know – or have reason to believe – the material was defamatory. This would possibly not protect an electronic service provider who in fact exercised some measure of editorial or 'publishing' control over bulletin board contents.

Other defences

Consent

Evidence of consent to publication is a full defence – although often difficult to prove, without signed statements. If you participate in the publication, for example by joining in a radio or TV discussion to put your side of the story, or by publishing your own statement alongside the offending version, then you may be held to have consented to publication taking place. However, the mere consent to be interviewed does not imply consent to specific libels. Consent can only be deduced from some positive act: silence does not imply consent, nor does the time-honoured phrase 'no comment'.

Death of the plaintiff

Libel is a purely personal action under UK law, and since the dead cannot sue personally, it is normally a complete defence to a libel action to establish that the person defamed is now dead. Even if the plaintiff was alive when the libel was published, but dies before the case is tried, (or even in mid-trial) the action instantly dies too, and cannot be continued by the plaintiff's relatives or heirs. It may still be possible, however, to commit a *criminal* libel against a dead person (see below, p. 175).

Limitation

It is a defence to an action for defamation to prove that it is out of time, or in other words has been started too late. Plaintiffs must issue their writs within 3 years of publication of the libel concerned (before 1986, the period was 6 years) – however, if the libel has been repeated, new 3-year periods start to run with each new publication. If the libel is not discovered until after 3 years has expired, the court may still allow an action to be commenced, but it must be within 1 year of the discovery. However, if a libel is not discovered for three years, it may be difficult to persuade a jury that it was libellous in the first place or, if it is, that much should be awarded by way of damages.

The current Defamation Bill proposes to reduce the limitation period to 1 year (although the court will retain its discretion to permit actions out of time).

SUMMARY CHECKLIST: DEFAMATION

IS IT DEFAMATION AT ALL?

- Is it a statement of fact, or an honest opinion?
- Has it been published yet? If not, is it too late to take it out, or tone it down?
- Is there any dangerous *innuendo*, or *inference*?
- Does it refer to an *identifiable* individual?
- Does it lower their reputation generally?
- Have we checked any 'fictitious' character names (for example in relevant directories)?
- Might this be repeating an *old* libel?
- Do we have an effective warranty against libel – or libel insurance?

ARE THERE ANY DEFENCES?

- Is the statement (and any innuendo) substantially true? Can we prove it?
- Is this all 'fair comment', or are there (untrue) allegations of fact?
- Is this an honest opinion, or is there any malice?
- Is it comment on a matter of public interest?
- Is the statement privileged in any way?
- Was any defamation innocent or unintentional?
- Is the person concerned still alive?
- Did they consent to publication?
- Is it too late to bring a libel action?

CRIMINAL LIBEL

Some libels are regarded as being so serious that they may not only be actionable in the civil courts, but may also be prosecuted in the criminal courts as a crime. It has been an offence at common law since the thirteenth century to publish written libels (particularly, in those days, about the king or the great officers of state) and it may still be possible to bring a prosecution today if prosecution is in the public interest, for example to prevent some public disturbance such as a breach of the peace. Punishment on conviction may consist of up to 1 year's imprisonment, or 2 years if the libel was known to be false, or a fine (or both), and either party may be bound over to keep the peace.

The crime consists in publishing a 'defamatory libel' (as opposed to a blasphemous or obscene libel) in written form – slander is not generally a crime (although public speakers may now commit other crimes, such as an incitement to racial hatred). A prosecution may be brought either where there is an actual likelihood of a breach of the peace, or at least where the libel is 'serious', rather than trivial or purely personal. Among the very few recent prosecutions were Sir James Goldsmith's prosecution against *Private Eye* in 1977, where there was some evidence of a sustained press campaign, and even bomb threats, and a (publicly funded) prosecution brought by Roger Gleaves in 1980 against the writers and publishers of the book and TV documentary *Johnny Go Home*. In the latter case, evidence of a previous conviction by Gleaves was not admissible in a criminal trial, and the truth of the allegations had to be proved all over again, as well as the fact that publication was in the public interest. Justification is not therefore a complete defence in cases of criminal libel – public interest must be established as well.

Because of the public interest and public order element, it is possible to commit a criminal libel against a whole *class* of people (unlike a civil libel). Nowadays, however, prosecutions for class libels against, for example, Jews, blacks, or gays, are more often brought under public order or race relations laws. It is also possible to bring a criminal prosecution for words published about the dead – but, again, only if the intention or likelihood was to provoke the dead person's heirs or relatives to commit a breach of the peace.

MALICIOUS FALSEHOOD

Some untruths may not, strictly speaking, be defamatory and (for example) lower you in the estimation of right-thinking members of society, but they may still cause you harm. To say of a publisher or a literary agent, for example, that they had retired from business and were therefore no longer looking for authors, would not be defamatory – people do retire occasionally. If it was untrue, however, it might cause them considerable financial harm, in the shape of lost business, and if it was said maliciously they may have an action for malicious falsehood. The violinist Stephane Grappelli found himself in exactly this position when his agents, after a misunderstanding over bookings, explained a series of cancelled concerts by stating falsely that he was 'very seriously ill in Paris and is unlikely ever to tour again'. It is not defamatory to describe someone as very seriously ill, but it was in that case a malicious falsehood.

In order to succeed in an action for malicious falsehood, you must prove:

- that the statement is untrue;
- that it was published maliciously ('malice', as in libel, includes any improper or dishonest motive); and
- that it is likely to (or 'calculated to') cause you financial loss.

Since likely financial loss is an important element of actions for malicious falsehood, interim injunctions may often be more readily granted than they are in libel actions, and legal aid may also be available. However, the court must be convinced there is a serious risk of financial loss, and there must be a strong suggestion of malice.

NEGLIGENT MIS-STATEMENT

If a statement is not defamatory, or a malicious falsehood, or otherwise illegal, but nevertheless causes harm to people who rely on it, it might still expose the publisher to an action for damages if it was made *negligently*. Suppose that a leading medical textbook seriously mis-states a recommended drug dosage, or that a specialist financial journal gives a subscriber the wrong investment advice in its regular Advice column. Would either of these mis-statements be negligent?

Negligence is a particular kind of civil wrong (known in English law as a tort). It consists, briefly, in the breach of a duty to take care in a way which causes damage to others. To prove that a particular statement is negligent, therefore, it is necessary to prove three things:

1 that the person making the statement owed you a duty of care;
2 that he or she breached that duty; and
3 that any loss or damage you suffered was caused by that breach.

DUTY OF CARE

There is no general legal duty to the whole world not to be careless. For a mis-statement to be negligent, it must be more than merely careless: the maker of the statement – the author or the publisher – must at the time the statement was made have owed the reader a specific legal duty of care. Such legal duties of care are not always easy to prove. They may arise in the context of a clear professional relationship (such as that between doctor and patient), or they may sometimes be assumed or implied in strongly similar circumstances, where any reasonable publisher (for example) would have foreseen the risk of injury to that particular reader, and taken suitable precautions to avoid it.

In the leading case of *Hedley Byrne v. Heller* (1964), the House of Lords confirmed as a general rule that:

if A assumes a responsibility to B to tender him deliberate advice, there could be a liability if the advice is negligently given.

The crucial word in that proposition is 'assumes'. In that particular case, an advertising agency was retained by a new client for a major advertising campaign, and took out space ads in national newspapers and booked TV advertising slots, all at the agency's own financial risk. Understandably, the agency sought financial references from the new client's bank, which the bank duly gave, but 'without responsibility'. The references turned out not to be reliable and the agency lost a large amount of money. The House of Lords held that a duty of care could exist where a 'special relationship' was created, which might happen in the following circumstances:

- where the party seeking information or advice was 'trusting the other to exercise such a degree of care as the circumstances required';
- where that trust was reasonable; and
- where the other gave the information or advice 'when he knew or ought to know that the enquirer was relying on him'.

However, in that particular case, the bank had clearly given the advice 'without responsibility', and in the view of the House of Lords that disclaimer was sufficient to avoid liability – they had *not* 'assumed' responsibility.

In the case of a publisher who publishes statements for the whole world to read, it would be difficult to establish a specific legal duty of care unless it could be shown that there was a 'special relationship' with a particular reader, or group of readers. This is unlikely to exist in the circumstances of trade publishing, but it may possibly exist in the case of some specialist, professional or STM publishers, who give information or advice to a limited, specific market knowing that those people might reasonably be expected to rely on it. This might particularly be so in the context of a specific Advice service (or column) – the second of our two original examples – where answers to subscribers' queries are held out as being authoritative; a reader or subscriber relying (and known to be relying) on the skill and judgement apparently being offered might well – in the absence of any disclaimer – be able to prove that a sufficient duty of care existed, and claim damages for negligence if he or she suffered loss when the advice turned out to be wrong.

In the first of our two examples above, however – where a mis-statement is published in a textbook circulating generally to a wide readership – it is unlikely that any individual reader would be able to establish a similar duty of care, and negligence would be much harder to prove.

DISCLAIMERS

Some publishers seek to discourage negligence claims by printing general disclaimers of liability at the front of their books. Such disclaimers are usually unpopular with authors since they imply a lack of confidence in the text, and they are probably of limited legal effect. Even if it can be established that they formed part of the contract of sale (and disclaimers in small print tend not to be noticed at the time) they are still subject to the test of 'reasonableness' under the Unfair Contract Terms Act 1977 (see p. 248). A court might well find in all the circumstances that the disclaimer was unreasonable – particularly if the publisher could easily have insured against the risk.

A specific disclaimer given in circumstances similar to the *Hedley Byrne* case above, however, might be effective if it made it clear that no responsibility for the statement(s) was being assumed.

OBSCENITY

INTRODUCTION

It is not a crime for an author to write obscene material, but it *is* a crime for a publisher (or anyone else) to publish it. It is also an offence for anyone to have it in their possession, with a view to publication for profit. Although authors are often asked in their publishing contracts to warrant that the material they produce is in no way obscene or indecent, this only gives a limited contractual remedy to the publisher against the author: the criminal offence will still be committed by the publisher and, in some cases, by the distributor and it is they who will be prosecuted and possibly fined or sent to prison. Publishers should therefore take every possible precaution themselves against publishing obscene or indecent material, however innocently. This applies as much to text as to photographs or other illustrations, and increasingly to computer images (for example, on the Internet) as much as to printed matter.

OBSCENE PUBLICATIONS

Although the criminal offence of publishing an obscene libel is of some antiquity (obscenity having originally been dealt with under ecclesiastical law) what is or is not 'obscene' has never been defined very clearly. The law is now largely contained in the Obscene Publications Act 1959, and the test of obscenity is now contained in section 1 of that Act. Section 1 provides that an article, or any distinct item contained in an article, is obscene:

> If its effect . . . is, if taken as a whole, such as to tend to deprave and corrupt persons who are likely, in all the circumstances, to read, see or hear the matter contained or embodied in it.

'Deprave' and 'corrupt' are pretty strong words. They mean something considerably worse than simply shocking or disgusting, and one conviction (of the *Oz* 'School Kids' issue) was overturned in 1971 because the trial judge had wrongly directed the jury that obscenity could mean merely 'repulsive, filthy, loathsome, indecent or lewd'. An article is not obscene simply because it is repulsive or filthy. The prosecution must prove that its tendency is strong enough actually to deprave and corrupt a significant proportion of its likely audience: in other words, to pervert or corrupt their morals sufficiently for it to constitute a public menace. Furthermore, the entire article 'taken as a whole' must have that tendency, not just one small bit of it.

It is important to note that obscenity is not just about sex. Anything tending to deprave or corrupt may be obscene, including material encouraging the taking of dangerous drugs, or glorifying violence, particularly if it is expressly targeted at children or adolescents. But sex usually creeps in somewhere.

OBSCENITY OFFENCES

Publication

It is an offence under section 2 of the Obscene Publications Act 1959 to publish an obscene article. 'Publish' includes distribution, circulation, sale, hire or even free gift or loan. It also includes (under the 1990 Broadcasting Act) TV and broadcasting.

Possession

The 1964 Obscene Publications Act added a further offence of having an obscene article for publication for gain, which now extends the threat of criminal penalties to printers, distributors, wholesalers, shopkeepers and booksellers. There may, however, be a defence of innocent dissemination where the person did not inspect the articles and had no reason to suspect they might be obscene (see below, p. 181).

Under section 85 of the Criminal Justice and Public Order Act 1994, publication of obscene matter was made a Serious Arrestable Offence, which means that a police superintendent may authorise the holding of suspects for up to 36 hours without access to legal advice or even notifying relatives. On conviction for either offence (publication or possession), a sentence of up to 3 years imprisonment, with an unlimited fine, may be imposed.

There is also a summary 'forfeiture' procedure under section 3 of the Act, under which a constable, on a warrant from a local magistrate, may enter and search premises for articles which he or she has reason to believe are obscene and being kept for publication for gain, which may then be forfeited unless the owner can show cause why they should not.

DEFENCES TO OBSCENITY

Public Good

No defence of literary or artistic merit had existed prior to the 1959 Act. It is now a defence under section 4 of the Act to prove:

that publication of the article in question is justified as being for the public good on the ground that it is in the interests of science, literature, art or learning, or of other objects of general concern.

'Other objects' includes sociological, ethical, and educational merits, but must fall within the same general area as those listed. Mere therapeutic relief of sexual tension (seriously argued in one case) is *not* an object of sufficiently general concern.

The burden of proof is on the publishers, but they may call expert witnesses in their support. Penguin Books used the defence of public good successfully shortly after the Act was passed, in the 1961 trial of D. H. Lawrence's *Lady Chatterley's Lover*, and a succession of expert witnesses – including the Bishop of Woolwich – testified to the literary and sociological merit of the work 'taken as a whole'. Expert evidence may even be admitted to establish that a work, far from promoting or glorifying obscenity, deliberately shocks and disgusts so much that the likely audience will only be repelled: this defence was used (ultimately successfully) by Calder & Boyars Ltd in 1969 to defend the book *Last Exit to Brooklyn*, which contained graphic depictions of drug abuse, senseless violence, and sexual perversion. It seems likely now that any serious work of literature will have a strong defence, however graphic, and more recent works, such as Brett Easton Ellis's *American Psycho*, have not even been prosecuted.

Innocent dissemination

Under section 2 of the 1959 Act and section 1 of the 1964 Act it is a defence for someone found in possession of an obscene article to prove that:

1 they had not examined the article; *and*
2 they had no reasonable cause to suspect it was obscene.

Both conditions must be satisfied – once a wholesaler or bookseller has actually examined (in other words, personally inspected) an article it will be no defence to claim that they did not realise that it was obscene. This defence is therefore more likely to protect printers and distributors than booksellers, most of whom 'examine' their stock at some point, even if only to look at the cover or read the blurb.

INDECENT PHOTOGRAPHS

Although something which is 'indecent' is by definition less offensive than something which is 'obscene', special considerations apply to publications containing indecent pictures of children. Under the Protection of Children Act 1978 it is an offence to take, permit to be taken, distribute or show, possess with a view to distribution, or advertise, any indecent photograph of a child under the age of 16. The Criminal Justice and Public Order Act 1994 has extended the definition of 'photograph' for these purposes to include any 'pseudo-photograph', for example, a computer generated image (it has also made offences under the 1978 Act Serious Arrestable Offences – see above, p. 180).

Whether or not a photograph is 'indecent' under the 1978 Act is to be decided by a jury according to 'the recognised standards of propriety'. These standards may of course change, which makes the task for publishers of illustrated or children's books of keeping within the law particularly difficult. The circumstances of the photography or the publication, or the motivation of the photographer, are all irrelevant: in one 1988 case, despite the fact that the 14-year-old girl concerned had clearly consented to the photographs being taken (in order to further her fashion career), and was photographed in the presence of her family and boyfriend, two or three of the photographs – showing her lightly clad, in underwear only, and 'in a provocative pose' – were held by a jury to be indecent. At times of public concern about computer pornography and child abuse, it would be wise to take advice before publishing photographs of children that a jury might feel were indecent.

POSTING INDECENT OR OBSCENE MATTER

Under section 11 of the Post Office Act 1953 it is an offence to send any indecent or obscene article by post. It is also an offence under section 4 of the Unsolicited Goods and Services Act 1971 to send unsolicited material describing human sexual techniques, or unsolicited advertisements for such material.

BLASPHEMY

Despite calls for its abolition, there is still a common-law misdemeanour of publishing a blasphemous libel. As with defamatory, obscene and seditious libels, blasphemous libels were originally punishable because of the threat they posed to public order and the established institutions of the state, including the established Church. As late as 1917 it was still being said that blasphemous words were punishable 'for their tendency to endanger the peace then and there, to deprave public morality generally, to shake the fabric of society and to be a cause of civil strife'. It is unlikely that attacks on the Church of England would have that effect today, but the offence still exists.

Under English law blasphemy is limited to attacks on the *Christian* religion and it is arguable that the offence can only be committed against the tenets of the established Anglican Church (so that an attack on the beliefs of Baptists or Quakers, though probably anti-Christian, might not be blasphemous). It has never offered any protection to other religions such as Islam, and an attempt in 1991 to prosecute Salman Rushdie and the publishers of *The Satanic Verses* for blasphemy noticeably failed.

This antique law, left over from an age when scurrilous attacks on the Bible or Book of Common Prayer might provoke riots in the streets, was last used in 1979 in a private prosecution brought by Mrs Mary Whitehouse against the homosexual periodical *Gay News* and its editor, Denis Lemon, for publishing what she described as 'an obscene poem and illustration vilifying Christ in his life and in his crucifixion'. The poem, by Professor James Kirkup, and entitled 'The Love that Dares to Speak its Name', described a homosexual centurion's feelings at the scene of the Crucifixion, but did so in sexually explicit terms which would doubtless have been offensive to many Christians, although possibly not to the Christians who read *Gay News*. No evidence of literary merit was admitted (there is still no such defence for blasphemy) and the prosecution was not required to prove that there was any danger of breach of the peace (there clearly wasn't). It was not even necessary to prove that *Gay News* intended, in publishing that article, to shock or outrage Christians, but merely that they intended to publish it. In the view of the House of Lords, any publication might be blasphemous if it used indecent, intemperate or offensive terms likely to outrage and insult the religious feelings of the general body of Christian believers in society. This remains the test today. It is not necessarily blasphemous to attack or deny Christianity or the Church, if you do so in decent and temperate language, but it is blasphemous (whatever your intentions) if you do so scurrilously or offensively. *Gay News* was fined £1,000 (a suspended sentence against the editor was overturned on appeal).

Although there have been no further prosecutions since 1979, the crime of blasphemy still exists. Until it is abolished, therefore, authors and publishers should be careful what they say about God and Christ, Christianity and the established Church, if they are planning to say it in indecent, offensive or intemperate terms.

SEDITIOUS LIBEL

Publishing a seditious libel is analogous to treason, although a milder form of offence. Like obscenity and blasphemy, the offence exists largely to control publications directed against the peace and good order of the state, and its institutions. It will not be seditious merely to criticise the Queen, or other institutions such as Parliament (few newspapers would survive if it were), but it may be if there was a seditious *intent*, for example to incite people to violence against the monarchy or to create anti-Parliamentary disturbances, and there is also a *likelihood* that public disorder will result. Although it was argued in 1991 that Salman Rushdie's *The Satanic Verses* provoked hostility between Muslims and other citizens, it was held not to be seditious because there was no evidence that it constituted an attack on the state itself or its institutions.

INCITEMENT TO RACIAL HATRED

Most public order offences, including race relations offences, are now dealt with under the Public Order Act 1986. It is an offence to stir up racial hatred by, among other things, using threatening, abusive or insulting words or behaviour, publishing, displaying, distributing or possessing written material which is threatening, abusive or insulting, or distributing or showing or playing a recording of visual images which involves the use of threatening, abusive or insulting words or behaviour. Each offence may be punished on conviction by up to 2 years imprisonment or an unlimited fine, or both.

Note in each case the requirement that the medium used should be 'threatening, abusive or insulting'. There must also be either:

- a positive *intention* to stir up racial hatred; *or*
- a *likelihood* that it will be stirred up.

'Racial hatred' is defined in the 1986 Act as meaning 'hatred against a group of persons in Great Britain defined by reference to colour, race, nationality (including citizenship) or ethnic or national origins'. Note that religious or other social groups are not included as such – the purpose behind the legislation is to prevent *racial* discrimination, not discrimination generally. It was held in 1983, however, that an attack on the long-established Sikh community could be considered an attack on an 'ethnic' rather than merely religious group and much the same might be said of an attack on Jews.

OFFICIAL SECRETS

Despite calls for more open government, and the Citizen's Charter, the UK still has no Freedom of Information Act, and in many respects we still live in a secret society. Under the Official Secrets Act 1911 and 1989 it is an offence to publish several categories of official government or state information if publication may be prejudicial or damaging to the safety or interests of the state. In practice, this tends to affect investigative newspaper and TV journalists more than book publishers, but memoirs of former civil servants, especially those involved with the security services, can often run a serious risk of legal action. This may not only be prosecution under the Official Secrets Act, but also civil action for breach of government confidentiality, as the *Spycatcher* case showed (see below, p. 186).

THE 1911 ACT

Although intended to apply to the spying activities of foreign enemy agents, section 1 of the 1911 Official Secrets Act still makes it an offence

if any person for any purpose prejudicial to the safety or interests of the State:

(a) approaches, inspects, passes over or is in the neighbourhood of, or enters any prohibited place within the meaning of this Act; or

(b) makes any sketch, plan, model or note which is calculated to be or might be or is intended to be directly or indirectly useful to an enemy; or

(c) obtains, collects, records or publishes, or communicates to any other person any secret official code word, or password or any sketch, plan, model, article or note or other document or information which is calculated to be or might be or is intended to be directly or indirectly useful to an enemy.

A prohibited place might include a power station, as well as more obvious military establishments, and an 'enemy' may include potential as well as actual enemies of the UK. 'Any person' might in theory include internal saboteurs or even journalists and authors, but the section has not successfully been used against non-spies, and an attempt by the Attorney-General in 1978 in the 'ABC' case to prosecute *Time Out* journalists Duncan Campbell and Crispin Aubrey under section 1 for a story including security revelations by a former soldier was thrown out by the trial judge as being 'oppressive' (they were given lighter sentences under section 2 – now replaced by the 1989 Act).

The 1989 Act

Section 2 of the 1911 Act, so widely drafted as to include almost anything, was replaced, on the recommendation of the Franks Committee, with specific classes of restricted information in the 1989 Official Secrets Act. They include, among others:

• security and intelligence;
• defence;
• international relations;
• information which might facilitate a criminal offence.

In most cases the prosecution will need to prove that the author or journalist knew or had reasonable cause to believe that publication would be 'damaging', but this may vary, depending on the category of secret and the source: some secrets (for example intelligence revelations by serving or former intelligence staff) are considered self-evidently 'damaging'. Lesser information, perhaps acquired by a government contractor (who had not been put on written notice that it was secret) may not be, and a likelihood of damage would need to be proved.

D-NOTICES

The Defence Press and Broadcasting Committee was set up after the 1911 Act to issue advisory Notices (called D-Notices) to the media, both on general policy matters and on the security implications of particular pieces of information. The notices are for guidance only, and have no legal status or authority.

BREACH OF GOVERNMENT CONFIDENTIALITY

Juries are not always as willing as governments would like to convict under the Official Secrets Acts, and where diaries or memoirs are concerned civil actions for breach of confidence are increasingly used to try and stifle publication on the grounds that every minister or government employee has a duty not to reveal government secrets. An injunction might be granted if there is still a risk to national security – however, Jonathan Cape were allowed to proceed with publication of the *Crossman Diaries* in 1975 on the grounds that by then the revelations were too old to be dangerous.

The Attorney-General was more determined in 1985 and 1986, however, when attempting to suppress publication of former MI5 officer Peter Wright's memoirs, *Spycatcher*. While proceedings for breach of confidentiality were under way in the Australian courts, several UK newspapers began to publish extracts. In a succession of actions, the government obtained interim injunctions against the *Guardian*, *Observer*, and *Sunday Times* but meanwhile the book was published in the USA and became freely available throughout the rest of the world. The House of Lords finally lifted the injunctions in 1988 on the grounds that there could no longer be any public interest in suppressing 'secrets' that had become so widely public. As a final humiliation, the European Court of Human Rights later ruled that maintenance of the injunctions after general publication had taken place was an infringement of the right to freedom of expression contained in Article 10 of the European Convention.

CONTEMPT OF COURT

Publishing comments on matters which are currently being tried, or about to be tried, in the courts can carry a risk of a fine or even imprisonment for contempt of court. In the *Spycatcher* case (above) the *Sunday Times* was held to be in contempt of court for publishing extracts despite injunctions already granted against the *Guardian* and *Observer* (even though those injunctions were not in fact addressed to the *Sunday Times* directly). It is, of course, contempt of court to disobey any court order.

Under the Contempt of Court Act 1981, a person may also be guilty of contempt by publication where the publication creates a *substantial* risk that *active* court proceedings will be *seriously* impeded or prejudiced.

Proceedings are 'active' from the moment a case is scheduled for trial, or an arrest is made. Note that there must be a *substantial* risk of *serious* prejudice. Thus, the more distant the trial or the more peripheral the material published the less likely that a contempt will have been committed.

Under section 3 of the 1981 Act it is a defence for a publisher to prove that at the time of publication they did not know proceedings were active, provided they took all reasonable care, and had no reason to believe otherwise.

An additional 'public interest' defence is now available under section 5 of the Act, which provides that a publication made as, or as part of, a discussion in good faith of public affairs (or other matters of general public interest) is not to be treated as contempt of court if the risk of impediment or prejudice to particular legal proceedings is merely incidental to the discussion.

SUMMARY CHECKLIST: OTHER RISKS

- Is this a malicious falsehood?
- Is it negligent to make this statement? Do we owe any duty of care to particular readers?
- Might this be obscene? Taken as a whole, would it deprave or corrupt?
- Are we publishing it, or in possession of it?
- Can it be justified as being for the public good (for example on grounds of literary merit)?
- Are we disseminating it innocently?
- Would a jury think this photograph was indecent?
- Is this material blasphemous? Is it scurrilous or offensive about Christianity, or the Anglican Church?
- Is this a criminal or seditious libel, or an incitement to racial hatred?
- Might this breach the Official Secrets Act, or any duty of government confidentiality?
- By publishing this now, would we be in contempt of court? Would publication by us seriously prejudice active court proceedings?

Copyright infringement 8

We saw in chapter 2 that copyright in the UK is not merely a personal licence to copy; its value lies primarily in the right to control (and if necessary, prevent) copying by others. In this chapter we will set out in detail exactly which activities a copyright owner may control in this way, and what remedies UK – and international – law provides against infringers. We will need to look in turn at the following things:

- the primary 'restricted acts' under UK law, such as copying itself;
- secondary infringements such as possession or dealing with infringing copies;
- defences such as Fair Dealing, and the permitted acts which will not infringe;
- where infringement does occur, the civil and criminal remedies available in the UK against infringers;
- the legal protection available for UK works overseas, and for foreign works here.

PRIMARY INFRINGEMENT

Section 16 of the 1988 Act provides that copyright owners have the exclusive right to do the following 'restricted acts' in relation to most copyright works in the UK (but not always artistic works):

1 to copy the work;
2 to issue copies of the work to the public;
3 to perform, show or play the work in public;
4 to broadcast the work or include it in a cable programme service;
5 to make an adaptation of the work, or do any of the above things in relation to an adaptation.

Anyone who does any of these restricted acts to a relevant work without the licence of the copyright owner will infringe copyright in the work, unless one of the exceptions applies (see below p. 198).

The key restricted acts for publishing purposes are (1) (2) and (5), but before we go on to consider these in more detail, two further general points need to be made:

Taking a 'substantial part' may infringe

Any of the acts listed above may infringe copyright if they are done either in relation to the work as a whole, or to any 'substantial part' of it. It is therefore not necessary for an infringer to copy (for example) the entire work, as long as a substantial part is copied. This of course rather begs the question: what is a substantial part?

The 1988 Act itself gives no guidance, but in a long line of decided cases the courts have held that what is substantial is a question of fact and degree in all the circumstances, and may depend as much on the *quality* of what is taken as on the quantity. One or two lines of text taken from a 500-page textbook might not be significant enough to amount to a substantial part of the whole thing, but centrally important dramatic lines from a novel or play might well be. Thus, as little as four lines from Rudyard Kipling's poem 'If' constituted a sufficiently substantial part in the 1920s when used without consent in a Sanatogen advertisement, and a few bars of music have similarly been held to be a substantial part of a popular tune such as 'Colonel Bogey': a key issue is often whether the part taken is commonplace or insignificant or whether it includes some identifiable, distinctive flavour of the work. In the much-quoted words of one judge in 1916: 'What is worth copying is prima facie worth protecting.' If it is valuable enough to an infringer to be worth taking at all, it may well be important enough to be a substantial part.

Infringement may be indirect

Any of the above infringing acts may be done indirectly as well as directly. Thus, copying a copy (or a copy of a copy) may infringe copyright just as much as copying directly from the original. In most cases of copying (for example from a book or journal) what is copied is not the author's original, but the authorised published edition, which is itself of course a copy.

Equally, copyright may be infringed by authorising (even impliedly) the infringement of others. There must, however, be a direct causal link between the 'authorisation' and the infringing act(s) which resulted. So, the sale and supply of recording equipment with a high-speed copying feature expressly advertised as suitable for home taping might in some circumstances infringe, even though the infringements would actually be done by others, but the mere sale of blank tapes by itself would probably not. Manufacturers of photocopying machines do not 'authorise' copyright infringement merely by selling and supplying their machines, but a university library or a business which installs a machine and permits multiple copying knowing that most if not all of the copying will infringe copyright and does nothing to prevent it, may well be held to have 'authorised' those infringements.

COPYING

Although anti-piracy slogans such as 'Copying is Theft' are not always strictly accurate, copying the work, or a substantial part of it, without permission and in the absence of one of the exemptions is probably the most common primary infringement. It often accompanies other infringements such as issuing copies to the public; indeed it would usually be difficult to do some of the other restricted acts without someone having copied first. A copy may still infringe even if its making is transient or incidental to some other use of the work.

Copying is widely defined in the 1988 Act (section 17) to mean reproducing the work 'in any material form' and this is expressly stated to include storing the work in any medium by electronic means. Any reproduction of any work in physical or retrievable form can therefore be caught under the definition: although there are as yet very few UK cases on the point, it is likely (as with recent US decisions) that uploading a work on to a bulletin board on the Internet and downloading from it on to an individual user's PC, would both involve 'copying' under UK law.

Whatever the medium, however, there must be some objective evidence that copying actually took place, and that the alleged infringing copy was derived directly or indirectly from the work in question. It will not often be possible to produce first hand witness evidence of copying, of course (unauthorised copying is not usually done in public) – a court will therefore in many cases be prepared to make a presumption that copying must have taken place where:

- there is sufficient objective similarity between the work and the alleged copy;
- the alleged infringer had access to or knew of the original;
- no (credible) counter-evidence is produced to suggest that the alleged copy might have resulted from independent skill and effort (or been taken from some other source).

Under these circumstances there will be a strong imputation that copying must have occurred, and in the absence of any defence (see below) this is likely to amount to copyright infringement.

Intention

It does not matter that the infringer did not consciously intend to copy; all the primary acts of copyright infringement are offences of strict liability, requiring no evidence of guilty knowledge or intent. An apparently innocent state of mind is no defence – neither is ignorance (for example, that the work in question was still in copyright, or even that it existed) and neither is honest mistake, such as a genuine belief that the copying in question was licensed by the copyright owner.

Evidence of this kind will of course be taken into account, and may provide a defence to any award of damages if there was no reason to believe the work was in copyright at all (see p. 197), but it will not otherwise prevent the acts concerned amounting to infringing acts. However blameless you think you are, if you in fact copy without permission you are very likely to infringe copyright.

Plagiarism

There is a common misconception in some circles that copying someone else's work can somehow be legalised by the strategic alteration of a few words and phrases. This is entirely wrong, and highly dangerous. The mere fact that few passages are reproduced exactly, word for word, will not necessarily be sufficient to prevent what is copied from being a substantial part of the whole, particularly if the copying is extensive and blatant. It will also not give any protection against infringement of the separate copyright in the author's compilation of material, including the selection and arrangement of topics and headings. The question to be asked is very simple indeed: did copying actually take place? If it did – whether of the text, or the compilation – then no amount of subsequent tinkering with the wording or the arrangement will save the activity from being copyright infringement – provided that at least some substantial parts have been taken. The fact that all the material *could* have been obtained from elsewhere will also not alter the position if the infringer chose instead to save the time and effort and skill involved and copy from an existing compilation. In the 1985 case of *Geographia Ltd v. Penguin Books*, the selection and arrangement of map details including colours was accepted as protectable, although on the facts the copying was insufficiently substantial.

This is not to say of course that existing material and common sources cannot be relied upon in creating a new work – provided that they are not copied. It may also be permissible to reproduce limited extracts in the context of fair dealing for the purposes of criticism and review, but these must be accompanied by a sufficient acknowledgement (see below). There have often been borderline cases where there is a marked similarity between two works, and it is clear that much of the material in the new work has been derived from the thoughts and ideas in the existing one. Even without any acknowledgement this may be perfectly legal (if a little unprofessional) – there is no copyright in ideas. However, over-reliance on any single existing work is generally inadvisable, and even though there may be no direct evidence of intentional copying, provided that sufficiently substantial parts have been taken a court may still be willing to infer that copying – however inadvertent – must have taken place.

Artistic works

The 1988 Act provides that the definition of copying in relation to an artistic work includes:

- making a three-dimensional copy of a two-dimensional work; and
- making a two-dimensional copy of a three-dimensional work.

A carving or sculpture which is copied from an original photograph may thus infringe copyright in the photograph even though the new work has added an extra dimension, and three-dimensional toys based on two-dimensional cartoon characters may similarly infringe copyright in the original graphic works. Conversely, a two-dimensional photograph or painting may infringe copyright in a three-dimensional work.

ISSUING COPIES TO THE PUBLIC

Under section 18 of the 1988 Act the issue to the public of copies of any work is a restricted act, and copyright in the work will be infringed if it is done without the copyright owner's consent.

'Issue to the public' is defined as the putting into circulation of copies not previously put into circulation, in the UK or elsewhere (for computer programs, this is defined as the UK or any other EU member state) – so first publication would count as issue to the public, but not subsequent re-circulation of copies which have already been published (even abroad). Under the Act issue to the public specifically does *not* include:

- any subsequent distribution, sale, hiring or loan of copies already circulating (even abroad); or
- any subsequent importation of those copies into the UK.

Note that 'copies' are referred to in the plural, though there seems no particular reason why the issue to the public of a single copy should not infringe copyright also, in appropriate circumstances. However, it is likely that at least one physical copy of the work itself must actually be put into circulation, so that merely advertising or collecting orders will probably not of themselves amount to issue to the public and there must be some evidence that the circulation which takes place is (at least potentially) to the public at large rather than to a small circle of friends or acquaintances.

Rental

Although subsequent acts of importation, or distribution, sale, hire or loan, are generally exempted as described above, rental of certain works is not. At present, section 18 of the 1988 Act covers only rental of sound recordings, films (including videos) and computer programs and such rentals will constitute issue to the public. There is no general 'rental right' for literary works other than computer programs (such as books) at the moment other than the financially limited Public Lending Right covering loans from public libraries (see p. 54). There will be a more general rental right in the UK, however, when the UK

implements the terms of the EU Rental Right Directive: on this generally, see
p. 55.

PERFORMING, BROADCASTING AND CABLE TRANSMISSION

Performing, showing or playing in public

Performing, showing or playing most works (but not artistic works) in public is a
restricted act, which will infringe copyright if done without permission.
'Performance' includes delivery of lectures, addresses, speeches and sermons
and can include presentation via any method of sounds or images, including
sound recording, films, broadcast or cable programmes as well as live recital.
The audience does not need to be large, but in order to be 'public' must consist
of more than a purely domestic or private gathering (even if some guests are
present).

The Act (section 19(4)) provides a limited exemption for those (such as TV or
cable companies) whose electronic media for transmitting sounds or images are
used by others (such as publicans, or club secretaries) for infringing
performances: in such cases the person by whom the visual images or sounds
are sent, and in the case of a performance the performers, shall not be regarded
as responsible for the infringement. They may however be caught by other
sections (see below).

Broadcasting and cable transmission

Broadcasting the work or including it in a cable programme service are both acts
restricted by copyright, in every kind of work except a typographical
arrangement.

A 'broadcast' means a transmission by wireless telegraphy which:

- is capable of being lawfully received by members of the public; or
- is transmitted for presentation to members of the public.

A 'cable programme service' is defined (in section 7 of the Act) to mean a non-
wireless telecommunications service either for reception at two or more places
or for public presentation: it could involve sending visual images, sounds or any
'other information' (such as data).

MAKING AN ADAPTATION

Making an adaptation of a literary, dramatic or musical work (not, incidentally,
of an artistic work) is an act restricted by copyright. Doing it without the
copyright owner's consent will amount to copyright infringement unless one of
the exceptions (such as fair dealing – see below) applies.

However, adaptations for the purposes of copyright law are narrowly defined. What amounts to an 'adaptation' under UK law is defined in section 21 of the 1988 Act in relation to different kinds of works:

Literary and dramatic works

In relation to a literary or dramatic work, an adaptation means one of the following:

- a translation (normally from one human language to another – for translations of computer codes, see below);
- a dramatisation of a non-dramatic work (turning a novel into a screenplay, for example) or the converse: a conversion of a dramatic work into a non-dramatic work;
- a picturisation (conveying the story or action by means of pictures, in a form suitable for reproduction in a book, newspaper, magazine or similar periodical).

Musical works

An adaptation in relation to a musical work means an arrangement or transcription of the work.

Computer programs

In relation to a computer program, section 21(3)(ab) of the 1988 Act (inserted by the Copyright (Computer Programs) Regulations 1992), provides that an adaptation means 'an arrangement or altered version of the program or a translation of it', and section 21(4) provides that a 'translation' includes:

(i) a version of the program in which it is converted into or out of a computer language or code or into a different computer language or code.

SECONDARY INFRINGEMENT

As well as the key primary infringements of copyright set out above, sections 22 to 27 of the 1988 Act provide for further, secondary infringements. They include:

- importing an infringing copy;
- possessing or dealing with it;
- providing means for making it.

There are also secondary infringements of transmitting a work via a telecommunications system, permitting the use of premises for an infringing performance, and providing apparatus for one.

IMPORTING AN INFRINGING COPY

Section 22 provides that:

> the copyright in a work is infringed by a person who, without the licence of the copyright owner, imports into the UK otherwise than for his private and domestic use an article which is, and which he knows or has reason to believe is, an infringing copy of the work.

Guilty knowledge

Note that the person must *know* (or have reason to believe) that the article is an infringing copy – unlike primary infringements, which are all offences of strict liability (see above), it is an essential element of all secondary infringements that the alleged infringer should have known – or can be presumed to have known – the full significance of what he or she was doing. Proving – or inferring – such 'guilty knowledge' is a question of fact in each case: some defendants (such as rival publishers or experienced book importers) may be presumed to be more familiar with copyright transactions than others. Where there is some doubt whether importers have the necessary knowledge or not, it is usually advisable to remove any doubt by putting them on formal written notice that what they are doing is an infringing act. This is normally done by a letter before action – after receipt of such a letter it is not then open to them to claim that they had no idea that the copies concerned were infringing copies.

'Infringing copy'

An infringing copy is quite widely defined in section 27 of the Act to include as well as actual imports copies that have not yet been, but are 'proposed to be', imported into the UK. Those copies may also include not only those which – if made in the UK – would have infringed the copyright itself, but also (under section 27(3)) those which would be in breach of an *exclusive licence* agreement relating to that work (reversing the notorious case of *CBS UK Limited v. Charmdale Records Distributors Limited* (1980) where an exclusive licensee for the UK was unable to prevent parallel importation of copies from the USA into the UK which breached his exclusive territorial licence but which had not been made in infringement of the copyright itself).

There is, however, a significant limitation on an exclusive UK licensee's rights to prevent parallel importation in section 27(5) of the Act, which makes it clear that any such rights will not be enforceable against imports from other member states of the EU, so that they will be subject among other things to the free movement of goods provisions in Article 30 of the Treaty of Rome:

> Nothing in sub-section (3) shall be construed as applying to an article which may lawfully be imported into the UK by virtue of any enforceable Community right within the meaning of section 2(1) of the European Communities Act 1972.

This also extends to computer programs: subsection 3A now provides that a copy of a computer program which has previously been sold in any other EU member state, by or with the consent of the copyright owner, is not an infringing copy for the purposes of subsection (3).

For more on parallel imports and Europe, see chapter 12, pp. 284-5.

POSSESSING OR DEALING WITH AN INFRINGING COPY

Copyright may also be infringed by doing any of the following acts in relation to infringing copies without the consent of the copyright owner and (again) 'knowing or having reason to believe' that the copies are infringing:

- possessing them in the course of a business;
- selling or letting them for hire, or offering or exposing them for sale or hire;
- distributing them or publicly exhibiting them, both in the course of a business;
- distributing them other than in the course of a business, but still to such an extent as to affect prejudicially the copyright owner.

Possession may be by an agent or employee, but must be 'in the course of a business' (which the Act defines to include a trade or profession) – on the meaning of this phrase generally, see chapter 10, p. 243.

Note that sale or letting for hire need not be in the course of a business in order to infringe copyright, and neither need distribution if it is significant enough to affect the copyright owner prejudicially (so that handing out to a class of students course work books known to contain infringing copies of copyright text could well amount to infringement in itself, even though it is not in the course of business and the copying was done by someone else, if such distribution was likely – as it probably would be – to affect sales of the authorised editions prejudicially).

PROVIDING THE MEANS FOR MAKING INFRINGING COPIES

It is also an infringement of copyright in a work for a person, without the copyright owner's consent to:

- make;
- import into the UK;

- possess in the course of business; or
- sell or let for hire (or offer or expose for sale or hire)

an article 'specifically designed or adapted for making copies of that work', knowing (or having reason to believe) that it is to be used for making infringing copies. Specialised photocopying or recording equipment might be covered, but only if specifically designed or adapted for making copies of the particular work concerned: the section is more likely to cover unauthorised dealings with negatives or plates.

OTHER SECONDARY INFRINGEMENTS

It is also an infringement of copyright in a work to do the following acts without the copyright owner's consent:

- transmit it via a telecommunications system (other than by broadcasting or a cable programme service) knowing or having reason to believe that infringing copies will be made as a result;
- permit the use of premises for an infringing performance (unless whoever gave the permission believed on reasonable grounds that the performance would not infringe copyright);
- supplying infringing apparatus (such as film or recording equipment) knowing or having reason to believe that the apparatus was likely to be used to infringe copyright.

PERMITTED ACTS AND OTHER DEFENCES

If one or more of the infringing acts listed above is alleged, a number of legal arguments may be produced by way of defence. Here is a checklist of the likeliest possible defences:

SUMMARY CHECKLIST: LIKELIEST POSSIBLE DEFENCES

- the work concerned is not a copyright work at all (for example it is not a literary or other work, or it lacks the necessary originality – see p. 19);
- it is not a qualifying work by reason of first (or simultaneous) publication in the UK, or the author is not a qualifying person in the UK (see p. 34);
- it will not be protected under UK law for some other reason (for example, that it offends public sensibilities, or is fraudulent or otherwise unlawful – see below, p. 198);
- although it was a copyright work, the period of copyright protection has now expired and at the relevant time the work was in the public domain (note that copyright in some public domain works may now have revived following the EU's Duration Directive. On this, and the term of copyright generally, see p. 37;

- the person alleging copyright infringement is not in fact the copyright owner (or the owner's exclusive licensee – see p. 209);
- no copying took place, and the work which allegedly infringes copyright was in fact the result of independent skill and effort (see p. 190);
- if copying did take place, the material copied is not significant or extensive enough to amount to a 'substantial part' of the copyright work concerned (see p. 189);
- the copying or other acts done were permitted acts, such as fair dealing (see below, p. 199);
- whatever took place, the copyright owner consented.

Most of the above defences are dealt with elsewhere in this book, as indicated, but we will look below at public policy (briefly) and Permitted Acts (in some detail).

PUBLIC POLICY

Although the boundaries of copyright are primarily defined by statute in the UK, the 1988 Act contains a number of general saving provisions (at section 171) for other existing rights – for example that the rights and privileges of the Crown and Parliament will not be affected by any copyright, and that a similar exemption applies to:

- any rule of equity relating to breaches of trust or confidence; and
- any rule of law preventing or restricting the enforcement of copyright, on grounds of public interest or otherwise.

This last proviso leaves scope for the courts to refuse to enforce any copyright on grounds of public interest or public policy, if it conflicts with 'any rule of law'. Although the old cases denying copyright protection to blasphemous or 'irreligious' works are unlikely to be followed nowadays, the proviso probably still gives judges sufficient grounds for denying copyright protection to a work which has already been held to be defamatory or obscene or where there is some other strong public interest argument against giving protection – but probably only if publication would actually be unlawful. It might also enable them to prevent a criminal from profiting from a crime, or from relying on copyright to protect a work which amounts to a fraud on the public (in one nineteenth-century case, an action against a book pirate failed because the religious work copied claimed to be a translation from an eminent German authority when in fact it was nothing of the kind).

PERMITTED ACTS

There are certain kinds of copying – generally non-commercial in nature – which may be done without infringing copyright if they come under the definition of one of the Permitted Acts set out in the 1988 Act. It would be a complete defence to any claim of copyright infringement to establish that the activity complained of was in fact a Permitted Act, although as we shall see motivation may be relevant too (for example in questions relating to fair dealing). The Act provides a long list of Permitted Acts, many of which are quite narrowly defined: we will consider below those of most relevance to publishing.

Fair dealing

Copyright in a literary, dramatic, musical or artistic work, or a typographical arrangement, will not be infringed by any 'fair dealing' with those works for the following purposes:

- research or private study;
- criticism or review;
- reporting current events.

'Fair dealing' is not defined in the Act, but it is an essential pre-requisite of all three of the above defences. It is not enough therefore merely to prove that copying (for example) was done for the purposes of research: it must have been *fair dealing* for the purposes of research. It will not succeed as a defence to a claim of copyright infringement otherwise. We will look at what is or is not 'fair' in the context of each individual activity, but generally speaking an activity is unlikely to be regarded as fair dealing if its underlying motivation was commercial or in any way competitive with the copyright work concerned. Other factors may include whether the original work has been published yet, and how extensive – and how important – are the extracts taken as a proportion of the whole (and in some circumstances how frequent). Motivation, however, is often the key factor.

Research or private study

Fair dealing for the purposes of research or private study is a Permitted Act and will be a defence to any claim of copyright infringement. The research or private study must genuinely constitute fair dealing, however, first and foremost: in this context this probably limits the defence to personal activities (such as personal copying) rather than acts undertaken collectively. In the case of copying, as a general rule the person doing the copying must be the same person as the person doing the research or private study. He or she may possibly ask a friend or some other agent, such as a librarian, to do it for them, and there seems no reason why more than one copy cannot be made, as long as all the copying is for the personal research or private study of the individual concerned. It will almost certainly *not* be fair dealing if a librarian or teacher makes multiple copies on behalf of an entire class of students – even if individually they are all engaged in private study: this was confirmed as long ago as 1916 in the leading case of *University of London Press Limited v. University Tutorial Press Limited*, where the clear motive was not individual or personal, but a collective motive to save the users (examination candidates) from buying the original works themselves.

The 1988 Act also now makes it clear (in section 29(3)(b)) that copying by someone other than the individual researcher or student will not be fair dealing if:

> The person doing the copying knows or has reason to believe that it will result in copies of substantially the same material being provided to more than one person at substantially the same time and for substantially the same purpose.

The position of the adjective 'private' in the phrase 'research or private study' has occasionally been thought to be significant: it is sometimes argued that study must be private, but research need not be (and could therefore include commercial research). In the light of the decided cases, this would be a highly dangerous view: whether research is truly private or not, it must still first and foremost be fair dealing. A court would look at the user's real motive in copying (for example) the work concerned. If the copying was by a commercial organisation for the purposes of commercial research, particularly if one of these purposes was to save the organisation (or its staff or clients or customers) having to buy multiple copies of the copyright works concerned, it is very likely that a UK court would be unwilling to regard that use as fair dealing. US courts have reached a similar conclusion in the recent landmark *Texaco* decision, in which the Supreme Court held on appeal that large-scale internal copying of scientific journals and other copyright materials by a major oil company was not 'fair use': it is likely that on similar facts a UK court would take a similar view. This is particularly so since (as in the USA) a collective licensing scheme for commercial and educational copying is generally available – in the UK, operated on behalf of copyright owners by the Copyright Licensing Agency (see below, p. 204).

Fair dealing for the purpose of research and private study specifically does not now include decompilation of a computer program – this is now a separate permitted act (see below, pp. 206–7).

Criticism or review

Section 30 of the Act provides that fair dealing with a work for the purpose of criticism or review (of that work, or another work, or of a performance of a work) does not infringe any copyright in the work provided that it is accompanied by a sufficient acknowledgement.

As with fair dealing for the purpose of research or private study, there are a number of points to note:

- In order not to infringe, the acts done must not merely be for the purpose of criticism or review, but must constitute *fair dealing* for that purpose. Any improper motive – such as an obviously commercial motivation – will seriously weaken any defence of fair dealing at the outset. It will be a question of fact and impression in every case: in the *University of London Press* case referred to above, very extensive extracts were reproduced, with little or no attempt at 'critical' commentary, and the primary motivation behind the copying was clearly not critical at all but commercial.

- Fair dealing may be regarded as for the purpose of criticism or review, even though the criticism or review concerned may be of the theories or philosophy behind the work rather than its actual literary content or style, and, of course, the criticism or review need not be favourable. It must however have some significant element of bona fide comment, or assessment.
- The criticism or review must be accompanied by 'a sufficient acknowledgement'. This phrase is defined in section 178 of the Act to mean 'an acknowledgement identifying the work in question by its title or other description, and identifying the author' (unless the work is published anonymously, or is unpublished and the author cannot be identified). Crediting the title and the author will constitute sufficient acknowledgement, therefore; there is no requirement under the Act to credit the publisher or copyright owner (if different from the author), although there is some case authority to suggest that an acknowledgement is not truly sufficient unless it also in some way credits the status of the work as a copyright work. It is probably advisable to include as complete a credit as possible on each page where an extract appears, and a full copyright acknowledgement on at least one page, perhaps under the relevant acknowledgements section, or list of sources.

One test of what may amount to fair dealing in the context of criticism or review may be the current trade practice relating to permissions: this was expressly cited in the leading case of *Sillitoe v. McGraw Hill Book Company (UK) Limited* (1983), and evidence of trade practice may continue to be admissible in determining fair dealing in such cases. The Society of Authors and the Publishers Association maintain standing guidelines to those wishing to use extracts from other published works for the purposes of true criticism or review. The current guidelines allow up to 400 words from any single quote to be used for such purposes without permission or fee, or 800 words for any two or more extracts from the same work (no single extract being more than 300 words). In the case of poems, the limit is 40 lines or up to 25 per cent of the work as a whole, or a series of extracts amounting to the same.

Reporting current events

Fair dealing with a work (other than a photograph) for the purpose of reporting current events does not infringe any copyright in it provided that it is accompanied by a sufficient acknowledgement (see above). The requirement of a sufficient acknowledgement does not apply to non-print reporting via sound recording, film, broadcast or cable programme.

The events being reported must be current, but the work copied or otherwise used need not be: it may count as fair dealing to reproduce part of an existing literary work (such as a political study, or a scientific report) for example, if it becomes relevant in reporting future current events. However the purpose must be the immediate one of 'reporting' those events, not some wider or more long term editorial purpose.

Note that these provisions apply to all works, *except* photographs.

Incidental inclusion of copyright material

Copyright in any work is not infringed by its incidental inclusion in an artistic work (such as a photograph), or in a sound recording, film, broadcast or cable programme. This is sometimes referred to as 'passing shot use'. The inclusion must, however, be truly 'incidental', which would probably exclude most deliberate acts designed specifically to add value, for example by dubbing in background music (deliberate inclusion of musical and allied works is now expressly ruled out by section 31(3) of the Act). Some other deliberate uses (such as the quotation of a few lines of a literary work by a character in a film) might nevertheless still count as 'incidental inclusion', in some circumstances, provided they amount to no more than passing shots.

Educational use

Sections 32 to 36 of the 1988 Act provide several somewhat limited exceptions to copyright infringement, designed to cover activities which are regarded as permissible under the general heading of 'education'. In the UK, these categories of permitted educational use are narrowly defined, so that much of the copying which goes on in schools and colleges (particularly if it is multiple copying) will not be permitted use under the 1988 Act and will still require the consent of the copyright owner. This can now be licensed under collective licensing schemes run by the Copyright Licensing Agency (see below, p. 204). This is in marked contrast to the copyright laws of some developing countries (at least, developing in the copyright sense) where 'educational use' has been notoriously widely defined to enable faculties – and the local photocopy shops – to reproduce entire text books more or less with impunity. This kind of educational piracy or wholesale copying (for example, of carol books for school choirs) is not possible in Britain under UK law, and what the law permits is strictly defined. The following acts are permitted:

Things done for the purposes of instruction or examination (section 32)

This is a very limited exception. The copying must be done in the actual course of instruction or teaching, or preparation for it. It must be done by the teacher or student concerned, and must not be via any reprographic process (such as photocopying or electronic copying). Actual examination use is also permitted, such as for the purpose of setting the questions, communicating them to the students or answering them – this extends to reprographic copying but not of musical works. Any subsequent use of a permitted copy under this section (including selling or hiring it) will lose the protection – and will be treated as infringing use.

Anthologies for educational use

Again, this exception (in section 33) is extremely limited. The passage taken must be 'short', and must be in an anthology designed for educational use, which otherwise consists mainly of public domain material, and must be accompanied by a sufficient acknowledgement (see above). No more than two excerpts from the same author may be used in collections published by the same publisher within any 5-year period.

Performing and recording by educational establishments

Section 34 provides that a performance of a literary, dramatic or musical work at an educational establishment (and in the course of its activities) by teachers or pupils will not count as a public performance for copyright infringement purposes, provided that the audience consists entirely of other teachers or pupils 'and other persons directly connected with the activities of the establishment' – this may include some parents, for example if they are also school governors, but not others: an 'open' audience of parents and other guests will almost certainly be a (potentially infringing) public performance.

The playing or showing of a sound recording, film, broadcast or cable programme under the conditions set out above would also not count as playing or showing the work concerned in public.

Section 35 provides that educational establishments may also record broadcasts or cable programmes, or copy such recordings under certain circumstances, without infringing copyright; however, this exemption does not apply where there is a licensing scheme available, as there currently is, so licences would now be required from the Education Recording Agency (ERA).

Reprographic copying

Section 36 of the Act provides that reprographic copies (which include copies made by electronic means as well as photocopies) may be made of passages from published literary, dramatic or musical works by an educational establishment for the purposes of instruction, but *only* if:

- not more than 1 per cent of any work is copied in any quarter; and
- no licences are available for such copying (about which the person copying knew or ought to have been aware).

Any subsequent commercial dealings with a permitted copy under this section (including sale or hire) will be treated as infringing acts.

Educational licences for hard-copy reprographic copying are currently available in the UK from the Copyright Licensing Agency, who regularly grant such licences on behalf of publishers and copyright owners and have done so for several years: it would be difficult nowadays for any teacher or librarian to claim that they did not know, or have any reason to believe, that such licences were available. No licensing scheme for electronic reprographic copying (often known as 'electrocopying') is yet available (but has been under consideration for some time and, if introduced, is likely to be widely advertised in educational circles).

Details of the Copyright Licensing Agency are set out in appendix B. The collective licences which it offers will cover multiple copying within defined limits depending on the terms of the particular licence. The licence will bring with it an indemnity from the Copyright Licensing Agency against any legal action by the relevant individual copyright owners, provided the terms of the licence are complied with.

Library and Archive copying

'Fair dealing', for example for the purposes of research or private study, may well not cover all the legitimate copying a librarian needs to do. Sections 37 to 44 of the 1988 Act therefore provide certain additional exemptions, for librarians of 'prescribed libraries'. For some purposes, this covers all libraries in the UK, but for others excludes any library 'conducted for profit'. Under the Copyright (Librarians and Archivists) (Copying of Copyright Material) Regulations 1989 made under the Act, this would exclude any library or archive which forms part of, or is administered by, a body established or conducted for profit. For those purposes, this would almost certainly rule out research libraries in major oil companies (or law libraries run by law firms).

Articles in periodicals

Librarians of prescribed libraries (see below) may copy an article in a periodical without infringing copyright in the text, or any illustrations, or the typographical copyright, provided the following conditions are met:

1 the librarian must be satisfied that the copies are required for the purposes of research or private study, and will not be used for any other purpose;
2 no person may be supplied with more than one copy of the same article (or with copies of more than one article from any single issue of a periodical);

3 a copy may be supplied only to a person satisfying the librarian that his or her requirement is not related to any similar requirement of another person;
4 the user must be charged a sum not less than the cost of making the copies (including a contribution to the general expenses of the library).

Libraries 'conducted for profit' are not prescribed libraries for these purposes.

Parts of published works

A similar copyright exemption exists for copying of parts of published works other than articles by librarians at prescribed libraries – again, libraries conducted for profit are excluded. The conditions are virtually identical to those set out above, applying to copying from periodicals, save that no person is to be supplied with a copy of 'more than a reasonable proportion' of any work (what is a reasonable proportion is not defined, but would clearly not include copying the whole work).

Supply of copies to other libraries

All UK librarians, whether their library is conducted for profit or not, may copy and supply to another librarian an article from a periodical or the whole or part of any literary, dramatic or musical work, unless at the time of the request they knew ('or could by reasonable enquiry ascertain') the name and address of the copyright owner. Again, only single copies may be made, and the other library must pay at least the cost price.

Replacement copies

All UK librarians may copy items from their holdings in order to preserve them, or to replace copies from other libraries which have been lost, damaged or destroyed. This exemption does not, however, apply where it is reasonably practicable to purchase a copy of the item in question to fulfil that purpose.

Copying unpublished works

All UK librarians may copy unpublished works deposited with them, such as letters or manuscripts, without infringing any copyright. The conditions are similar to those listed above. The exemption does not apply if the librarian is aware (or ought to be) that the work had been published before being deposited, or that the copyright owner has prohibited copying of the work.

It will be seen that these statutory library exemptions are all fairly limited in scope, even where the library concerned is a prescribed library. Permitted copying is almost always restricted to single copies (which would exclude multiple copying of newsletters or journals to students or other users). In addition, in many cases the librarian must be 'satisfied' about the purpose for which the copies are to be supplied. This probably means that the librarian is at least expected to make reasonable enquiries of users and be reasonably satisfied with the response. This may be achieved by verbal questioning, but where a librarian (or the librarian's employer) is concerned about the risks of legal liability for copying which turns out to infringe (since copyright is infringed by the person making the copies not the person making the request), it may be advisable for the librarian to obtain a signed declaration from the user before the copying is done. There is provision in section 37(2) of the 1988 Act for a statutory declaration, which may be relied on in situations where a librarian is required to be satisfied as to any matter, and which will have the effect of transferring legal liability to the user, unless the librarian is aware at the time the declaration is made that it is 'false in a material particular'. The 1989 Regulations contain a prescribed form of statutory declaration for these purposes.

It is therefore possible for a librarian to avoid legal liability for single copying which turns out to infringe copyright. It is not, however, generally possible to avoid the risk of legal action by copyright owners for multiple copying in breach of copyright unless permission for that copying has been obtained from the copyright owner or under a collective licensing scheme operated on the owner's behalf, such as those offered by the Copyright Licensing Agency (see above p. 204).

Parliamentary and judicial proceedings

Section 45 of the Act provides that copyright is not infringed by anything done for the purposes of Parliamentary or judicial proceedings. The Act defines 'Parliamentary' to include not only the UK Parliament but also the European Parliament. Judicial proceedings are also widely defined to include, for example, tribunals. However, the copying must be done for the *purposes* of those proceedings, so that a solicitor copying evidence as part of pleadings prior to a trial will be protected, but a teacher or librarian copying Parliamentary or case reports for information or teaching purposes might well not be.

Sections 46 to 50 provide further exceptions regarding the proceedings of Royal Commissions and statutory inquiries, public records and other material open to public inspection or on an official register, and certain copying done by the Crown or under statutory authority.

Lawful use of computer programs

The Copyright (Computer Programs) Regulations 1992 provided new permitted acts in relation to computer programs, under which any 'lawful user' – who already had a right to use the program – may:

- make any necessary back up copy of it;
- 'decompile' it, where necessary to create an independent program to run with it, or with some other program (not substantially similar to the program being decompiled)
- and copy or adapt it (for example, in order to correct errors)
(new sections 50A–50C of the 1988 Act respectively).

Designs and typefaces

Under sections 51 and 52, it does not infringe copyright in a design document or model (for anything other than an artistic work or typeface) to make any (presumably three-dimensional) article to that design, or copy such an article, or (inter alia) issue it to the public. Artistic works which have been licensed by the copyright owner to be copied 'by an industrial process' and marketed (such as character illustrations licensed for merchandised goods) may be copied by making and exploiting similar goods without infringing copyright after a period of 25 years from the year the original articles were first marketed. This section does not, however, permit copying or exploiting the artistic works concerned in any other way.

Under section 54, it does not infringe copyright in the design of a typeface (which is an artistic work) to do the following things:

- to use it in the ordinary course of typing, composing text, typesetting or printing;
- to possess an article for the purpose of such use; or
- to do anything in relation to material produced by that use.

This is despite the fact that such use may be based on an infringing copy. There may however still be a liability for secondary infringement, such as importing or possessing an infringing copy of the typeface design itself.

Transferring copies in electronic form

Where a copy of a work in electronic form – a software program, or a text on CD-ROM – is purchased with an express or implied licence to copy or adapt it (for example, permitting a back-up copy), then where the purchaser is freely permitted to sell or transfer it to someone else, that someone else may also copy or adapt it in the same way, without infringing copyright. A right to make a back-up copy, or any other licensed copy, can thus be passed on from seller to purchaser without the need for further licensing. However, any additional copy retained by the seller after the transfer of the licensed copy has taken place will be treated as an infringing copy.

Copying anonymous or pseudonymous works

For works made after 1 August 1989, copyright will not be infringed by any acts done at a time when:

- it is not possible 'by reasonable enquiry' to identify the author; *and*
- it is reasonable to assume copyright has expired or that the author died at least 70 calendar years earlier.

Complex transitional provisions apply to pre-1989 works. In addition, the above does not apply to Crown copyright works, or copyright works of certain international organisations.

Copying abstracts (section 60)

Section 60 of the Act permits the copying (or issuing to the public) of abstracts which accompany published periodical articles on scientific or technical subjects. Such abstracts are a common feature of medical and other scientific journals, and are frequently copied. The abstract must be primarily an abstract rather than anything more (such as an extended editorial): it must have the function of describing or summarising ('indicating') the contents of the article. The article must also have a 'scientific or technical' subject – although this sounds as if it might have rather a narrow scope, it may well be wide enough to cover abstracts of any similar specialist or professional articles, even in the social sciences or arts generally, provided they were pure abstracts accompanying the articles concerned.

The exception does not apply if there is a licensing scheme available for such use: there is not, at the time of writing, and the Copyright Licensing Agency seems to accept for the time being that the copying of abstracts under section 60 is generally permissible.

Other permitted acts

Other permitted acts under the 1988 Act include the following:

- things done in reliance on a registered design (section 53);
- use of notes or recordings to report current events (section 58);
- public reading or recital of reasonable extracts (with a sufficient acknowledgement) (section 59);
- representation of certain artistic works on public display (section 62);
- copying an artistic work in order to advertise its sale (section 63);
- subsequent works made by the same artist (section 64);
- specified rentals of sound recordings, films and computer programs (section 66);
- incidental recording for the purposes of a broadcast or cable programme (section 68);

- private photographing of a broadcast or cable programme or recording it for the purposes of time shifting (sections 70 to 71);
- reception and re-transmission of a broadcast in a cable programme service (section 73).

CIVIL AND CRIMINAL REMEDIES IN THE UK

What do you do if someone infringes your copyright? Perhaps equally importantly: what might they (and a court) do to you if you infringe theirs? In this section we will look at who can sue, and who can *be* sued, in UK courts, what civil remedies (such as damages) might be available to them, and in what circumstances, and finally – but increasingly importantly – what *criminal* penalties might apply.

WHO CAN SUE?

The copyright owner

Perhaps self-evidently, all copyright infringements are actionable by the copyright owner. It must be the correct copyright owner, however – as we saw in chapter 2, a typical publication such as a book or CD-ROM might contain several different copyright works, and there may be several different copyright owners: in order to bring an action for infringement, the copyright owner must be the owner of the particular copyright which has been infringed. So, if an illustration has been copied without permission, the owner of artistic copyright in that illustration may sue for infringement, but probably not, for example, the owner of literary copyright in the accompanying text – they are different copyrights, and likely to be owned by different people. The position would be the same with any separate, but associated, copyright – such as a compilation of the book as a whole, or an underlying computer program. If the text (or compilation, or computer program) was copied too, of course, then all three owners may have actions, but not otherwise.

The owner must also own the copyright at the correct *time* (in fact, two separate times):

- at the actual time when the infringement occurred. A subsequent copyright owner (such as a beneficiary under a will, or an assignee) cannot sue for infringements which took place before he or she became the owner; *and*
- when the writ is issued: you will have no cause of action if you no longer own legal (or at least equitable) title to the copyright.

Joint copyright owners

Although a joint copyright owner cannot exploit the copyright without the consent of the others, any joint copyright owner can take legal action for infringement of the relevant copyright without needing to join the others in the proceedings (although the others, of course, may wish to join in).

Exclusive licensees

Section 101 of the 1988 Act provides that an exclusive licensee has the same rights and remedies as the copyright owner and can therefore sue for copyright infringement in the same way. Any infringer can be sued, except the copyright owner themselves.

The infringement must have occurred after the licence was granted, and while it was in force. The infringement must also fall within the terms of the particular exclusive licence concerned, of course – so that an exclusive licensee of English-language volume rights may bring an action against an infringing English-language paperback, but not against a Russian translation or a multimedia version.

Although an exclusive licensee may commence proceedings (and for example seek an injunction), once the action is under way the copyright owner must be joined as a plaintiff (or added as a defendant) unless the leave of the court is obtained. The court will usually only grant leave in exceptional circumstances – as in 1972, for example, when Bodley Head were granted leave to pursue an action on their own since the copyright owner – Solzhenitsyn – could not do so in Russia where the book concerned was banned.

Non-exclusive licensees, and other parties such as agents, have no right to take proceedings for copyright infringement in their own name.

Presumptions on title

With old publishing records hard evidence of copyright ownership may be difficult to come by. The court will assist plaintiffs in such cases by making a number of presumptions, spelt out in sections 104 to 106 of the Act. In each case, unless the contrary is proved:

- anyone whose name appears as the author on published copies of a work will be presumed to be the author;
- any such author will be presumed not to have written the work in the course of employment, or subject to Crown or other copyrights;
- where no author is named, but a publisher is identified, that publisher will be deemed to be the copyright owner, provided that the work otherwise qualifies for UK copyright protection on the basis of its country of first publication (see pp. 35–6);
- where the author is dead or unknown (and cannot be ascertained by reasonable enquiry) it will be presumed that the work is original, and that the plaintiff's claims as to first publication are correct;

- where the work is a computer program, and is published bearing statements crediting a particular copyright owner, or relating to first publication in a particular country or issue to the public in specified year, those statements will be presumed to be correct.

WHO CAN BE SUED?

Section 16(2) of the 1988 Act provides that copyright in a work is infringed by a person who without licence of the copyright owner does, or authorises another to do, any of the acts restricted by copyright. As we saw above, these restricted acts may be primary infringements such as copying, or issuing copies to the public (above pp. 190 and 192), or secondary infringements such as importation or possession (pp. 195 and 196). Any 'person' who does, or authorises, any such acts, as defined, without permission may thus be sued. This therefore includes:

Natural persons

(Human beings) who do, or authorise, any of the restricted acts (on the meaning of 'authorise', see above, p. 189). In a publishing case, there may be several different infringements, such as copying, issuing copies to the public, importing, possessing, selling, hiring or distributing, and each person will be separately and personally liable for their own infringements. Several co-defendants may therefore be sued at once, including authors and publishers, printers, wholesalers and bookshops, even though the causes of action may be different.

Employees will often be personally liable even if they were acting in the course of their employment (in that case *both* employee and employer may be liable) and so will directors and agents.

Legal persons (such as companies)

In the case of many small companies the one or two directors in charge to all intents and purposes *are* the company. So, although many of the infringements would have been done by the company and it will therefore be necessary to sue the company, it will be advisable to sue the directors personally as well (since small companies may conveniently cease trading, whereas directors tend to survive).

Joint infringers (or 'joint tortfeasors')

A common, concerted design by two or more persons to infringe may lead to both (or all) of them being sued jointly (even if one of them is outside the UK).

WARNING LETTERS

The first step in many actions for copyright infringement – indeed actions of any kind – is the sending of a warning letter. This is normal practice, and may give both sides the opportunity to sort the matter out (fairly) amicably without having to resort to costly and time consuming litigation. If a standard business letter does not produce the desired result, a more formal solicitor's letter, threatening specific legal action (and therefore called a letter before action) might concentrate minds sufficiently to stop the infringement and settle the matter on mutually acceptable terms. Whether or not a warning letter was sent may also have an impact on the question of costs later on: if there is time, such letters are therefore advisable.

Where the infringement is a primary infringement – such as copying (see p. 190) – there is no legal requirement to send a warning letter before commencing legal proceedings: indeed, there may be very strong reasons for *not* warning the infringer what is about to happen (see below, p. 215). With secondary infringements such as possession or dealing, however, it is necessary to establish that the infringer *knew* (or ought reasonably to have known) that the acts concerned were infringing acts (see p. 195), and for this reason it may be necessary to send a formal warning letter at the outset, putting the infringer on legal notice, which can then be produced at the trial as hard evidence of guilty knowledge.

Drafting warning letters requires some care: defamatory statements and malicious falsehoods must be avoided (see chapter 7), and in the case of letters sent to third parties such as distributors, any unlawful interference with contractual relations (see p. 65).

INJUNCTIONS

An injunction is a discretionary court order, either commanding someone to do something or (more commonly) ordering someone to *stop* doing something and forbidding them from doing it in the future, or at least until the injunction is lifted. The latter, negative, version is often the most important and most urgent legal remedy a plaintiff will seek against a copyright infringer: once the infringement is discovered what the copyright owner usually wants most of all is for the defendant to be ordered to stop (or in some cases not to start: for example not to publish). Questions of financial compensation, though important, are usually less urgent and can be left to be dealt with by a suitable award of damages at the trial (see below, p. 213): an injunction, however, may be an urgent priority.

There are five criteria which a court will apply in deciding whether to grant an interim, or pre-trial injunction (set out in a 1975 leading case known as *American Cyanamid*):

1 Is there a serious issue to be tried? An injunction will not be granted where the plaintiff does not have at least an arguable claim, which would carry a real and substantial prospect of success at any trial;

2 Would damages be an adequate remedy? If they would, then an injunction will normally not be granted (unless there is a serious likelihood that the defendant will never pay). A good example of this would be a permissions dispute, where the copyright owner concerned regularly grants permissions to others in similar circumstances, for fixed scales of fees.

3 Where does the balance of convenience lie? If the disruption which granting an injunction will cause to the defendant is greater than the disruption which the plaintiff claims will be caused by continuing (alleged) infringement, then an injunction may well not be granted. If, for example, the effect of an injunction would be to force the defendant to take an entire edition off sale, losing not only the likely domestic market but also key co-edition deals, then the damage to the plaintiff which *not* granting an injunction will cause will need to be very considerable indeed to outweigh that.

4 Preserving the status quo. All other things being equal, a court may well simply seek to preserve the status quo: this may best be served by granting an injunction, or in some cases by *not* granting one.

5 Relative strength of each parties' case. This may help the court to decide, but only where one party clearly has a very much stronger *prima facie* case than the other.

Having weighed the above, the court may still refuse an injunction if it appears inequitable to grant one – for example if the plaintiff has delayed unreasonably. It is entirely at the court's discretion, depending on the facts in each case. If an injunction is granted, a court will usually require as a condition of granting it that the plaintiff gives the defendant what is called a *cross-undertaking* as to damages. This will protect the defendant against any loss or damage incurred as a result of complying with the injunction – for example by taking a book off sale on the day before publication – should the plaintiff's claim turn out to have been unfounded when it is finally adjudicated on, at the trial. Where the plaintiff is unable to give a sufficient cross-undertaking, the court may refuse to grant the injunction.

DAMAGES

It is not necessary in order to win an action for copyright infringement to prove financial (or any other) loss. If copyright infringement is proved, some damage will be assumed. There is a general burden of proof on any plaintiff to prove any *specific* loss or damage, but apart from that a court will usually be willing to make a general award of damages to compensate the plaintiff for what has happened. The basic aim is to restore the plaintiff to the position he or she would have been in had the infringement not occurred.

Not surprisingly, it is not always easy to arrive at a scientific method of quantifying the plaintiff's loss, particularly in publishing actions. Any one or more of the following criteria may be adopted:

- *Loss of profits*: a court will take into account any reasonable expectation of profits, either based on evidence of previous publications or on reasonable commercial forecasts. Loss of likely subsidiary rights revenue (such as a US deal) will be as relevant as lost home sales, although a court will not compensate a plaintiff for possible future profits which are purely speculative. There is also a general duty on all plaintiffs to take any reasonable steps to mitigate their loss where possible.
- *Damage to business*: compensation will often be given for general injury done to a plaintiff's business or trade, over and above lost sales.
- *A fair licence fee*: where the plaintiff normally grants licences for the use of the copyright material concerned, a more reasonable starting point for assessing damages might be to calculate a fair licence fee which might have been levied had the defendant sought a licence in the usual way. Evidence of current levels of licence fees in the market concerned will be borne in mind: the court may still award a higher figure if this calculation does not seem to go far enough to compensate the plaintiff properly.
- *Additional damages*: under section 97(2) of the 1988 Act, a court may award additional damages, as the justice of the case may require – bearing in mind all the circumstances, but in particular, the *flagrancy* of the infringement, and any *benefits* gained by the defendant.

It is important to note that damages are not available in copyright actions where at the time of the infringement the defendant did not know, and had no reason to believe, that copyright subsisted (at all) in the work concerned (section 97(1)) – however, other remedies, such as injunctions or an account of profits, may still be available in the court's discretion.

OTHER REMEDIES

Account of profits

This is an equitable remedy, available only as an *alternative* to damages (you cannot have both) where it seems more appropriate – once the financial information is known – to assess the profit the defendant earned from the infringement. It is unlikely that a plaintiff would opt for an account of profits unless the known profits were considerably more substantial than the sum a court would be likely to award in damages.

Delivery up

Section 99 of the 1988 Act entitles a copyright owner to apply to the court for delivery up of infringing copies which someone has in their possession, custody or control in the course of their business (innocently or otherwise). Proof of guilty knowledge is only required in the case of articles – such as machinery – specifically designed or adapted for making (infringing) copies. Under section 114 of the Act, the copies may be forfeited to the copyright owner, or destroyed, or otherwise dealt with as the court thinks fit.

Seizure

Copies which are found 'exposed or otherwise immediately available for sale or hire' (section 100) may be seized by the copyright owner without the need for any court order – however, there are serious practical restrictions: the local police station must be notified before any such raid takes place, no force may be used, and nothing may be seized from the infringer's permanent or regular place of business (since the section is primarily aimed at market stalls selling bootleg tapes).

Confiscation by customs

Under section 111 of the Act, owners of copyright in a published literary, dramatic or musical work may give written notice to the Commissioners of Customs & Excise to treat infringing printed copies as prohibited goods for up to 5 years. This gives some scope for customs seizures where a tip off is received well enough in advance, but only applies to such works in *printed* form (and not therefore to computer software). There are however parallel provisions covering sound recordings and films.

Imports from elsewhere in the European Economic Area may be immune from prohibition under the free movement of goods provisions of the Treaty of Rome (see chapter 12, pp. 284–5).

Anton Piller orders

Named after the (1976) case in which they were first used, these are pre-trial court orders requiring a defendant to give immediate access to premises without notice and allow property – such as incriminating documents – to be inspected and in some cases taken away by the plaintiff (generally the plaintiff's solicitor). Needless to say such an order (which is not just confined to copyright actions) is a drastic measure and its execution is closely regulated by the court. Generally speaking, *Anton Piller* orders may be used only where such access is urgent and essential and where the plaintiff's case is very strong. There must also be a substantial risk that the defendant might destroy such evidence given advance warning.

Mareva injunctions

Also named after a (1980) case, *Mareva* injunctions may be granted in urgent circumstances by a court to prevent a defendant from removing assets (such as stock, or money) out of the country – or otherwise putting them beyond the court's jurisdiction – in order to avoid judgment. The plaintiff must have a strong arguable case and there must be a significant risk that the assets concerned may be dispersed.

CRIMINAL PENALTIES FOR COPYRIGHT INFRINGEMENT

As well as the more familiar civil remedies which copyright owners may seek to obtain against infringers, such as injunctions and damages, the 1988 Act also provides *criminal* penalties of fines or imprisonment for a number of specific criminal offences. These are largely contained in section 107(1) of the Act. Under that section, a person commits an offence who, without the licence of the copyright owner, does any of the following acts in relation to an article which he or she knows (or has reason to believe) is an infringing copy of a copyright work:

1   makes it for sale or hire;
2   imports it into the UK, otherwise than for private or domestic use;
3   possesses it in the course of a business with a view to committing any act infringing the copyright;
4   in the course of a business:
    • sells it or lets it for hire;
    • offers or exposes it for sale or hire;
    • exhibits it in public; or
    • distributes it; or
5   distributes it otherwise than in the course of a business to such an extent as to affect prejudicially the owner of the copyright.

There are also separate offences under section 107(2) of the Act, of making or possessing an article specifically 'designed or adapted' for making copies of a work, knowing (or – again – having reason to believe) that article is to be used to make infringing copies for sale or hire in the course of a business, and, under section 107(3), of the public performance of a literary, dramatic or musical work, or the playing or showing of a sound recording or film, where the person responsible knew (or had reason to believe) that copyright would be infringed.

Persons convicted of these offences are liable to criminal penalties including fines, terms of imprisonment ranging from up to 6 months (in the Magistrates' Court) to 2 years (in the Crown Court). Further, under section 110 of the Act, directors or other senior officers of a company may be prosecuted personally if a relevant offence by the company is proved to have been committed with their 'consent or connivance'. Note, in all these cases, that proof of actual guilty knowledge or intent is not always necessary: evidence that the accused had 'reason to believe' infringement was occurring or would take place may also secure a conviction. In many cases, this may be established simply by sending a warning letter (see above, p. 212).

There are provisions in sections 108 and 109 for delivery up of infringing copies, and for police search warrants.

Until now, these criminal provisions have not attracted a great deal of legal attention, being seen as more relevant to the activities of obvious pirates and market traders selling bootleg tapes and CDs than to reputable individuals or companies. However, magistrates in recent years have proved more willing to hear such cases, even where the defendant argues that serious issues of copyright law and fair dealing are raised which ought to be heard in the High Court (and the High Court may well agree – it refused to strike out on these grounds criminal proceedings brought in 1994 by the Design & Artists Copyright Society DACS against arts publisher Thames & Hudson, although that prosecution was subsequently withdrawn). Given the – relative – speed and cheapness of proceedings in the Magistrates' Court, and the significant criminal penalties available – potentially giving individuals as well as companies a criminal record – the criminal provisions of the 1988 Act may turn out to have considerable relevance to copyright owners seeking remedies against infringers, even where the alleged infringer may be a substantial and reputable company.

INTERNATIONAL COPYRIGHT PROTECTION

UK copyright works are not only protected in the UK, under domestic UK law, but to a large extent internationally too. Equally, a great many foreign copyright works are protected here. This happy state of affairs is not the result of any all-embracing international copyright law, but has been arrived at piecemeal, over the years, by a combination of bilateral treaties between the major copyright nations, and, increasingly, multilateral Conventions to which most of the significant trading nations of the world now belong. We will look at these treaties and Conventions in more detail below. It is however essential to bear in mind from the outset that these arrangements are no more than treaties – in the case of many nations (including the UK) they may well have no legal effect unless and until the country concerned implements them as part of its own domestic law. Some countries are better – and quicker – than others about implementing their international treaty obligations; for example, despite being a founder signatory of the Berne Convention in 1886 (see p. 15) the UK did not comply fully with its Berne obligations to protect moral rights of authors until the 1988 Act, and the USA (having only acceded to Berne in 1988) still has not done so. The UK also still has no *droit de suite*, granting artists a share in any re-sale profits, although it is provided for by Article 14 *ter* of Berne. So, whatever the treaties say, if you want to know what actual copyright protection is available in a particular country at any given time, the only way of finding out reliably is to look at their own domestic copyright law.

THE BERNE CONVENTION

The most important international copyright convention today is the Berne Convention. Signed in 1886 by a handful of mainly European states and still going strong over a century later, it has now been acceded to by well over 100 countries, including every EU member state and Russia, the USA and China. It has of course been revised over the years: the latest (Paris) Act dates from 1971. Not all members have yet acceded to the Paris Act: in cases of doubt, it is advisable to check with the World Intellectual Property Organisation (WIPO), which administers Berne and other intellectual property conventions (their address is set out in appendix B).

The levels of copyright protection required by Berne were strongly endorsed by the final (Uruguay) Round of the General Agreement on Tariffs and Trade (GATT), in particular in the associated TRIPS agreement (dealing with the Trade Related aspects of Intellectual Property Rights) which has now been adopted as a minimum international copyright standard by GATT's successor body, the World Trade Organisation.

For those who belong, the Berne Convention has a number of fundamental principles:

- a wide range of original 'literary and artistic works' are protected, defined to include 'every production in the literary, artistic or scientific domain, whatever may be the mode or form of its expression' – dramatic and musical works, films and photographs are expressly included and most member states now also protect computer programs (usually under literary works). Translations, adaptations and compilations are also covered;
- it is open to member states to require (as the UK does) that protected works must have been fixed in some material form (see p. 19);
- protection shall extend equally to works of authors who are *nationals* of a Berne member state, and to works of non-nationals which are *first published* in a member state. First publication includes simultaneous publication within 30 days (for the UK position, see p. 35);
- authors shall enjoy, in Berne countries other than the country of origin, copyright protection for their works amounting to 'national treatment': in other words, the same rights which those other countries grant to their own nationals (and governed by the same domestic laws);
- protection must not be subject to any formalities (such as registration) and must extend from the moment a work is created – or at least fixed in material form – for the rest of the life of the author and at least a further full calendar 50 years (within the EU this period was harmonised up to life plus 70 years as from July 1995: see p. 37). In the case of simultaneous publication in several Berne countries granting different terms of protection the 'country of origin' shall be the one granting the *shortest* term;

- authors shall have independent moral rights of paternity and integrity in their works (see chapter 3, pp. 48 and 45).

Generally speaking, authors shall have the exclusive right of authorising reproduction (and translation) of their works, but certain copying, for example fair dealing in the UK (see pp. 199–202) may be allowed provided it 'does not conflict with the normal exploitation of the work and does not unreasonably prejudice the legitimate interests of the author' (this wording appears verbatim in a number of member states' copyright laws, but is often widely interpreted to cover copying activities such as large-scale educational copying which would be regarded as flagrant infringement in the UK). There are further exemptions, set out in an Appendix to the Paris Act, allowing in certain circumstances 'developing countries' to apply compulsory translation licences for limited periods 'for the purpose of teaching, scholarship or research' for works not otherwise available in the local language: these have also been a source of much controversy. A developing country is one regarded as such 'in conformity with the established practice of the General Assembly of the United Nations', but this strict rule has often been somewhat stretched.

THE UNIVERSAL COPYRIGHT CONVENTION (UCC)

At the end of the Second World War neither of the two new super powers, the USA and Russia, belonged to the Berne Convention. The new United Nations, and its educational and cultural arm UNESCO, were keen to bring the US particularly within the international copyright community, but the relatively long copyright term of life plus 50 years, and the ban on any registration formalities, among other things, proved continuing obstacles to US accession to Berne. UNESCO therefore sponsored an alternative Convention, the UCC, which was signed in 1952 and which the US, UK and a number of other major copyright nations joined (although the UK did not finally sign up until 1957).

There is one important formality, but on the whole the level of copyright protection required by the UCC is somewhat lower:

- works protected are broadly similar, and a similar 'national treatment' principle applies. Protection again is on the basis of either the author's nationality or the country of first (or simultaneous) publication;
- the minimum period of copyright protection is however the life of the author and 25 years only. In some cases this may be 25 years from first publication;
- formalities (such as copyright registration) are permitted, but will be regarded as complied with if all published copies carry what has become known as the 'UCC copyright notice' – the copyright ©, the name of the copyright owner, and date of first publication – in no particular order, but 'placed in such manner and location as to give reasonable notice of claim of copyright' (Article III);
- there are developing country provisions similar to those in the Appendix to Berne.

Between 1952 and 1989 (when US accession to the Berne Convention came into effect) most UK published works carried the UCC copyright notice on their title pages, expressly in order to comply with UCC requirements and thereby secure effective copyright protection in the USA, a key English language market. Since US accession to Berne, such formalities should no longer be strictly necessary for the purposes of US protection (but registration may still be desirable, though – see below), but there are still countries which subscribe to the UCC but not to the latest (Paris) Act of Berne and most publishers will therefore probably continue to print the UCC wording. It is normally set out thus:

© Hugh Jones 1996

The word 'copyright' is sometimes added before the ©, but is not strictly necessary.

COPYRIGHT PROTECTION IN THE USA

For most of the nineteenth century, the USA granted little or no copyright protection to the works of foreign authors (indeed, such foreign copyrights were not recognised at all until the Chace Act of 1891). As a result the works of European authors and composers such as Dickens and Gilbert & Sullivan were freely and frequently pirated in America, despite personal lecture tours and simultaneous 'authorised' performances. The Chace Act did finally provide copyright protection for foreigners, but only to citizens of those countries which either granted national treatment to US works or granted reciprocal protection under an international (bilateral) treaty. Thereafter, UK works could be protected in the USA, but (until fairly recently) subject to registration and renewal formalities. US copyright protection is still a formidably complex area of law. It is impossible in a book of this scope to do more than provide a brief overview of the current position: it cannot be stressed too strongly that for reliable answers to specific queries it is highly advisable to seek the advice of a specialist attorney.

US domestic copyright law was significantly revised by the passage of their current copyright law, the Copyright Act of 1976. The Act came into force on 1 January 1978: as a consequence, one of the first and most important questions to ask is whether the work concerned was created before or after 1978.

Works created before 1978

Before the 1976 Act came into effect, US copyright protection did not depend on the life of the author, but lasted for a fixed term of 28 years, calculated from the date of first publication, with a possible renewal for one further 28-year term: making 56 years in all. Protection also depended on compliance with a number of formalities (not as a prerequisite for copyright itself, but as requirements to institute litigation for infringement):

- an approved copyright notice (usually ©) printed on all copies published in the US;
- registration of the copyright at the Copyright Office;
- deposit of copies (a single copy in the case of foreign works);
- formal renewal at the end of the first 28-year term;
- compliance with the notorious '*manufacturing clause*' (section 16 of the 1909 Act) which required that all copies published in the US should be typeset, printed and bound wholly within the limits of the US.

The last formal requirement in particular – a fairly blatant piece of protectionism – prevented many UK works from being protected at all in the USA, until the UK became a signatory to the UCC in 1957: from that point on, the only formality required in order to protect newly created UK works in the USA was the UCC copyright notice. On the whole, however, with one or two exceptions, existing UK works continued to be unprotected unless the full range of domestic formalities had been complied with.

Works created after 1978

For works created on or after 1 January 1978, the 1976 Act provided a new term of copyright protection, in line with the UK and other Berne countries, of life plus 50 years (this is likely to be increased shortly to match the new European period of life plus 70 years). For works which, as of 31 December 1977 were in either their original or renewal terms of 28 years, the 1976 Act provided that the second term of 28 years be extended by an extra 19 years, to 47 years – making a total of 75 years from first publication. Those copyrights already in their second, renewal, term at the time were automatically extended; those copyrights still in their first term had to be renewed in their 28th year in the normal way (but would automatically get the new 47-year renewal term). Special provisions applied to works of unknown authorship and works 'made for hire' (works made in the course of employment, or under certain commission arrangements). Copyright was not revived in pre-1978 public domain works.

Certain registration formalities continued to exist, including the UCC copyright notice for foreign works, but the 'manufacturing clause' was considerably reduced in scope and finally expired in July 1986.

US implementation of the Berne Convention and GATT

Following the Berne Convention Implementation Act of 1988, the USA finally acceded to the Berne Convention, with effect from 1 March 1989. Thereafter in the spirit of Berne membership all formalities, at least as a pre-requisite to copyright protection, were swept away, and even the basic UCC copyright notice was no longer required. It is likely however, that UK works will continue to bear the UCC notice for some time to come, since among other things it will continue to provide evidence against any defence of innocent infringement under US law (which might otherwise reduce any damages). Indeed, copyright registration itself is still advisable in some circumstances for evidential purposes, and to maximise available damages, and to secure attorney's fees in actions for infringement.

Despite Berne membership, the USA did not immediately grant retrospective copyright protection to all existing works of other member states: this did not happen until 1 January 1996, following US adherence to the 1994 GATT/TRIPS agreements (see p. 218). As of 1 January 1996, foreign works of Berne or GATT member countries – which includes the UK – which were still then protected in their country of origin, but which had entered the public domain for failure to comply with formalities in the USA, were restored to copyright protection for whatever remained of their domestic copyright periods. In the case of UK and other EU works, this meant up to an additional 20 years. US protection for such 'Restored Copyrights' may be secured until 31 December 1997 by filing a Notice of Intent to Enforce with the US Copyright Office or by serving a Notice directly on those concerned: those US publishers previously exploiting the work in reliance on its (then) public domain status (called Reliance Parties) have a 12-month sell-off period in which to dispose of remaining stock.

Trade marks and passing off   9

TRADE MARKS

INTRODUCTION

Although copyright can be a powerful form of legal protection for published (and unpublished) works, there may be some key words, names or phrases, or other distinguishing signs (such as a logo), which have an established goodwill or reputation of their own in the market place and which may be protected independently as trade marks under UK law. They may include titles of books or journals, names of authors (such as Wisden or Beatrix Potter), or names of characters ranging from Peter Rabbit to Judge Dredd. They have become increasingly important to the publishing trade in recent years as a means of protecting properties with merchandising potential, but it is important to recognise that they are not just a useful means of protecting characters in children's books, and licensing T-shirts and novelty soap, but may also be an extremely valuable form of protection for database, reference and general publishing and all kinds of distinctive publishing marks. Publishers, authors and agents should at all times consider the trade mark implications of the material they are handling, for two reasons:

- to protect as soon as possible names or other signs with valuable trade mark potential;
- to avoid infringing any existing trade marks.

WHAT IS A TRADE MARK?

Under section 1(1) of the Trade Marks Act 1994 (revising the (much) earlier 1938 Act):

A trade mark means any sign capable of being represented graphically which is capable of distinguishing goods or services of one undertaking from those of other undertakings.

This is a much wider definition than under previous law, and should now make it easier to register many marks which were not previously registrable:

- *'Any sign'* Although 'sign' is not defined, section 1(1) of the 1994 Act goes on to specify that a trade mark may consist of 'words (including personal names), designs, letters, numerals or the shape of goods or their packaging'.
- *'Capable of being represented graphically'* This could now include not only two-dimensional marks, but three-dimensional *shapes* (such as the famous Coca-Cola bottle), *sounds* capable of being reduced to musical notation, such as advertising jingles, and even possibly *smells* (presumably on the basis of the formula or some other written description).
- *'Capable of distinguishing goods or services'* This is a central requirement of any trade mark, and we will return to this later. For the present, note that the mark, in order to be registered, does not need to distinguish goods or services already, as long as it is *capable* of doing so, and the proprietor can demonstrate a bona fide intention to use it at the time the application is made.

WHAT MAY BE REGISTERED?

Under present UK law, all the following familiar publishing signs might well be registrable as trade marks, *provided* the trade mark Examiner is satisfied that they are capable of distinguishing the relevant goods or services from others:

- single letters, or sets of initials;
- single words;
- proper names;
- names of authors;
- names of characters;
- titles;
- phrases or slogans;
- logos and other designs;
- the distinctive shape or size of a publication.

Logos or designs (known as 'devices') are often more distinctive than ordinary words or phrases, and therefore easier to register: the first trade mark registered in the UK was the Bass triangle, and the Guinness harp was close behind (this must tell us something about the British).

As a general rule, words or other marks may *not* be registered if they are purely *generic*, or *descriptive* of the goods in question, and which (in the words of the 1994 Act):

- 'designate the kind, quality, quantity, intended purpose, value, geographical origin (or) time of production' of goods or services or which;

- consist exclusively of signs which have become *customary* in the language or practices of the trade.

However, such objections may be overcome with sufficient evidence of distinctiveness or use.

WORDS AND PHRASES

Given the above guidelines, the words most likely to be capable of registration as trade marks are those with no obvious descriptive or generic link with the product, which can be used and accepted as distinctive with no risk of confusion. The best trade marks are often *invented* words: meaningless but punchy and with no generic connection to anything at all, such as Kodak, Persil, Typhoo or Lego.

Known or existing words can be used, if completely unassociated with the product – 'Mars' for chocolate, for example. Composite words may also be registered successfully if 'invented', such as Coca-Cola and Prontaprint. A common surname or a geographical name may not be registered, however, without very strong evidence of distinctiveness – Buxton spring water managed to overcome this objection, but only after strong evidence of distinctiveness in the market place, and several years' continuous use.

Phrases and slogans may be registered, but not if generic, and again usually only after substantial evidence of distinctiveness. 'Have a Break' was therefore refused, but 'It's finger-lickin' good!' was accepted.

TITLES

Although many titles may lack the necessary substance and originality to attract copyright protection, book, journal, or other titles may be registered as trade marks. However, it may be difficult in the case of a single edition of a book to establish a sufficiently strong association or reputation in the market – serial publications such as directories, newspapers or magazines are more easily registered. *How to Appeal Against Your Rates* therefore failed, but *Bradshaw* and *Eagle* both succeeded. The (extremely) generic book title *Science and Health* was not surprisingly refused registration. The applicants (Christian Scientists) did however secure registration for Mary Baker Eddy's signature, and for a distinctive device mark.

If no registration has been obtained (either because the application has failed or none has been made) a title may still be protected by an action for 'passing off' (the closest English law has so far come to an unfair competition action). There must, however, be a *real* likelihood of confusion, and also evidence of actual damage or loss, before a passing off action will succeed against a rival title: for more on this see below, p. 230.

AUTHORS' NAMES

It would be difficult to secure trade mark registration of an author's name unless there was very strong evidence indeed that it had become accepted as distinctive in its own right, part of the book's goodwill. This normally only applies to serial publications or to established works which have run to several editions. Wisden or Roget would be good examples, as would Beatrix Potter.

A nom-de-plume would also be difficult to register, but the established user may well have an action for passing off against others using the same name. Similarly a signature (of a cartoonist, for example) may be hard to register if the name is simple or common and confusion may result. (It should not be forgotten that an author has a statutory moral right in some circumstances to prevent false attribution to him or her of work which the author did not write (see chapter 3, pp. 53–4). There may also in some circumstances be an action for defamation (see chapter 7).)

NAMES OF CHARACTERS

As Sir Arthur Conan Doyle found with Sherlock Holmes there is no general right to prevent a fictional character's name being used by other authors in their own works. Disputes more commonly arise over unlicensed character merchandising and the courts are increasingly adapting the law to take account of this. A decade ago, the owners of 'Judge Dredd', 'Abba' and 'Kojak' all failed to secure injunctions for passing off against unlicensed merchandisers since they were not themselves merchandising in that way and there was no real risk of public confusion between the unlicensed goods and the legitimate rights owners. More recently, however, character merchandising has become widespread and the courts seem to be increasingly willing to protect such rights. In a recent case, the owners of 'Ninja Turtles' (which were merchandised almost entirely by licensees) were able to establish that the public were being misled into thinking that unlicensed T-shirts had come from the UK proprietors of the Ninja Turtles brand. Though the reputation of Ninja Turtles was very recent (a matter of months), thanks to massive TV exposure it was well established enough for the unlicensed merchandising to constitute passing off (see below, pp. 230–2).

HOW TO REGISTER A TRADE MARK

Trade mark registration under the 1938 Act used to be a notoriously cumbersome procedure, often taking over two years, but in recent years – particularly since the 1994 Trade Marks Act – times (and costs) have been considerably reduced. Provided there is no significant opposition, it is now possible to secure UK registration for a registered trade mark in well under a year. It is normally advisable to seek advice from a specialist trade mark lawyer before commencing an application, and for the application itself it is customary to use the services of a trade mark agent.

The procedure under the 1994 Act is very much as before. Applications should be made to the Trade Marks Registry, who will need the following information:

- details of the applicant (for example, whether an individual, partnership or company, and whether or not resident in the UK);
- the particular goods or services for which the applicant is seeking to register the trade mark (see below);
- if a particular typeface, or a logo/device is involved, a representation of the proposed mark
- a statement that the applicant (or the applicant's licensees) is already using the mark in relation to the specified goods or services, or intends to do so

Classes of goods and services

Trade mark protection is given for *classes* of goods and services. There are 42 classes in all, ranging from chemicals and drugs to clothing, games and playthings, and (of course) beer. Books are included under paper, printed matter, etc., in Class 16. One of the most important things to grasp about trade marks is that protection is normally *only* given for specified classes. However, one application can now be filed covering several of the 42 possible classes.

Advertisement and opposition

Once an application has been examined by the *Trade Marks Registry*, it is advertised in the Trade Marks Journal in order to enable other interested parties to oppose it if they think it will conflict with an existing mark (or prior application) of theirs, or otherwise cause confusion. Oppositions must be filed within 3 months of advertisement. If the opposition cannot be settled the matter will be resolved at a hearing, at which both sides may be represented.

Assuming that there is no opposition, or that any opposition is defeated, registration will then be granted for the particular classes of goods and services concerned. Trade mark registration now lasts for 10 years initially, but may be renewed again and again indefinitely. Many marks are not renewed, but the most famous are renewed regularly. Unlike copyright, therefore, which expires 70 years after the year of the author's death, trade mark protection may be perpetuated forever – as long as your mark is not challenged (for example, for becoming generic) and you – or your agent – remember to pay the renewal fees.

There is no legal requirement, incidentally, to use the ®, although most proprietors find it a useful warning that their mark has been registered. There is certainly no requirement on authors, or editors of dictionaries, to use the ® sign whenever the word occurs: such advertising is the responsibility of the proprietor. One often also sees the letters ^{TM} in a circle: this has no legal significance whatsoever and merely indicates that the person using the mark regards it as a 'trade mark' whether it is registered or not.

PROTECTION OF TRADE MARKS

The proprietor of a trade mark is in a very strong commercial position. Once the mark is registered, the proprietor acquires what amount to virtual monopoly rights over exploitation for that particular mark applied to the particular goods or services concerned. There may however be provision for individual words, or other elements, of the registered mark to be disclaimed – so that while 'Peter Rabbit' may be registered as a single mark, the individual words 'Peter' and 'Rabbit' may need to be disclaimed since individually they are too common, and non-distinctive of the particular goods concerned, to be protected. The Registry cannot, however, now insist on disclaimers as they have to be offered voluntarily.

TRADE MARK INFRINGEMENT

Section 10(1) of the 1994 Trade Marks Act provides that:

A person infringes a registered trade mark if he uses in the course of trade a sign which is identical with the trade mark in relation to goods or services which are identical with those for which it is registered.

Section 10(2) further provides that infringement may take place where the signs, or goods or services, used are not identical but *similar*, but where there nevertheless exists a likelihood of confusion on the part of the public, including the likelihood that the public will associate the infringing mark with the registered trade mark. You are, however, unlikely to infringe another mark unless you are using the word or device concerned *as a trade mark yourself*.

Under section 10(3), infringement can occur if the mark is used on *dissimilar* goods in a way which 'takes unfair advantage of' or is 'detrimental' to the mark. Comparative advertising may be permitted, however, and section 10(6) of the Act now provides that any descriptive or generic use of the mark in that context will not infringe if it is 'in accordance with honest practices in industrial or commercial matters' (to the extent that 'honest practices' have any place in publishing, we await with interest the courts' interpretation of this phrase).

Proprietors of trade marks are vigilant about any unauthorised use of their marks, and often write standard threatening letters to publishers when they spot 'their' word or other mark in, say, a book title. No infringement occurs however if the use is purely descriptive – as perhaps in a reference to someone 'hoovering' a carpet or to the presence of background 'muzak'. You may even succeed in having an existing registration revoked if you can establish that the word concerned has become a generic term in its own right (inclusion in *The Oxford English Dictionary* is useful evidence, despite the editorial disclaimers one sometimes sees in dictionaries). A good example of such legitimate 'descriptive' use occurred in the recent (1995) Scottish case of *Bravado Merchandising Services Limited v. Mainstream Publishing (Edinburgh) Limited*, where the registered owners of the trade mark 'Wet Wet Wet' (the name of a pop group) failed to prevent a publisher – Mainstream – from marketing a book entitled *A Sweet Little Mystery – Wet Wet Wet – The Inside Story*. In the view of the court, such a use as a book title was purely descriptive, and therefore did not infringe: 'it would be startling if books could not be published about persons or products simply because their names had been registered'.

Where trade mark infringement does take place, however, the normal legal remedies will apply, including:

- an injunction to restrain infringing acts;
- an award of damages, or an account of profits;
- new provisions for delivery up of infringing goods, material or articles.

EU AND INTERNATIONAL TRADE MARK PROTECTION

Registration of a trade mark in the UK only gives protection within the United Kingdom, and until fairly recently, if trade mark protection in other territories – such as the USA – has been required it has been necessary to pursue separate registrations in each individual territory, under the local laws concerned. For an international publishing business seeking worldwide protection, this can prove expensive – however, it is often worthwhile for distinctive international publishing marks, such as *Encyclopaedia Britannica*, and *Grove's* Dictionaries of Music, particularly as an added deterrent to piracy.

Community trade mark

As of 1 April 1996, it is now possible to file one trade mark application to cover all the countries of the European Union including the UK: this may either be done at individual national trade mark registries, or via the new community Trade Mark Office in Alicante, Spain. Advertisement and opposition procedures are similar to those under UK law, and the period of protection will also be 10 years. Although the new system is untested at the time of writing, it promises to simplify registration formalities and costs for the whole territory of the EU, and also to simplify enforcement, since infringement of a community trade mark may be pursued centrally in one national court rather than (as at present) separately in each member state where infringement has occurred. A judgment in one member state may be enforced throughout the EU.

International trade marks

Following the Madrid Agreement, it is possible to file an application for approximately 30 international territories by means of one single application, which will then be forwarded and co-ordinated by the World Intellectual Property Organisation (WIPO) in Geneva. The UK is not yet a member of the Madrid Agreement at the time of writing, and to take advantage of the system a publishing business would need to have a presence in one of the territories concerned.

Some measure of international protection is also available outside the EU under the Madrid Protocol but so far only half a dozen states have ratified the Protocol, and although the UK is a member the necessary provisions have not yet been implemented into UK law. At the time of writing, therefore, the proposed International Trade Mark system does not yet provide a viable alternative to separate registration in individual territories, which will probably continue to be advisable for some time to come.

PASSING OFF

THE TORT OF 'PASSING OFF'

Even without a registered trade mark, it is still possible over a period of time to acquire goodwill in a distinctive name or title, or in the distinctive style, design or general physical appearance of goods (known as their 'get-up'). Under common law, such trading goodwill will be protected, against rival traders who may seek to use it unfairly in order to enhance sales of their own (usually more recent) product. The general principle of law was stated as long ago as 1896 in the leading 'Camel Hair Belting' case, as follows:

> The principle of law may be very plainly stated, that nobody has any right to represent his goods as the goods of somebody else.

Prior to that case, it might have been thought that 'Camel Hair Belting' was just about as generic a product description as it was possible to have, and that any rival trader seeking to start selling belting made out of camel hair could not legally be prevented from using the same generic description. However, 'Camel Hair Belting' had by the time of the action acquired such established goodwill, and such a distinctive reputation, in the market place that the action for passing off succeeded. Many publications, or lists, acquire a similar goodwill in their name or physical get-up – famous labels such as Puffin or Wordsworth Classics, or arguably distinctive get-ups such as the Dorling Kindersley laminated white cover designs, would be similarly protectable under the law of passing off. Such common-law protection is not ideal (as we shall see, it requires proof of actual loss, among other things) and many of our trading partners, in Europe and the USA, deal with the matter somewhat more logically under fully fledged unfair competition laws. If the evidence is strong enough, however, our action for passing off can be an effective way of preventing such unfair competition under both English and Scots law.

In the more recent 'Advocaat' case (1980) Lord Diplock identified five characteristics which must be present in order to create a valid cause of action for passing off:

(1) a misrepresentation;
(2) made by a trader in the course of trade;
(3) to prospective customers of his or ultimate consumers of goods or services supplied by him;
(4) which is calculated to injure the business or goodwill of another trader (in the sense that this is a reasonably foreseeable consequence); and
(5) which causes actual damage to the business or goodwill of the trader by whom the action is brought or which will probably do so.

The weakness of passing off actions under English Law is that, as a general rule, they will not succeed unless there is hard evidence of actual (or likely) loss or damage. There must also be a *real* likelihood of confusion in the market place – this can usually be established by small market surveys, but these take time and are not always conclusive.

The publishers of the well-established 'What's New In . . .' series of magazines secured an injunction against *What's New In Training Personnel* since in that case the risks of confusion, to public and advertisers alike, were great. But the *Morning Star* failed to obtain an injunction against the *Star* newspaper (according to the judge, 'only a moron in a hurry' would have been confused), and the *Evening Times* in Glasgow failed to prevent a newspaper of the same name starting up in London.

Most publishers, of course, go to considerable lengths to create and establish their own distinctive name and get-up, but there are always those who will seek to cut corners by linking their product unfairly to the goodwill established by someone else. Any new publisher launching a weekly trade journal for booksellers and publishers in the UK under the title *The Bookseller*, particularly if it used a similar design and get-up to the established organ, would almost certainly face an action for passing off – however there might equally be an action for passing off against a publisher who tried to launch a new publication called, for example, *The Electronic Bookseller* if the get-up was confusingly similar and there was an implication – as there probably would be – that the new product was being launched by the publishers of *The Bookseller*, or under license from them, and carried with it their considerable reputation and goodwill.

If there is a real likelihood of confusion, and some evidence of loss, a passing off action may well succeed. It is, however, a question of fact in every case. Encounter Limited (the publisher of the current affairs magazine *Encounter*) succeeded in one case in obtaining an injunction against Quartet Books Limited, preventing them from publishing a series of monographs entitled 'Quartet Encounter', on the basis that anyone seeing the books would conclude that this was a joint enterprise between *Encounter* and Quartet: in the words of the judge, 'I cannot conceive of anybody who just sees the book lying about at the booksellers coming to any other conclusion.'

On the other hand, where there really is no credible risk of confusion in the market place, an action for passing off will fail: in the 1987 case of *Mothercare UK Limited v. Penguin Books Limited* a passing off action to restrain the use of the words 'mother care' in the title of a book Mother Care/Other Care published by Penguin Books Limited failed. In the view of the Court of Appeal, the requirement for a successful passing off action, that there should have been a misrepresentation (see above, p. 231) had not been established and the court 'was wholly unable to see any basis for saying that there was a misrepresentation in the title of the book. The book, taken as a whole, did not begin to suggest that the book had been issued or sponsored by, or was in any way associated with Mothercare'.

REMEDIES

Where passing off is established, the most effective remedy a plaintiff will usually seek is that of an injunction, and the usual considerations will apply (see above, p. 213). Damages, or an account of profits, will also be available in appropriate cases.

Sales and marketing

V

Sale of goods and consumer protection 10

SALE OF GOODS

INTRODUCTION

Publishing is all about selling – or so, at least, every marketing director would tell us. Many other topics with legal significance are involved in the publishing process, of course, as we have seen – copyright, for example – but in a very real sense the act of publishing *is* the act of selling. No-one who has been to Frankfurt could ever be in any doubt about that. However, this chapter is not about selling rights (for this, see chapter 5), but about selling the thing itself – the book, or the journal, the CD-ROM, or the on-line service. What happens in legal terms when X sells something to Y? Are any legal duties and obligations imposed on the seller, and are there any exceptions? Are there any specific duties owed to the public? What is the position of wholesalers and retailers?

Lawyers have traditionally called this area of law Sale of Goods, although for much of the high street or mail order selling which publishers do, Consumer Law is now a more helpful label. Even when the publication concerned is not 'sold' as such, but distributed free of charge (for example, a controlled-circulation newspaper paid for by advertising revenue) many of the same legal principles apply. We shall take a look at these basic principles in this chapter, and in the next chapter we will examine the special rules applying to advertising.

SALE OF GOODS AND CONSUMER RIGHTS

'Sale of goods' has a wonderfully Victorian ring to it: indeed, for most of this century the governing Act was the Sale of Goods Act 1893. That Act was passed in an age of *laissez-faire* economics when a man's word was his bond and merchants did not expect (or want) the law to interfere with free trade or freedom of contract. Freedom (or 'privity') of contract was a fundamental principle of English law. All things being equal, with one or two exceptions, what the parties to a contract chose to agree between them was entirely a matter for them, and was not for the law to disturb. This applied to contracts for the sale of goods – such as books – just as much as to any other kinds of contracts. It assumed, however, that the parties were dealing on more or less equal terms, and that in the case of contracts of sale there was a reasonably fair balance between the buyer and the seller.

Before the 1893 Act, the balance had become heavily weighted in favour of the seller. Although some regulation of weights and prices of basic commodities such as beer and bread had existed since the Middle Ages, the basic rule of mercantile law was *caveat emptor*: let the buyer beware. The law would not protect a buyer from a bad bargain unless there was some obvious impropriety, such as fraud or duress, and buyers were expected to satisfy themselves about the suitability or quality of goods they were buying before buying them. Once the deal was struck, that was that: they must abide by their contract, however bad. This was all very well in the days when buyers could go to market and inspect what were then relatively straightforward goods like horses or sacks of wheat for themselves, but as the Industrial Revolution developed, two things happened:

1 goods became more complex and their defects became less visible – so that buyers often found they had to rely on the seller's *description* of the goods; and
2 goods were increasingly mass produced, so that buyers were no longer making individual contracts which they could negotiate with each seller, but forced to deal on industry-wide terms and conditions, drafted entirely from the seller's point of view.

Increasingly, even Victorian businessmen required certain minimum guarantees about the goods they were buying – for example, relating to ownership, or the condition or suitability of the goods when finally delivered.

The 1893 Act went a long way towards restoring a fair balance between buyers and sellers. In particular, it introduced into all contracts for the sale of goods certain implied terms – for example, implied conditions that the goods would be fit for their purpose and of 'merchantable quality'. Although the 1893 Act has now been (almost) entirely superseded and amended by more recent legislation, many of these implied terms still form an important part of modern UK law. We will look at all of them below, in their modern context.

In today's consumer society, therefore, the law no longer assumes that well-informed buyers go about striking arm's-length bargains with individual sellers. That may be the commercial reality in some cases (a sale of stock between two publishers, for example), but in others the buyer (of a computer, for example, or even a toaster) may be negotiating at a distinct disadvantage, and may need more protection. We will therefore need to consider two different kinds of sale:

• Sales between businesses (where the contract will usually prevail, subject to some important provisos, which we will consider below); and

- Sales to the public, or 'consumer sales' (where the 'contract' may be hard to identify, and different provisions may now apply).

Both are now highly regulated, but in different ways. The original Sale of Goods Act 1893 has itself been amended by more modern 1979 and 1994 Acts, and has been added to by (among others) the Misrepresentation Act 1967, the Unfair Contract Terms Act 1977, and the Consumer Protection Act 1987. Supporting it all is a highly consumer-orientated European Commission, which has been responsible in recent years for a steady flow of Directives and other measures from Brussels on topics such as Product Liability, Data Privacy, and Misleading Advertising, all designed to protect the interests of consumers throughout the European Union.

Remedies for unsatisfied buyers, or consumers, may now therefore be found in a number of different places:

- in the terms of individual contracts;
- in civil liability for torts such as negligence or misrepresentation;
- (increasingly) in specific statutory duties, many of which are now duties of strict liability.

Let us start at the beginning, however, and consider what duties – and remedies – may exist under the contract of sale itself.

CONTRACTS OF SALE

What does the law understand by a sale? Consider some publishing examples:

- A publisher's rep visited a bookseller a couple of weeks ago, and the bookseller ordered several titles. The rep described one as being particularly suitable for a degree course taught at the local university, and the bookseller ordered 30 copies. The publisher has now supplied the books, but the bookseller has not yet paid for them.
- A bookseller sells a copy of a book to a customer, who says it is required for a particular series of knitting patterns. The blurb refers to those patterns, but in fact the book is defective and the vital pages are missing.
- A publisher sells copies of a textbook on wholesale terms to an educational supplier. The supplier has its own standard terms and conditions.
- A UK publisher agrees to sell 20,000 copies of a new title to US co-publishers, in their imprint. The US publishers need the copies by a particular date, and make it clear that time is of the essence.
- A publisher mails out a brochure, with details of a medical database on CD-ROM. A regular update service is also advertised. A doctor orders, and is sent, the CD-ROM, but the service fails to materialise.

In all these examples, the essence of the transaction is a contract for the sale of goods, and (in the last case) for services. But when is each contract complete, what are the terms and conditions of each one, and does the law imply any terms of its own? Equally importantly, if the buyer has any rights under the contract, against whom can those rights be enforced? In the case of the knitting book for example, is it the bookseller's fault that the book is defective: and does this mean that the bookseller is obliged to give a refund? Or is the publisher (who published it) or the printer (who manufactured it) liable to the buyer? Who is liable to whom, and when?

Contracts for the sale of goods

Some of these questions can be answered by first finding out whether a contract exists at all, and if so what kind. Contracts, as we saw in chapter 4 are fundamental to the publishing business, but may also essentially be very simple things. They may be created whenever X makes a promise to Y, and Y promises something of value in return: on that basis, all the above examples would clearly be contracts. They are also contracts of *sale*, because in return for an agreed price, it is intended that the buyer will get not only physical possession of the goods, but also the legal ownership of the goods (what lawyers call the 'property' or 'title' to the goods).

They are therefore different from contracts of hire, or contracts for services only, for an important part of the bargain is that the buyer will become the new legal owner. In the words of section 2(1) of the 1979 Sale of Goods Act, they are contracts 'by which the seller transfers or agrees to transfer the property in goods to the buyer for a money consideration called the price'. They are therefore covered by the Sale of Goods Acts, and this has a number of important results.

Contract terms

What are the terms of each contract? Do they have equal weight, or are some more important than others?

Terms of a contract may be *express*, that is specifically set out and agreed by the parties at the time, or they may be *implied*, for example by a previous course of dealing between the parties, or by representations made by one party to the other, and on which the other party relied. Some terms may also be implied by statute: we will come to several important examples of these below.

Some terms may also be more important than others. A *condition* is a term which is fundamental to the bargain, which goes to the root of the whole contract. The price is often the best example, but terms relating to quantity and schedule might equally be conditions. Breach of a condition by a seller normally entitles the buyer to repudiate the whole contract, reject the goods completely, and ask for his or her money back. A *warranty*, by contrast, is much less important. Despite the frequent appearance of the word 'warranty' in publishing contracts, in law a warranty is merely collateral to the main purpose of the contract. Breach of a warranty will not entitle a buyer to rescind the contract entirely or reject the goods, but will merely provide an action for damages.

OWNERSHIP AND TITLE

In a contract for the sale of goods, perhaps the most fundamental condition is that the buyer will acquire good title to the goods – in other words, become the legal owner, unhindered by any rival claims from elsewhere. This assumes, of course, that the seller owns the goods in the first place (and has not, for example, stolen them or have them on hire purchase). The normal rule in such cases (known to lawyers as the *nemo dat* rule) is that you cannot give better title than you yourself possess (*nemo dat quod non habet*: one cannot give what one does not have). If you don't own goods, then a person buying them from you won't own them either. There are exceptions to this general rule: where, for example, the owner has consented to the sale or has impliedly authorised the sale by his conduct. Sale by a commercial agent would normally pass good title. Sale 'in market overt' also used to be an exception to the *nemo dat* rule: but this was abolished (alas) by the Sale of Goods (Amendment) Act 1994.

A seller who remains in physical possession of goods with the buyer's consent after a sale is completed (for example to repair them, or warehouse them) might also be capable of passing good title by delivering them to a new, second buyer: as long as the new buyer received the goods in good faith and without knowledge of the first buyer's rights. So if a bookseller sells the last signed copy of a Booker prize-winning novel to buyer A, who pays the price but leaves it in the shop to be collected later and the bookseller meanwhile re-sells it and hands it over to buyer B, buyer B might well become the new owner. Buyer A would of course have an action for the return of his or her money and possibly a claim for other damages, but would not be entitled to claim ownership of the book itself.

Similarly, a publisher who in similar circumstances sold a particular consignment of bound or sheet stock twice over would effectively pass legal ownership to the innocent final customer to whom the stock was actually delivered. In both cases, the seller (however dishonest) was in possession with the owner's consent, and can therefore pass on good legal ownership to someone buying in good faith.

Although this has the effect of protecting innocent book-buyers, it may leave publishers at some risk if they deliver stock on sale or return to a retailer and the retailer either fails to pay, or – worse still – goes bankrupt. Many publishing distribution contracts therefore contain express terms, known as 'retention of title clauses', which clearly stipulate that, even after they are delivered to the retailer, legal ownership of the goods remains with the publisher until they are paid for (or, in some cases, all outstanding debts are paid). If a major chain of bookshops (for example) calls in the receivers, such clauses are designed to ensure that relevant unsold stock can be reclaimed from the bookshelves by the publishers concerned, and will not belong to the bookshop's creditors.

Nevertheless there are often practical difficulties in claiming title to specific stocks when they have become mixed with other stocks on the buyer's premises (how do you identify those which are yours?) and it may prove difficult to rely on a retention of title clause unless it is very carefully drafted.

IMPLIED CONDITION OF GOOD TITLE

With one exception, which we deal with below, section 12(1) of the 1979 Sale of Goods Act provides that in every contract of sale there is:

> an implied condition on the part of the seller that . . . he has a right to sell the goods.

This is so, whether the contract refers to the matter or not. There is a corresponding implied condition in contracts for future sales. Note that the 1979 Act implies a *condition* of good title into every such contract, not merely a warranty. This means that a buyer who does not get the legal title he or she bargained for may rescind the whole contract – understandably enough.

In addition to the condition of good title, section 12(2) also provides additional *warranties* that:

- the goods are (and will remain) free of any legal charges or 'encumbrances' which may restrict their use; and
- the buyer will enjoy 'quiet possession' of the goods

What happens if you wish to sell the goods, but are genuinely uncertain as to whether you have the full legal right to do so? Can you sell 'such title as I may have'? Where there are difficulties in proving title, buyers may be quite willing to bear that risk as a commercial risk, particularly if you and they have dealt with each other regularly before. Section 12(3) of the 1979 Act provides for this situation, and provides specifically that the implied conditions and warranties above will not apply to such limited sales: there will in such cases only be limited warranties, for example that any charges and encumbrances which *are* known are disclosed to the buyer before the contract is made.

SUMMARY CHECKLIST: LEGAL OWNERSHIP IN SALES

To recap so far: to find out who owns particular goods, the questions to ask might be as follows:

- Does a contract of sale exist?
- Does the seller own the goods in the first place?
- If not, has the owner impliedly (or actually) authorised the sale?
- If not, does the seller possess the goods with the owner's consent, and does the buyer buy in good faith?

- Is there a valid retention of title clause?
- Is there any other restriction on title (for example, a sale of only 'such title as I may have')?

If we apply these criteria to our first contract of sale example (at p. 237, above), where the publisher has supplied the books, but the bookseller has not yet paid for them, it is likely that the publisher will have owned the books, and that a contract of sale exists. However, if there was a valid retention of title clause, the bookseller might not yet own the books. Even so, if (as is likely) the bookseller had physical possession of the books with the owner's consent, the bookseller might still effectively pass on legal ownership to a customer who bought one of them in good faith.

SALES BY DESCRIPTION

The seller's description of the goods may be such an important factor in the buyer's decision to buy, that it should in fairness be treated as a term of the contract. Accordingly, under section 13(1) of the Sale of Goods Act 1979:

> Where there is a contract for the sale of goods by description, there is an implied condition that the goods will correspond with the description.

Note that the implied condition applies only where the sale is *by* description, in other words where the description forms a significant part of the bargain, and is not merely incidental. So where a bookseller describes a text to a customer as being suitable for a certain syllabus, that might well be a sale by description. What if the jacket blurb carries a similar claim, but the bookseller, when asked, expresses no opinion on the subject? The customer's contract of sale is with the bookseller, not the publisher, so the description in the blurb would not become a term of the contract if the bookseller carefully remained distanced from it, or refused to endorse it. What if the book in question is *simply* selected, taken to the check-out till, and sold, without the printed description being referred to? This is a common situation in busy retail shops, particularly supermarkets. Probably, now, section 13(3) of the 1979 Act would apply, which provides that:

> a sale of goods is not prevented from being a sale by description by reason only that, being exposed for sale or hire, they are selected by the buyer.

Under such circumstances any description on the goods themselves would give rise to the implied condition under section 13(1), and if the goods did not comply with that description the buyer would be entitled to rescind the contract and reject the goods. The publisher might also be guilty of a false trade description under the Trade Descriptions Act 1968 (see chapter 11).

Equally, a description would also bind a publisher who sold direct to a customer by mail order, if it formed a significant part of the bargain. Quite apart from the Trade Descriptions Act implications, it would also constitute an implied condition of the contract of sale itself.

Sales by description might also bind a publisher selling stock, for example to a bookseller or wholesaler. The buyer could reject the goods if they did not comply with the description, even if the buyer had suffered no loss. This would be so, even if the buyer had inspected a sample – under section 13(2) of the 1979 Act:

> If the sale is by sample, as well as by description, it is not sufficient that the bulk of the goods corresponds with the sample *if the goods do not also correspond with the description* (my italics).

MISREPRESENTATION

If a description cannot be incorporated as an implied term into the contract of sale itself, a seller might still be liable under the general law of tort for any misrepresentations made to the buyer, if the buyer relied on them and suffered loss or damage as a result.

Misrepresentations may be fraudulent, negligent or innocent:

- *Fraudulent misrepresentation.* Since the last century it has been established law that sellers will be guilty of fraud (strictly speaking, the tort of deceit) if they cause loss or damage to buyers by intentionally misleading them with statements of fact knowing them to be untrue or not caring whether they are true or false. Not surprisingly, most of the cases involve used cars. In most cases, where fraud can be proved, the buyer may rescind the contract (so as to be restored to his or her original position), or alternatively claim damages.
- *Negligent misrepresentation.* Even in the absence of actual fraud, the Misrepresentation Act 1967, section 2(1), now provides that a buyer will still be entitled to damages, or to rescind the contract, if a misrepresentation was made negligently. Negligence however implies a duty of care, and may be difficult to prove: on negligence generally, see p. 250.
- *Innocent misrepresentation.* In the absence of either fraud or negligence, where the misrepresentation was entirely innocent, the buyer's only remedy would normally be to rescind the contract. However, if this was no longer possible – for example, because the goods had been destroyed – a court may award damages in lieu, under section 2(2) of the 1967 Act.

SUMMARY CHECKLIST: DESCRIPTIONS, AND MISREPRESENTATION

- Is there a sale by description?
- Do the goods correspond with that description?
- Has there been any misrepresentation?

In our first contract of sale example (p. 237) the sales rep described one book as particularly suitable for a local degree course, and the bookseller ordered on that basis: the sale would probably therefore be a sale by description, and if the books did not correspond with the description the bookseller could rescind the contract (for breach of an implied condition) and return the books.

MERCHANTABILITY AND SATISFACTORY QUALITY

Under section 14 of the 1893 and 1979 Sale of Goods Acts all sellers of goods who sold in the course of their business were bound by an implied condition that those goods would be of 'merchantable quality'. Since the term implied was a condition rather than a mere warranty, so that buyers were entitled not only to damages but to reject the goods entirely, there was considerable argument in the courts over what was or was not 'merchantable'. The factors which might be taken into account clearly included fundamental defects in quality, such as exploding 'Coalite' (in one case) and a plastic catapult which broke and blinded a boy in one eye (in another case), but minor and less obvious defects were less clear, particularly if they were aesthetic rather than purely functional. The definition of 'merchantable quality' provided an objective standard of sorts, based on a buyer's reasonable expectations under all the relevant circumstances, but reflected the Victorian idea of goods as trading commodities which merchants bought (and might wish to re-sell) rather than consumer goods for the buyer's own use. This emphasis has now been changed by the Sale and Supply of Goods Act 1994, and the test now is one of 'satisfactory quality', with clearer guidance as to the factors which may be taken into account.

IMPLIED TERMS OF SATISFACTORY QUALITY

Section 14(2) of the 1979 Act, as amended by the 1994 Act, now provides as follows:

(2) When the seller sells goods in the course of a business, there is an implied term that the goods supplied under the contract are of satisfactory quality.

(2A) . . . goods are of satisfactory quality if they meet the standard that a reasonable person would regard as satisfactory, taking account of any description of the goods, the price (if relevant) and all the other relevant circumstances.

Note that, for the 1979 and 1994 Acts to apply, the seller must be selling 'in the course of a business'. The implied term will not apply to purely private sales. For most publishers, booksellers and distributors most of their sales transactions will clearly be in the course of a business. This applies equally to sales of stock between publishers, consumer sales in bookshops, or mail order sales. However, it is not necessarily enough to establish that the seller *is* a business – the sale itself must be 'in the course of' *that* business. It may be necessary to examine the transaction more carefully in borderline cases, for example when a publisher sells off a company car or a bookseller disposes of a computer. Arguably, neither of those transactions would be in the course of the seller's particular business. In the case of the car, this might particularly be so if it were a private car only occasionally used on company business. It will be necessary to look at all the relevant factors – particularly, perhaps, whether the sale appears in the accounts (and tax return) of the business concerned.

'SATISFACTORY QUALITY'

Under the 1994 Act, quality factors which may specifically be taken into account (among others) include the following:

- fitness for all the purposes for which goods of the kind in question are commonly supplied;
- appearance and finish;
- freedom from minor defects;
- safety; and
- durability.

Any one or more of these factors may now be relevant in deciding whether a reasonable person would regard the goods as satisfactory. Clearly, the first category is potentially the broadest, covering *all* the purposes 'for which goods of the kind in question are commonly supplied' – note, however, that the relevant purpose must be one for which such goods are *commonly* supplied, not some special or esoteric purpose not normally associated with the goods in question (for fitness for a special purpose, see below, p. 246). A scientific or technical textbook or CD-ROM with vital instructions missing so that it could not be used in teaching, or a cookery book without key ingredients or with the wrong quantities and therefore useless for cooking, would probably not be fit for all the purposes for which such books or CD-ROMs are commonly supplied, and since this would breach the implied condition that the goods would be of satisfactory quality the buyer would be entitled to rescind the contract, return the goods and ask for his or her money back.

'Appearance and finish' and 'Freedom from minor defects' now appear for the first time, confirming the result of a 1988 case where a string of minor defects in an expensive Range Rover were held to make it unmerchantable (although it was still basically roadworthy) – the buyer of a Rolls-Royce or a Range Rover is entitled to have higher expectations than the buyer of, say, a second-hand Lada whose only concern might be to get (relatively) safely from A to B. This flexible definition of what is or is not satisfactory quality must apply equally to publications. A buyer of an expensive multi-volume encyclopaedia might well be entitled to claim that it was not of satisfactory quality under the Act if the gold blocking on the spines came off after two weeks, whereas the buyer of a cheap paperback classic might be glad if the jacket stayed on at all.

'Safety' and 'Durability' may be of vital concern to consumers, and are also now expressly included on the recommendation of the Law Commission. 'Durability' probably only implies durability for a reasonable time, and 'safety' here probably only implies safety for reasonable or normal use – in one case involving pork chops which contained a harmful parasite, the buyer failed to prove that the chops did not reach the (then) standard of merchantable quality since the chops were only partially cooked, and normal cooking would have killed the parasite and made them perfectly safe to eat. Safety is clearly relevant for cars or electrical goods such as computer equipment – a CD-ROM containing a virus might not now be considered sufficiently safe to be of 'satisfactory quality'. Sellers also have statutory duties relating to safety under the Consumer Protection Act 1987, (below, p. 252).

Exceptions

The implied term of satisfactory quality will not apply in the following circumstances:

- where the defect is specifically drawn to the buyer's attention before the contract is made;
- where the buyer examines the goods before the contract is made (and that examination ought to have revealed the defect); and
- where the sale was by sample, and the defect would have been apparent on a reasonable examination of the sample.

Note that the vital revelation, or inspection, must have taken place *before* the contract was made. In the case of sales by sample, section 15 of the 1979 Act provides similar implied terms that the bulk will correspond in quality to the sample, and will be of satisfactory quality except for defects apparent on examination.

SUMMARY CHECKLIST: SATISFACTORY QUALITY

- Is the sale in the course of the seller's business?
- Would a reasonable person regard the goods as satisfactory?
- Are they fit for all the purposes for which goods of that kind are commonly supplied?
- Is their appearance and finish satisfactory?
- Are they free from minor defects?
- Are they reasonably safe, and durable?
- Was the defect brought to the buyer's attention before the contract was made?

- Did the buyer examine the goods before the contract was made? Ought that to have revealed the defect?
- Was the sale by sample, and would the defect have been reasonably apparent?

FITNESS FOR PURPOSE

In addition to the implied term that goods will be of satisfactory quality, there is a further implied condition imposed on the seller that goods will be reasonably fit for any *particular* purpose made known by the buyer. This implied condition is contained in section 14(3) of the 1979 Sale of Goods Act, which provides as follows:

> Where the seller sells goods in the course of a business and the buyer, expressly or by implication, makes known . . . to the seller . . . any particular purpose for which the goods are being bought, there is an implied condition that the goods supplied under the contract are reasonably fit for that purpose.

This will apply even though the purpose is unusual or esoteric, provided that the buyer has made that particular purpose known to the seller. It may be made known expressly, or by implication, but it must be clearly made known, so that the seller is in no doubt that that is the purpose for which the buyer requires the goods, and for which he or she is paying the price. Where the circumstances of the sale indicate otherwise, the implied condition of fitness for that purpose will not apply. For example, where the buyer would have made the purchase anyway, and was clearly not relying on the seller's professional advice – or where it would have been unreasonable to do so – any statement by the seller about fitness for purpose will probably be regarded as merely ancillary, and will not form part of the contract. So, where a student goes into a campus bookstore with a reading list, and selects a textbook on the list and buys it at the till, the purchase is clearly being made in reliance on the reading list, not on any extra encouraging remarks which the bookseller may add. In those circumstances if the book turns out to be unsuitable, the student's remedy – if he or she has one at all – would be against the lecturer who drew up the reading list, not the bookseller who sold the book, or the publisher who published it.

Suppose, however, that the student is clearly in some doubt, expressly asks the bookseller's advice as to whether the text is suitable for a specific course, and is advised that it is? In those circumstances, where the student clearly relies on the bookseller's skill and judgement, the bookseller will almost certainly be bound by an implied condition that the book is fit for that purpose.

A supply of software might be considered to be a supply of goods for these purposes, so that the same implied condition of fitness for purpose would apply: in a recent (1994) decision a bespoke software package ordered by St Albans City Council to calculate the basis of the community charge in its area, and which miscalculated the population in a way which led to revenue and funding losses of £1.3 million, was held not to be reasonably fit for the purpose for which it had been ordered, and was thus in breach of contract (since the Council was forced to deal on the computer company's standard terms and conditions, there was also an Unfair Contract Terms Act issue – see below, p. 248).

Publishers supplying goods or software direct would equally be bound in such circumstances, for example where a purchaser ordered a textbook, or a set of multiple-choice exam questions on CD-ROM, by mail order, making it clear to the publisher that it was required for a specified course. If the wrong book or CD-ROM is supplied, even though it may in all other respects be of 'satisfactory quality', there will be a breach of the implied condition of fitness for purpose and the buyer will be entitled to reject the goods. Equally, a publisher selling stock to a retailer or wholesaler, knowing that it is required for further distribution or re-sale, would probably be bound by a similar condition if the goods for some reason turn out to be impossible to re-sell.

The only way for the seller to avoid such liability would be to establish:

1 that no particular purpose was specified or implied (and was not already obvious, such as the 'purpose' of an umbrella or a hot water bottle); or
2 that no opinion was expressed as to the fitness for that purpose of the goods in question; or
3 that any unfitness which did appear stemmed from some other special circumstances unique to the buyer and not disclosed to the seller (or otherwise obvious) at the time – for example (as in one case) a perfectly good Harris Tweed coat which caused dermatitis to a lady buyer who did not disclose that she had abnormally sensitive skin.

SUMMARY CHECKLIST: FITNESS FOR PURPOSE

- Is the sale in the course of the seller's business?
- Has the buyer clearly made known a particular purpose?
- Was the buyer relying on the seller's professional advice or opinion?
- Did the unfitness stem from any other special circumstances, not disclosed at the time?

EXCLUSION AND LIMITATION CLAUSES

Is it possible to avoid or limit liability under such implied terms, for example by putting a clause in the contract in small print somewhere which specifically excludes or limits it? In most cases now, the answer is no – particularly where the exclusion clause attempts to avoid liability to consumers. However, some may still be permitted if they pass a test of 'reasonableness'. For disclaimers of liability for negligent mis-statements, see chapter 7, pp. 177.

Exclusion clauses (sometimes called exemption clauses) were once widely used (and abused) in standard form contracts, and some of the more notorious examples would attempt total, blanket avoidance of any liability to consumers for any loss, damage or injury, and even for death. In many cases judges have refused to enforce such clauses if they were not properly brought to the notice of the consumer at the time of the contract (as in the infamous phrase 'for conditions see timetable'), or were unduly onerous or exorbitant (such as a £3,783.50 time penalty charged by a photographic library for a two week delay in returning transparencies). In addition, because exclusion clauses were so destructive of the consumer's rights, they have generally been interpreted narrowly by the courts *against* the party trying to enforce them – so that a clause excluding liability for a breach of *warranty*, for example, would *not* avoid liability for any breach of a *condition*. This is known in English law as the '*contra proferentem*' rule, but even with this ammunition, courts have not always been able to prevent sellers from using exclusion clauses to avoid their proper obligations.

The Unfair Contract Terms Act of 1977 was therefore passed to regulate the scope of exclusion clauses and other unfair terms by statute. Some liabilities – for example, for death or personal injury – may now never be excluded and others may only be excluded in certain circumstances. These largely depend on whether the purchaser is buying as a *consumer*, or negotiating freely in the course of a business (such as a publisher buying stock from another publisher). The following rules may apply:

Liabilities which may never be excluded

Any clause attempting to exclude liability for the following will be void and unenforceable:

- death or personal injury resulting from negligence;
- breach of the implied condition of good title (see p. 240).

Where the purchaser buys as a consumer

Stricter liability applies in the most common consumer situations where the seller is dealing in the course of a business but the buyer is *not*. Under section 3 of the 1977 Act, any clause in a contract attempting to permit performance 'substantially different from that which was reasonably expected', or no performance at all (such as a 'force majeure' clause) will only be allowed if it satisfies a requirement of 'reasonableness'. What is or is not 'reasonable' depends on all the circumstances, including customs of the trade, the intention and knowledge of the parties and the relative strengths (or weaknesses) of their bargaining positions.

Section 3 also applies where the buyer (even though a business buyer) is obliged to deal on the seller's standard terms of business. Those companies whose negotiating strength means that buyers in effect have no choice but to deal on their standard terms should therefore bear in mind that those terms and conditions will now be open to legal challenge unless they are reasonable. This might apply to publishers, printers, or any other commercial suppliers, including computer corporations: in the 1994 case discussed above (p. 246), where bespoke software for a local council was held not to be fit for its intended purpose, an exclusion clause limiting liability to £100,000 (losses were £1.3 million) was held unreasonable under the circumstances. The local council was under severe time pressure, had a limited choice of suppliers (all of whom dealt on similar terms), and at the time the computer company concerned had product liability insurance of £50 million.

Under section 2, liability for any loss or damage (except death or personal injury) may be excluded, but again only if reasonable.

Equally importantly, under section 6, the main implied conditions under the Sale of Goods Acts – that the goods will correspond with any description, will be of satisfactory quality and fit for their purpose, and correspond with any sample – can *never* be excluded where the buyer deals as a consumer.

Following a 1993 EC Directive relating to unfair consumer contracts, the UK has now introduced the Unfair Terms in Consumer Contracts Regulations 1994. These extend the protection already given under the 1977 Act. What is or is not an 'unfair term' broadly mirrors the requirements of 'reasonableness' contained in the 1977 Act, but with a new requirement of *good faith*, which may depend among other things on the extent to which the seller has 'dealt fairly and equitably' with the consumer. An 'unfair term' now means any term which contrary to the requirement of good faith causes a significant imbalance in the parties' rights and obligations under the contract to the detriment of the consumer (Regulation 4(1)).

Following the 1994 Regulations, it now seems likely that unfair contract terms will be increasingly difficult to enforce. Indeed, under Regulation 6, the *contra proferentem* rule (see above, p. 248) seems finally to have reached its apotheosis: 'a seller or supplier shall ensure that any written term of a contract is expressed in plain, intelligible language, and if there is doubt about the meaning of a written term, the interpretation most favourable to the consumer shall prevail'.

Where the purchaser buys in the course of business

This covers the case of businesses contracting at arm's-length, as in co-publishing deals, or contracts with printers, agents or distributors. Here, where the bargaining positions are deemed to be somewhat better balanced (and insurance cover is more likely on both sides), more liabilities may be excluded. Liability for loss or damage (other than death or personal injury) may be excluded, but only if reasonable, and all the Sale of Goods Act implied conditions listed above (except the implied condition of good title) may be excluded, but again only if the relevant clause satisfies the test of reasonableness.

The 1994 Regulations do not apply to non-consumer sales. In addition, the Unfair Contract Terms Act 1977 does not apply to contracts relating to the creation, transfer or termination of a right or interest in any intellectual property (including copyright). It would therefore not apply to most author–publisher agreements.

CONSUMER PROTECTION

NEGLIGENCE, AND DUTIES OF CARE

So far, we have considered the remedies which a buyer of goods might have against a seller under a contract of sale. Some will be provided by the terms of the contract itself, and others under implied terms included by the Sale of Goods Acts, such as the implied terms of fitness for purpose or satisfactory quality. However, all these remedies depend on the contract of sale between the buyer and the seller. They will not protect anyone who is not a party to that contract. What happens if the defective goods cause loss or damage not to the buyer but to someone else – to the buyer's family or friends, colleagues at work, or even next-door neighbours? If the seller is not liable under the contract itself, does the *manufacturer* owe any general duty of care to such people, or to the public at large?

We have seen that, as well as contractual remedies, there may also be remedies in tort, for example for negligent mis-statement (above, p. 177) or for fraudulent or negligent misrepresentation (above, p. 242), where a duty of care can be shown to exist. Duties of care already exist between skilled or professional people such as lawyers and their clients, or between doctor and patient, and breach of such duties could well amount to negligence, but they were not generally regarded as existing between manufacturers and the general public. Not, that is, until 1932 and what is possibly the most famous case in English (and Scots) law: *Donoghue v. Stevenson*.

A shop assistant, Miss Donoghue, went with a friend of hers to a café in Paisley. The friend (not Miss Donoghue, notice) ordered ice cream for both of them, and ginger beer in a brown bottle. They had the ice cream, and drank half of the ginger beer, but hidden at the bottom of the ginger beer bottle were the decomposing remains of a snail. These remains came floating out with the latter half of the ginger beer at an inappropriate moment and – quite understandably – caused Miss Donoghue severe shock and gastro-enteritis.

Miss Donoghue had no action for damages against the café proprietor under the contract of sale, because the contract of sale was with her friend, not with her. The House of Lords held that, even so, the manufacturer owed a general duty of care to her as the ultimate consumer of the goods. In the immortal words of Lord Atkin:

The rule that you are to love your neighbour becomes in law – you must not injure your neighbour; and the lawyer's question, Who is my neighbour? receives a restricted reply. You must take reasonable care to avoid acts or omissions which you can reasonably foresee would be likely to injure your neighbour. Who, then, in law is my neighbour? The answer seems to be – persons who are so closely and directly affected by my act that I ought reasonably to have them in contemplation as being so affected when I am directing my mind to the acts or omissions which are called in question.

This duty of care is particularly strong when the goods are sold direct to the public in pre-sealed form such as canned or bottled goods – or perhaps today shrinkwrapped books or CDs – which cannot realistically be checked once they have left the manufacturer's warehouse.

As Lord Atkin put it:

A manufacturer of products, which he sells in such a form as to show that he intends them to reach the ultimate consumer in the form in which they left him with no reasonable possibility of intermediate examination, and with the knowledge that the absence of reasonable care in the putting up of the products will result in an injury to the consumers' life or property, owes a duty to the consumer to take that reasonable care.

It is a proposition which I venture to say no-one in Scotland or England who is not a lawyer would for one moment doubt.

In cases since 1932, this duty has been extended to friends, family, guests, borrowers, employees and even bystanders. However, it is up to the person injured to prove that such a duty of care exists, and that – where it does – the manufacturer is negligent in failing to comply with it. In cases involving self-evident defects such as snails in ginger beer bottles, this may be relatively easy (particularly now), but in other circumstances negligence on the part of the manufacturer may be harder to prove. It may require evidence of a failure in the production process, a design flaw, or defective instructions for use (where instructions are appropriate) and in many cases such evidence will be hard to obtain.

There may also be some difficulty in establishing negligence where the loss or injury is caused not by manufactured goods but by a statement of advice or assurance, even where the recipient has acted in reliance on that advice and suffered loss as a result: the difficulty will lie in proving that a duty of care already existed, or was assumed. Where a responsibility already exists, for example between professionals and their own clients, this will be fairly clear, and responsibility has been *deemed* to be assumed in some recent cases, for example involving negligent house surveys. But a business reference (such as a banker's, or employer's, reference) given to a third party, particularly with a disclaimer, might well not create a sufficient duty of care: there might perhaps be a general duty in such circumstances not to be dishonest or not to make statements which are known to be untrue, but otherwise it may be difficult to establish negligence based on a duty of care if the advice or opinion given turns out to be wrong. (On negligent mis-statement generally, see chapter 7, p. 177.)

For these reasons, some duties of care are now imposed on manufacturers directly by statute.

LIABILITY FOR DEFECTIVE GOODS

In one particular respect – that of product safety – the liability of producers and manufacturers for their products has increased dramatically in the UK and throughout Europe in recent years. Following the EC Directive on Product Liability of 1985, the UK passed the Consumer Protection Act 1987, which now imposes on producers and others considerably stricter liability for damage or injury caused by defective goods, without any need for the consumer to establish liability under a contract of sale, or to prove negligence or any other fault. Such strict liability is, of course, chiefly designed to cover those consumer goods with the greatest inherent dangers, such as cars, electrical goods, and – because of the risks to children – toys, but could equally well apply to a CD-ROM containing a virus, or even defective ink or paper if they were proved to have some harmful chemical side-effect.

Those liable under the Act include:

- producers of products (or extractors or refiners of natural products such as natural gas or oil);
- those who import products into the European Union; or
- those who sell goods under their own brand name (such as supermarkets).

Suppliers may also be liable as well as producers where they have supplied the defective goods to the producer (perhaps in the form of defective components) or to the final consumer (such as a retailer, if the producer is not readily identifiable).

What is 'defective'? A product is defective under section 3(1) of the 1987 Act:

if the safety of the product is not such as persons generally are entitled to expect.

'Safety' includes not only the physical safety of the consumer, but also covers any damage to property (although not loss of or damage to the defective product itself – if a CD-ROM blows up your computer, you may claim for the loss of your computer, but not for the cost of the CD-ROM itself).

Section 4 of the 1987 Act provides a number of defences. The strict liability under the Act may be avoided if:

- the defect was caused by compliance with any statutory or EU requirement;
- the defendant was not the actual supplier;
- the defective product was supplied privately or not for profit (for example, at a private dinner or church fete);

- the defect was not present when the product was supplied; or
- the state of scientific and technical knowledge at the time would not have enabled the producer to discover the defect.

In addition to these defences a producer of a defective product may also plead 'contributory negligence' on the part of the consumer – in other words, that the consumer's own negligence in using the product was at least partly to blame for the damage caused or injury suffered, and the damages awarded may be reduced accordingly.

SUPPLYING UNSAFE CONSUMER GOODS

As well as imposing strict liability for defective products on producers, the Consumer Protection Act 1987 also (in Part II of the Act) imposes *criminal* liability on *suppliers* of consumer goods which are not safe. Under section 10(1) of the Act, it is an offence, punishable by fine or imprisonment, to supply, offer or agree to supply, or expose or possess for supply, any consumer goods which are not reasonably safe (having regard to all the circumstances). 'Reasonably safe' means that there must either be no risk of death or personal injury, or at most a risk 'reduced to a minimum'. The Secretary of State may make safety regulations and issue notices covering specific goods from time to time. It is extremely unlikely that these would affect publications such as books and periodicals, which in themselves are unlikely to be unsafe, although they might become unsafe if, for example, they were sold to children with accompanying toys, games or other free gifts. It is also quite conceivable that an educational CD-ROM or multimedia package might contain unsafe items, particularly if aimed at young children.

Innocent retailers have a defence where they were unaware that particular goods were unsafe, or can establish that they took reasonable precautions and acted with due diligence (for example, by conducting random safety checks).

SUMMARY CHECKLIST: CONSUMER PROTECTION

- Does a duty of care exist?
- If so, does breach of that duty amount to negligence?
- Might the goods be defective goods?
- Is their safety such as the public is entitled to expect?
- Have unsafe consumer goods been supplied?
- Do any of the available defences apply?

Advertising and promotion

11

ADVERTISING

INTRODUCTION

There is a school of thought that if you invent a better mousetrap, the world will beat a path to your door. This may be true of mousetraps, and (perhaps) some essential professional texts, but as a general rule most publishers find it pays to advertise. As a result, as anyone who picks up a copy of *The Bookseller* will know, advertising is as prominent a feature of the publishing world as it is of any other major industry – perhaps more so – and can range from the modestly factual to the glossiest forms of hype. It is not, however, without its legal risks. We considered some of the general risks which accompany all published text, such as defamation and malicious falsehood, in chapter 7. In this chapter we will take a look at the laws which particularly apply to advertising and promotional techniques, and which govern what you say in advertisements, and how you say it.

All advertisers sooner or later face the same universal temptation: to over-state the value of the thing being sold. You know the sort of thing: brilliant author, uniquely authoritative (or hysterically funny/thrilling/raunchy) work, miraculously good value at this never-to-be-repeated pre-publication offer. In a world increasingly dominated by the media, consumers are probably immune to much of this, and most of it is harmless enough. If it is no more than generalised hype, the law treats it, rather crushingly, as a 'mere puff', and gives it no particular legal significance. But beware: look again at the above blurbs. Are you simply throwing in the adjective 'authoritative' (for example) as a mere puff, or are you actually stating – or implying – that your author or publication has specific authority (such as that of an examining board or Royal College)? Similarly, are you merely describing your product as being 'good value', or are you making a specific pre-publication offer? The difference could be highly significant. Where statements are made which *mislead* the consumer, into buying something which he or she would not otherwise have bought, publishers may find themselves breaking the law. And the *criminal* law is often involved in this area of publishing, with fines and even imprisonment for those who infringe. It is therefore very much in publishers' interests to take care how they describe their publications.

TRADE DESCRIPTIONS

Trade descriptions are covered by the Trade Descriptions Act of 1968. The Act applies between businesses, as well as to consumer advertising, and it covers statements relating to services (see below, p. 256) as well as to goods.

Under section 1(1) of the 1968 Act any person commits an offence:

who, in the course of a trade or business:
(a) applies a false trade description to any goods; or
(b) supplies or offers to supply any goods to which a false trade description is applied.

A trade description can include almost any feature or quality of the goods – their size, quantity, composition, manufacture, strength, accuracy, pedigree, official approval, testing or endorsement, or history, including previous ownership. Note however that, for the Act to apply, the description must be applied in the course of a trade or business: private sales are not covered.

How do you 'apply' a trade description, however, and when is a trade description a 'false' trade description?

Applying a trade description

A description can be 'applied' to goods by printing it directly on them (for example, as part of a jacket blurb), or by attaching it (perhaps via a label or sticker) or by marking it on to the packaging, or on anything in which, on which, or next to which the goods are placed, such as a spinner or other display unit, or adjacent point of sale material. Descriptions can also be applied, of course, by means of physically quite separate advertising, such as space advertising, leaflets, catalogues and price lists, provided that the description is used in a manner 'likely to be taken as referring to the goods'. In fact, a trade description does not even need to be applied in physical form at all – it can be an oral description by the person supplying the goods, or even implied from the mere fact of supply if goods of a particular description were specifically requested. Most publishing advertising would therefore be covered.

False trade descriptions

What is 'false'? Section 3 of the 1968 Act helpfully tells us that false means 'false to a material degree': this includes statements which, though not strictly speaking false, are, nevertheless, misleading. So to describe a car as having 'one lady owner' might be a false trade description, even if the statement was strictly true in the sense that, out of five previous owners, only one was a lady. In the publishing context, any of the following may potentially be false trade descriptions:

- New, comprehensively updated, 1996 edition
- 30,000 articles with 12,000 illustrations
- specifically written for the GCSE syllabus
- as approved by the Royal College of Surgeons
- Windows and Mac

It might also be a false trade description to promote and package a book as if it were written by one of your best-selling authors, when in fact it was largely written by someone else: HarperCollins were prosecuted for this reason in 1991 by Warwickshire Trading Standards Officers, for publishing an 'Alastair MacLean' novel, jacketed in a style very like all his other successful thrillers, which although based on his own sketches with the full consent of his estate was in fact substantially ghost-written after his death by another writer altogether (named Alastair MacNeill). It was clearly in the interests of Alastair MacLean's estate – and his reading public – that his final work-in-progress should be published, but the court took the view that to package and sell it as a full-length Alastair MacLean novel was a false trade description. Although doubtless good in its own right it was not in fact a book by him, but by someone else. It is worth bearing in mind, therefore, that however understandable the motives – and continued use of a famous author's name and a strong brand identity are powerful motives – books should not be described in a way which misleads the public.

The Act applies to trade descriptions relating to *services*, as well as goods, and there have been many cases – not surprisingly – resulting from statements made in holiday brochures about non-existent hotels, restaurants, beaches and other facilities. Such criminal liability, contained in section 14 of the Act, might however also extend to a publisher who advertised facilities relating to books, such as '14 days free approval' or 'postage and packing free' when in fact these facilities did not exist, or did not extend to the particular books in question. It might well also cover advertisements relating to a help-line service with a CD-ROM product which either turned out not to exist at all, or not to include the full cover advertised. Under section 14, however, (unlike section 1 above) the person making the false statement must either *know* it to be false, or make it *recklessly*.

Prosecutions, and defences

Local Trading Standards Officers (formerly called weights and measures inspectors) are given wide powers under the 1968 Act to investigate complaints, and bring prosecutions, make test purchases, enter premises and seize goods and documents. Penalties, if convicted, range from a fine of up to £5,000 on summary conviction to an unlimited fine and/or up to 2 years imprisonment on indictment.

It is, however, a defence to a charge of applying a false description to prove that the commission of the offence was the result of

- a mistake;
- an accident, or some other unavoidable cause;
- reliance on information supplied by someone else; or
- someone else's actions or omissions;

provided that it can also be proved that 'all reasonable precautions' were taken and 'all due diligence' was exercised to avoid the commission of the offence (section 24). A similar defence is available to suppliers, such as wholesalers or booksellers, who may (under section 24(3)) prove that they did not know, and could not with reasonable diligence have ascertained, that the goods did not conform to the description.

A special defence is also available under section 25 to those people such as magazine and journal editors who innocently publish advertisements placed in their publications by others, if they can prove that the advertisement was accepted and placed in the course of their business *and* that they were not aware (and had no reason to be) that publication would involve an offence under the Act. The defence would also cover an innocent advertising agency placing an advertisement on behalf of a client.

MISLEADING ADVERTISEMENTS

As well as the criminal powers available to Trading Standards Officers under the 1968 Act, regulatory powers to prevent misleading advertisements are also given to the Director General of Fair Trading, under the Control of Misleading Advertisements Regulations; 1988. The Regulations were passed in order to implement the EC's Misleading Advertisements Directive of 1984, and give the Director General the power to seek injunctions in the courts, preventing, or halting, the publication of most kinds of misleading advertisements, including press and magazine advertising, direct mailings, posters and leaflets. They do not however apply to TV, cable, or radio advertisements, which are regulated by separate, but similar, provisions under the Broadcasting Act 1990.

An advertisement is misleading under the Regulations if it:

- 'deceives or is likely to deceive' those to whom it is addressed, or those it reaches; and
- because of this, 'is likely to affect their economic behaviour' (for example, by persuading them to buy the product), or otherwise injure a competitor.

The question of what is 'likely to deceive' was considered in a 1989 case involving misleading advertisements for a 'wonder' slimming product called SpeedSlim. Mr Justice Hoffman, ordering an injunction, said:

An advertisement must be likely to deceive the persons to whom it is addressed if it makes false claims on behalf of the product. It is true that many people read advertisements with a certain degree of scepticism. For the purposes of applying the regulations, however, it must be assumed that there may be people who will believe what the advertisers tell them, and in those circumstances the making of a false claim is likely to deceive.

MISLEADING PRICE INDICATIONS

Price is, of course, one of the key factors in the decision whether to purchase, and sellers of products and providers of services (such as restaurants) have proved highly inventive over the years in thinking up new ways to mislead and deceive consumers about the true price of what they are buying. Spurious 'bargains', non-existent 'sales' or 'reductions' and 'inclusive' prices (which turn out after all to omit significant items such as VAT or service charges) have all achieved consumer notoriety in their time – although not perhaps so much in the publishing trade, where recommended retail prices were enforced under the Net Book Agreement until 1995 (for RPM and the former NBA generally, see chapter 12).

Misleading price indications are now covered by Part III of the Consumer Protection Act 1987, and the (1988) Code of Practice made under that Act. Price Marking Orders are also made periodically, to guide retailers. It is an offence under section 20 of the 1987 Act to give any consumer in the course of any business an indication which is misleading as to the price at which goods, services, accommodation or facilities are available. A pricing is 'misleading' (or may *become* misleading) if as a result the consumer might reasonably be expected to think any of the following were the case:

- the price is less than it actually is;
- the price applies generally, when in fact it only applies to a particular item (such as an individual title, or service);
- the price is inclusive, when in fact extra charges are made (such as VAT);
- the price is a special or temporary bargain, when in fact it is not (for example, a spurious 'sale' or pre-publication offer);
- the price compares favourably with other rival products, or recommended prices, when in fact the comparisons are false.

Under section 24 of the Act, it is a defence for a publisher or other manufacturer to show that a recommended price was generally in force which was not followed by the retailer concerned. There is also a defence of innocent publication for newspapers, magazines and others who regularly carry such advertising, and a defence of incidental publication, in a book, newspaper, magazine, or on film, TV or radio, in a form other than an advertisement. Finally, (as with offences under the Trade Descriptions Act) it is a general defence (under section 39) to show that you took all reasonable steps and exercised all due diligence to avoid committing the offence.

The 1988 Code of Practice gives further detailed guidance on matters such as price comparisons, statements about value or work, introductory offers and sales such as the National Book Sale or other special events, mail order advertising, and VAT, postage, packing and delivery charges. The Code, which is available from Trading Standards Offices, is intended for guidance only and does not create any separate offences, but may be taken into account in any prosecution under the 1987 Act.

COMPARATIVE ADVERTISING

One particularly dangerous temptation for advertisers is to indulge in what is known as 'comparative advertising' – advertising which makes direct comparisons (usually disparaging ones) with competitors' products: for example, that one make of batteries lasts longer than an identifiable rival battery, or that one car or computer is better value for money than another (illustrated) model. Magazines are prone to this, when comparing alleged circulation figures, actual readership, or advertiser satisfaction levels. The ASA's Advertising Code generally permits such advertising, 'in the interests of vigorous competition and public information', but makes it clear that

comparisons should be clear and fair. The elements of any comparison should not be selected in a way that gives the advertisers an artificial advantage.

This broadly tolerant view should not however mislead publishers into believing that comparative advertising is relatively safe. Very real legal dangers exist here – in particular, the following.

Trade mark infringement

If your advertisement shows, or otherwise uses, a rival's registered trade mark, you may be infringing that trade mark (on trade marks generally, see chapter 9). Under section 10(6) of the Trade Marks Act 1994, any such use:

otherwise than in accordance with honest practices in industrial or commercial matters shall be treated as infringing the registered trade mark if the use without due cause takes unfair advantage of, or is detrimental to, the distinctive character or repute of the trade mark.

Much comparative advertising, by its very nature, would arguably be likely to infringe the trade mark on this basis. Compliance, or non-compliance, with the ASA Code of Advertising Practice would also be likely to be taken into account by any court in deciding what (if any) 'honest practices' in the publishing trade were relevant and whether they had been followed.

Copyright infringement

If you reproduce a substantial part of a rival's copyright work – for example, packaging design, a title or logo, or distinctive typeface – in an advertisement without their permission, you may infringe their copyright in that work, and (subject to defences such as incidental inclusion, for example in a film) they would have the usual remedies for infringement (see chapter 8).

Malicious falsehood

If you publish an untrue statement, motivated by malice (or some other improper motive), and thereby cause loss or damage to someone else, you may be guilty of publishing a malicious falsehood or a trade libel (on this generally, see chapter 7, p. 176). The injured party may sue for damages and apply for an injunction: in one (1992) case between two computer companies, Compaq and Dell, the plaintiffs, Compaq, succeeded in obtaining an interim injunction on these grounds which prevented Dell from making untrue and misleading comparisons (particularly on dealer price) between the computer products of both companies.

Passing off

Although most comparative advertising seeks to *distinguish* one product from another, it is possible to refer to a rival's product in advertising in such a way that the public is given the impression that they are somehow approving or endorsing your own product, or that the products are linked, with the result that their own goodwill would be diluted and confusion would be caused. A good example of this was the 1985 case between McDonald's Hamburgers and Burger King, where McDonald's took action to prevent tube advertisements by Burger King bearing the words 'It's Not Just Big, Mac.' Although McDonald's failed on the ground of malicious falsehood, they succeeded in obtaining an injunction to prevent passing off, on the grounds that potential customers would be misled into thinking that there was an association between McDonald's successful Big Mac hamburger and Burger King, and that they could get a Big Mac at Burger King establishments. (For a further treatment of passing off, see chapter 9, pp. 230–2.)

Publishers would therefore be well advised to do all they can to make absolutely certain that statements made in comparative advertisements are fair comparisons, comparing like with like, that the quoted facts are true at the time of the advertisement, that they do not infringe any copyright or registered trade mark owned by rivals, and do not indulge in any form of passing off or in any other way mislead or confuse the public.

It is likely that there will shortly be new legislation in the UK dealing specifically with comparative advertising, in order to implement the EC Directive on Comparative Advertising. The Directive was due for implementation in member states throughout the European Union by 31 December 1995, but is currently still in the final stages of discussion. It is likely that UK implementation may take the form of amendment to the 1994 Trade Marks Act. Article 3 of the latest proposed text of the Directive provides as follows:

1   Comparative advertising shall be allowed only provided that it objectively compares the material, relevant, always verifiable, fairly chosen and representative features of competing goods and services and that it;

(a) does not mislead;

(b) does not create the risk of confusion in the market place between the advertiser and a competitor or between the advertiser's trade marks, trade names, other distinguishing marks, goods or services and those of a competitor;

(c) does not discredit, designate or bring contempt on the trade marks, trade names, goods, services or other activities of a competitor and does not principally capitalise on the reputation of a trade mark or trade name of a competitor;

(d) does not refer to the personality or personal situation of a competitor.

BRITISH CODES OF ADVERTISING AND SALES PROMOTION

In addition to the various legal controls mentioned above, the advertising industry has developed a parallel system of self-regulation, monitored and enforced by the Advertising Standards Authority (ASA). The ASA attempts to ensure that advertisements do not mislead, and are in the public interest, and may investigate complaints, publish findings and make references to the Director General of Fair Trading, requesting the Director General to seek injunctions preventing offending advertisements. The ASA may also request newspapers and other publishers not to accept particular advertisements. In addition, the ASA's Committee of Advertising Practice promulgates regular Codes of Practice: recently (February 1995) revised and re-named The British Codes of Advertising and Sales Promotion. There are separate Codes covering TV advertising.

The first Principle of the Advertising Code has become famous ('All advertisements should be legal, decent, honest and truthful') but there are many other provisions covering, among other things, safety, personal privacy, prices, free offers, guarantees, and comparisons with rival products (see above, p. 259). The Sales Promotion Code, similarly, provides for protection of consumers (especially children), competitions and prizes, and other promotions or incentive schemes. There are also separate Codes for alcohol and cigarette advertising.

The Codes have no independent legal force, and are written in fairly general terms, but evidence that an advertiser has not complied with one or other of the Codes is likely to be taken into account in any court proceedings. It is therefore very much in publishers' interests to do all they can to see that their advertising complies with the Codes, and that copies of the Codes – which are usually available free of charge from the ASA – are on every marketing and advertising department's shelves.

SUMMARY CHECKLIST: ADVERTISING

- Is this statement a mere puff, or is it a trade description?
- Is it a false trade description?
- Might we have a defence, if we took all reasonable precautions, and used all due diligence?
- Is this a misleading advertisement?
- Are we making a misleading price indication?
- Are we indulging in comparative advertising?
- Are we infringing any trade marks or copyrights (or using a well-known personality for implied endorsement without their consent)?
- Are we following the ASA Advertising Codes?

UNSOLICITED GOODS AND SERVICES

One of the more notorious promotional techniques of the 1960s was 'inertia selling', an aggressive system of sending products – and invoices – out to people who had not ordered them in the hope that some at least would be passive or compliant (or intimidated) enough to buy them. The public outcry that resulted led to the passing of the Unsolicited Goods and Services Act (1971), which now severely restricts such practices.

Under section 2 of the 1971 Act, it is now a criminal offence, punishable by fine, for anyone in the course of a trade or business to make a demand for payment for goods when:

- the goods are unsolicited; and
- they have no reasonable cause to believe they have any right to payment.

It is also a criminal offence under such circumstances to make threats of legal proceedings for non-payment, or threaten any other sanctions, such as unfavourable credit listings. However, in the (familiar) situation where a computer is not properly told (or refuses to believe) that an existing subscription has been cancelled, and keeps sending out publications, invoices and demands for payment, it was held in a 1973 case involving *Reader's Digest* that this did not constitute an offence under the 1971 Act, since the goods were not unsolicited but had been originally requested, and it could not be said that the publisher 'did not have reasonable cause to believe that there was a right to payment'.

The recipient of unsolicited goods is under no obligation to return the goods or look after them, and (under section 1) may:

use, deal with or dispose of them as if they were an unconditional gift . . . and any right of the sender to the goods shall be extinguished.

This is provided the sender sent the goods intending that the recipient could acquire them, (and did not, for example, send them by mistake) and provided the recipient had not in any way requested the goods, or agreed to acquire them or return them. The recipient can either do nothing for 6 months, or put the sender on 30 day's formal notice to come and take the goods away – if at the end of either period the goods have not been collected they will become the recipient's property in accordance with section 1.

Perhaps understandably, the practice is now considerably less common, but the penalties should still be borne in mind.

DISTANCE SELLING

Distance selling (like distance learning) is less exotic than the name implies: it simply means contracts negotiated at a distance, and would include mail order sales based on direct mail campaigns or telephone 'cold calling'. In the European Commission's view the development of new technology, such as tele-shopping, now requires increased consumer protection within the EU, particularly for personal privacy, and a proposed EU Distance Selling Directive reached a Common Position before the EU Council of Ministers in June 1995. Even in its latest revised form it would extend existing rights of consumers in the UK and throughout the European Union, and when implemented may limit many direct selling activities currently permitted under UK law.

The latest text of the Directive would provide increased regulation for all contracts negotiated at a distance. These are quite widely defined and would include not only products such as books and journals, but also services, although not financial services.

DISTANCE SELLING DIRECTIVE

Key features of the proposed Directive are as follows:

- Two means of communication, fax and automatic calling machines, may not be used at all for distance selling, without the prior consent of the consumer. The original draft also included communication by telephone, and electronic mail but these prohibitions (which would have outlawed all 'cold calling' without prior consent) were dropped after heavy political opposition. Why faxes should now be prohibited, without consent, but not telesales, is unclear. Communications to companies or persons acting in the course of their employment (such as a book buyer) would not be prohibited.
- All contract solicitations must comply with 'the principles of good faith in commercial transactions', and the commercial purpose of the solicitation must be clear. It must also be made clear whether the costs of using that

particular distance medium, especially to place an order or secure the service, are to be borne by the consumer.

- At the same time as the sales pitch is made, clear and unambiguous information must be supplied to the consumer, including arrangements for payment, delivery and performance, any additional transport charges or VAT charges and the consumer's right of withdrawal.
- There are provisions against inertia selling, similar to the UK's own Unsolicited Goods and Services Act 1971 (see above, p. 262). In particular, failure to reply shall not constitute consent, and the consumer in most cases shall have the right to do as he or she pleases with the unsolicited goods. Samples or promotional gifts are allowed, provided it is made clear that they are completely free with no obligation for the consumer.
- If no time limit for performance is expressly stipulated in the contract, performance must begin not more than 30 days from the day following that on which the consumer forwards his or her order.
- No later than delivery of the goods, full contract information must be sent in writing to the consumer, including all payment terms and conditions, including any guarantees and after-sales service.
- The consumer shall have a guaranteed right of withdrawal for not less than 7 working days after the product or service is received.
- The consumer must have the right to dispute any payment where fraudulent use has been made of a credit card.

The Directive is likely to be adopted during the course of 1996: member states are currently given a further 2 years in which to implement it.

DATA PROTECTION

Most publishers – and many retailers – maintain substantial databases of personal information, for example about authors, customers and subscribers. There is nothing necessarily sinister about this – most well-run businesses will want to research and mail to their markets regularly – but such data can be misused, particularly where it consists of *personal* data about individual people, and particularly when it is stored electronically (as it increasingly is). UK law already regulates such computerised personal data under the Data Protection Act 1984, and it is likely that even further controls will shortly be introduced throughout the EU under the Data Protection Directive. Databases such as directories are currently given copyright protection under UK law, although this will be subject to a higher test of originality after January 1998 (see Chapter 2, pp. 19–20).

THE DATA PROTECTION ACT 1984

The 1984 Act governs 'personal data', which is data that is

- held on computer; and
- relates to living, identifiable people

Manual databases, such as card-index systems or paper files, are not covered by the Act (although they may soon be following the Directive, see below), and data which does not relate to an identifiable, living human being is also not covered. Certain categories of data are exempt, and need not be registered:

- data required by law to be made public;
- data held for reasons of national security;
- data used only for calculating and paying wages or pensions (and, presumably, royalties);
- data held only for distributing articles or information to the addressees concerned (or recording that distribution) and containing only essential particulars such as names and addresses;
- data held for personal use, or relating to unincorporated clubs.

Otherwise, unless the data held fits into one or other of the above categories, all those who hold and use personal data ('data users') must be registered with the Data Protection Registrar, and comply with the general data protection Principles set out in the Act. To hold personal data while unregistered is a criminal offence under the Act, punishable by fines.

Section 21 of the Act gives all individuals the right to be informed by data users of any personal data held by them, and supplied with copies. If the individual suffers loss as a result of the data being inaccurate, lost or destroyed, or disclosed or allowed to be accessed without authority, he or she may have a right to apply to the Registrar (or a court) to have the data corrected or deleted, and to compensation, including damages for any distress caused (sections 22 and 23). A data user may, however, have a defence if it can prove that it took all reasonable care to prevent the inaccuracy, loss, destruction or access.

THE DATA PROTECTION DIRECTIVE

The Data Protection Directive – Directive 95/46 on the protection of individuals with regard to the processing of personal data and on the free movement of such data – was adopted on 24 October 1995. Member states have three years in which to implement the Directive – in other words any necessary revisions to UK law must be in place by 24 October 1998. In view of the implementation timetables for the Duration and Rental Directives, UK implementation may take some time. However, the Home Office has now circulated a Consultation Paper, inviting comments on how the UK should implement the Directive.

Unlike the 1984 Act, the Directive covers 'personal data' not only held on computer, but also held *manually*. Personal data may only be processed with the *consent* of the individual concerned (the 'data subject'), or where it is necessary to fulfil a contractual obligation to the data subject to protect his or her vital interests, or to comply with national or EU law, or in the interests of public authority. Any commercial, or other, interests of the data controller are likely to be overridden by the interests of the data subject. In addition, any 'consent' given by the data subject:

- must be 'informed' consent; and
- may be withdrawn at any time.

Consent is only 'informed' consent if the data subject has been given all relevant information, for example about the structure and purpose of the data, who is processing it and who it is being sent to. This may pose serious practical problems for some publishers who use databases including personal data – although publishers of professional directories may be able to establish sufficient 'informed' consent with the support of the relevant professional bodies.

Some particular categories of 'sensitive' personal data may not be processed *at all*, except by certain non-profit making associations or foundations, unless the data subject consents, or there is manifestly no infringement of privacy or fundamental freedoms:

- data covering race or ethnic origins;
- data relating to political (or other) opinions, religious, or philosophical beliefs;
- details of trade union membership;
- data on health or sexual life.

Member states may lay down exceptions to these general rules, for example where criminal convictions are concerned, or to protect press freedom.

The data subject must be given access to the data, on request, and has the right to rectify – or remove – any inaccurate or incomplete data he or she may find. Access may be restricted only where it is necessary for reasons of national security, defence or public safety, or in pursuance of criminal proceedings or a monitoring or inspection function performed by a public authority.

The UK must implement the Directive by October 1998, and a number of amendments to UK law will be required, for example, relating to disclosure of information, prohibitions on processing data relating to race, politics and religion except in limited circumstances, and exemptions such as those covering press freedom.

SUMMARY CHECKLIST: PROMOTION AND DATA PROTECTION

- Are we promoting unsolicited goods or services?
- If so, do we have reasonable cause to believe we are entitled to payment?
- Are we engaged in distance selling?
- If we are using fax or automatic calling machines, do we have the consumer's prior consent?

- If not, are they acting in the course of their employment?
- Are we observing the principles of good faith in commercial transactions?
- Are we holding 'personal data' electronically?
- If so, should we be registered with the Data Protection Registrar?
- Do we have the individuals' 'informed consent'?
- If not, does the Data Protection Directive apply?

Distribution and export

12

We looked in chapters 10 and 11 at the contracts which normally govern the sale of finished books and other manufactured products in the UK, and at the general law affecting consumer protection and advertising. We have seen that the law still attaches great importance to individual contracts, but increasingly regulates trading behaviour in the UK by means of statutory liability, especially where consumers are concerned. We have also seen how many of the statutes and other regulations now originate, not from Westminster, but from Brussels. In this final chapter, we shall turn a lot more of our attention to Europe. Distribution and the free movement of goods and services are key concerns of the European Union. So, also, are the goals of free, unrestricted, competition, and the famous 'level playing field'. Any publisher selling or distributing in the UK and Europe needs to bear these economic priorities very much in mind: agreements or trading behaviour which are found to be contrary to EU law, for example because they are monopolistic or otherwise anti-competitive, may be heavily penalised, and UK law is moving in the same direction. This may affect distribution agreements, purchasing agreements and sales agency agreements, and potentially all commercial licensing of intellectual property, both within the UK and throughout Europe.

TRADE AND COMPETITION

Competition is a natural, some would say an essential, feature of healthy markets, and publishing is often highly competitive. Small publishers have a way of turning into larger publishers, however – or being acquired by them – and large publishers may be able in time to influence, or even dominate, their particular market either by themselves, or as one of a group. Such groups can wield considerable market power. This is not in itself a bad thing: market power can encourage healthy rationalisation, and can benefit the consumer in many ways (by improving distribution, for example). It can cause legal difficulties, however, if it is used in an anti-competitive way, or leads to what are known as 'anti-competitive practices'. Anti-competitive practices can start quite informally, for example, over lunches between marketing directors, and may at first be nothing more than a (fairly) innocent exchange of views and gossip. When competitors have lunch, however, economists (and lawyers) start to feel nervous. From such humble beginnings, price fixing agreements may result, or divisions of local territories or market sectors, agreements on discounts or other terms of trade or other measures designed to restrict competition. Agreements or practices which restrict competition are very likely to be prohibited under UK and EU competition law, and are very likely to be unenforceable. They may even lead to large fines.

In these circumstances, great care needs to be taken when entering into commercial agreements, especially 'horizontal' agreements between companies competing at the same level, but also where there are 'vertical' arrangements operating at different levels up and down the distribution chain, for example between suppliers and agents or exclusive licensees.

We will look first at the relevant UK law, and then consider the growing area of EU competition law.

UK COMPETITION LAW

RESTRAINT OF TRADE

Since the early fifteenth century, the courts have refused to enforce contracts which are in unreasonable restraint of trade. Any such contract is *prima facie* void under English law. Each contract, of course, 'restrains' trade in some way, since it limits what one or both of the parties may do in the future, but it is only *unreasonable* restraints which will not be enforced. These most often occur in the context of restrictive covenants, for example, seeking to control rival activity by former employees, or former proprietors, of a publishing business, and may also occur with exclusive distribution or purchasing agreements.

An attempt to restrain a former marketing director from working in the same capacity for any comparable publishing company for the next 5 years would almost certainly be in unreasonable restraint of trade, for example – not only because of the *breadth* of the restriction (which would rule out a large proportion of the likeliest job options) but also because of the unreasonably long *time* during which the ban would operate. A restraint on working for any direct competitor for 12 months, on the other hand, might be regarded as reasonable, and therefore enforceable, but any attempt to impose wide-ranging bans over long periods may well be difficult to enforce, particularly if they would significantly limit the capacity of the person concerned to earn a living at all.

Anyone wishing to enforce restraints of trade will need to prove three things:

1 that he or she has a legitimate interest worthy of protection (protecting the goodwill of the business, for example);

2 that the restraint is reasonable between the parties themselves (and does not, for example, last for an unreasonable length of time or restrict too wide an area of activity); and

3 that it is reasonable in the public interest.

Even if an individual contract may be enforceable between the parties, however, any business activity resulting from it which affects competition may still be caught by UK legislation such as the Restrictive Trade Practices Act, and Resale Prices Act, and also – as we shall see later – by the competition provisions of the Treaty of Rome.

RESTRICTIVE TRADE PRACTICES ACT 1976

Certain kinds of restrictive agreements relating to goods or services may be registrable under the 1976 Act. Such agreements will be void and unenforceable unless they are registered with the Office of Fair Trading. The Act applies to agreements between two or more parties carrying on business within the UK, under which any two or more parties (not necessarily the *same* two or more parties) accept certain restrictions. In the most common situation, for publishers, of agreements relating to goods, the restrictions include any restrictions on the following:

- the prices to be charged, quoted or paid;
- recommended or suggested resale prices;
- the terms or conditions of supply or acquisition;
- the quantities or descriptions of goods to be produced, supplied or acquired;
- the production or manufacturing processes to be used;
- the persons or classes of persons, or the geographical areas or places to be supplied, or acquired from.

Information agreements may also be covered, for example agreements between publishers to notify each other of impending price rises.

The 1976 Act covers informal 'agreements' or arrangements, whether or not legally binding, as well as formal contracts, provided that they effectively impose restrictions on the conduct of two or more parties. However, there must be some evidence of an agreement, some element of mutual undertaking or collusion. Parallel behaviour which is purely coincidental is not covered.

It is not necessary to prove that the agreements or arrangements actually restrict competition – simply that they restrict the conduct of the parties. The 1976 Act is formalistic and the test for its application has nothing to do with whether there is an effect on competition. It may therefore extend equally to classic cartels between competitors as well as to more innocent behaviour.

At least two separate legal entities must be involved. This includes individuals, companies and trade associations. For the purposes of the 1976 Act, internal agreements between companies in the same group, such as those between parents and subsidiaries, will probably not be caught, but an agreement between two separate companies (even though it concerns supplies to one of their subsidiaries) will be. Agreements entered into by trade associations are almost by definition registrable, since they are deemed to have been made by all the members, who are similarly deemed to have accepted the restrictions. This would cover bodies such as the Publishers and Booksellers Associations.

Certain categories of agreements are exempt, for example statutory and certain employment agreements, certain exclusive distribution agreements, and most forms of intellectual property licences. Copyright agreements are normally exempt under Schedule 3 of the 1976 Act: the whole purpose of copyright is to be restrictive, after all, and a vertical copyright licence largely restricts the commercial behaviour of only one party. The rules however are extremely complex and great care is needed in interpreting them. As a general rule, the exception will only be available where the *only* restrictions that are accepted are ones which relate to copyright. Similar rules apply to other intellectual property rights. Mixed agreements cannot benefit from the exemption.

When an agreement is registrable, there is a duty to register particulars of it as soon as possible with the Office of Fair Trading. Particulars must be registered *before* the proposed restrictions are put into operation, and in any case not longer than 3 months after the date of the agreement. An agreement cannot be registered out of time. In cases of doubt, the parties may notify the OFT provisionally via a 'fail-safe' procedure. New rules came into effect in March 1996 avoiding the need to submit for registration agreements subject to an EU block exemption, and certain agreements where the aggregate relevant annual turnover in the UK of both parties does not exceed £20 million on the date of the agreement.

The Director General of Fair Trading has a statutory duty to refer registered agreements to the Restrictive Practices Court, unless they are not significant enough to merit a reference. In practice, the vast majority of registrable agreements benefit from a dispensation that they are not of such significance as to justify a referral. In some instances the parties agree to amend their agreement in such a way as to obtain such a dispensation.

In the event of a reference, the parties may abandon the agreement, or the relevant restrictions, or else defend it before the court as being in the public interest. There are a number of specific defences (called 'gateways'), such as protection of the public against injury, the encouragement of exports, or the reduction of unemployment: the broadest gateway is the defence that removal of the restriction 'would deny the public as purchasers, consumers or users of any goods other specific or substantial benefits or advantages enjoyed or likely to be enjoyed by them'. In practice, very few restrictive agreements survive a reference to the court: one of the few was the Net Book Agreement (now no longer in force – see below, p. 272).

It is important to appreciate that an agreement which is registrable under the 1976 Act can arise in almost any circumstances, from distribution and joint venture agreements to an agreement to engage a self-employed author.

RESALE PRICES ACT 1976

With only two exceptions (books, and proprietary medicines) collective resale price maintenance (RPM) in the UK is illegal. Section 1(1) of the Resale Prices Act 1976 makes any agreement or arrangement between suppliers unlawful that boycotts, or discriminates against, dealers who have resold, or who resell goods in breach of an RPM condition. In the case of books, the Office of Fair Trading is currently reviewing whether circumstances have changed since the exemption was granted in 1962, and following the collapse of the Net Book Agreement in 1995, it is likely that the exception for books will be removed; medicines may not be far behind.

Individual (as opposed to collective) RPM is not illegal as such under the 1976 Act, but under section 9(1) of the Act:

> Any term or condition in a contract between a supplier and a dealer which purports to establish a minimum price for the resale of goods within the UK is void.

Certain classes of goods may however be exempted by the Restrictive Practices Court on public interest grounds, via 'gateway' defences: the only two to have succeeded are books under the Net Book Agreement (now gone) and medicines supplied to the NHS. Both exemptions may now prove to be short lived.

THE NET BOOK AGREEMENT

Although the Net Book Agreement was declared not to be against the public interest in 1962 when the court found that abolition would lead to '(1) fewer and less well-equipped stock holding book shops; (2) more expensive books, and (3) fewer published titles', there have been further references since 1962, and at the time of writing another is currently under way: following the collapse of the NBA in 1995 it appears likely that the Restrictive Practices Court will reverse its 1962 ruling and formally remove the public interest exemption, which would make it virtually impossible under UK law to re-introduce a similar Agreement in the future. For the EU competition implications, see below, pp. 274–86.

FAIR TRADING ACT 1973

The Fair Trading Act provides for 'monopoly situations', and other uncompetitive practices, to be referred to the Monopolies and Mergers Commission for investigation. A monopoly situation exists where at least 25 per cent of goods of any description supplied in the UK are supplied by (or to) a single person, company or group. Note that monopolies can be purchasing monopolies as well as selling monopolies. Under section 6 of the 1973 Act, two or more separate companies acting together may create a 'complex monopoly situation' if they:

so conduct their respective affairs as in any way to prevent, restrict, or distort competition in connection with the production or supply of goods of that description.

Reference to the Monopolies and Mergers Commission is normally made by the Director General of Fair Trading, or by a relevant minister. Recent references have included the wholesaling of newspapers and periodicals (1978 and again in 1992), collective licensing via collecting societies (1988) and CD pricing (1994) – all of which, in some cases with modifications, were found not to be operating against the public interest. Where monopoly situations are found to operate against the public interest, orders may be made to terminate agreements, to ban discrimination, tie-ins or refusals to supply, to control prices, and to remove any other practice operating against the public interest.

COMPETITION ACT 1980

The Competition Act 1980 provides for the investigation and control of 'anti-competitive practices' in the UK. Under the Act, persons (or companies or groups) engage in anti-competitive practices if they pursue in the course of business a course of conduct:

> which has, or is intended to have, or is likely to have, the effect of restricting, distorting of preventing competition in connection with the production, supply or acquisition of goods in the UK.

The supply of services is also covered under the Act. However, where a firm, or group of firms, has less than a 25 per cent share of the relevant market, or an annual turnover of less than £10 million, the Act will not apply.

A term which is registrable under the 1976 Act is not subject to investigation under the 1980 Act.

Investigations are normally carried out by the Office of Fair Trading; the OFT often commences an informal investigation, and in many cases the mere threat of an investigation is sufficient to encourage companies to stop a particular practice, or at least modify it. A formal undertaking may be offered to avoid an investigation. If this approach is not possible, or does not work, a more formal investigation may be carried out, and possibly a reference to the Monopolies and Mergers Commission. If the practice concerned is found to harm the public interest, undertakings may be required, and, if these are not given, orders may be made prohibiting the continuance of the practice and remedying any damage caused.

SUMMARY CHECKLIST: UK COMPETITION LAW

- Is this contract in restraint of trade?
- Is it a restrictive agreement under the Restrictive Trade Practices Act 1976?

- Does it impose restrictions on two or more separate parties?
- Is it exempt from registration?
- If not, has it been registered with the OFT (and in time)?
- Are we in a 'monopoly situation' under the Fair Trading Act 1973, with at least 25 per cent of the relevant market?
- If so, is there any risk of a reference to the Monopolies and Mergers Commission?
- Are we engaged in an 'anti-competitive practice' under the Competition Act 1980 (with 25 per cent of the relevant market, or less than £10 million annual turnover)?

EU LAW

As pointed out earlier, freedom of competition, free movement of goods and single market integration are key concerns of the European Union. Although, as already pointed out, UK competition law is moving increasingly into line with EU law, there may be circumstances where the UK authorities are unwilling or unable to take action against some kinds of anti-competitive behaviour themselves, in which case a direct complaint to the European Commission may be made. The Commission, which has extensive investigative powers and powers of search, may make its own investigations, and if an infringement of the EU competition rules is found the anti-competitive practice will be prohibited. The European Commission has extensive fining powers.

The European Union competition laws are contained in the EC Treaty, which is the latest revised version of the Treaty of Rome. Competition matters are largely dealt with in Articles 85 and 86 of the Treaty, dealing respectively with anti-competitive agreements and abuses of a dominant market position. Articles 30–6 deal with the free movement of goods.

ARTICLE 85: ANTI-COMPETITIVE AGREEMENTS

Article 85(1) prohibits agreements and concerted practices which either actually or potentially have, or are intended to have, a negative effect on competition and which are significant enough to affect trade between member states. Under Article 85(1):

> the following shall be prohibited as incompatible with the common market: all agreements between undertakings, decisions by associations of undertakings and concerted practices which may affect trade between Member States and which have as their object or effect the prevention, restriction, or distortion of competition within the common market.

The Article sets out examples of some of the kinds of agreements or practices which are prohibited – the list includes those which:

- directly or indirectly fix purchase or selling prices or any other trading conditions;
- limit or control production, markets, technical development, or investment;
- share markets or sources of supply;
- apply dissimilar conditions to equivalent transactions with other trading parties, thereby placing them at a competitive disadvantage;
- make the conclusion of contracts subject to acceptance by the other parties of supplementary obligations which, by their nature or according to commercial usage, have no connection with the subject of such contracts.

Under Article 85(2) any such prohibited agreements or decisions are automatically void – unless they are exempt under Article 85(3) (see below, p. 276).

In practice, rules very similar to the EU competition rules will apply to agreements where the other party is based in a country which is a member of the European Economic Area, EFTA or other countries having free trade or association agreements with the EU, such as the countries of former Eastern Europe.

A number of key terms need to be further defined.

Agreements

Article 85 regulates agreements, decisions and concerted practices. Agreements can be informal understandings and 'gentlemen's agreements' as well as written contracts – the European Commission and the Court of Justice have consistently given a wide interpretation to these terms. It is the economic *effect* of the agreement which is important, rather than its form.

Between undertakings

'Undertakings' include all natural and legal persons who, or which, are capable of carrying on commercial or economic activity. This would of course include companies, but also individuals, trade associations, state-owned corporations, and even some government bodies, at least insofar as they carry on economic activities. It is therefore quite likely that UK government agencies actively licensing copyrights on a commercial basis, such as HMSO or the Ordnance Survey, would be regarded as undertakings for the purposes of Article 85 (and Article 86 – on which see below, p. 280).

Which may affect trade between member states

It is not necessary to establish that inter-state trade has actually been affected, or even is about to be: all that is required is that it should be reasonably foreseeable that it might be affected. An agreement between two UK companies or groups, or a UK trade association (such as the Publishers Association) might well be considered to have a potential effect on trade between member states, for example if it makes the domestic market harder for others to enter – this would particularly be so in the case of an industry-wide agreement intended to operate across an entire national market.

In the case of the former Net Book Agreement, however, the European Court of Justice did criticise the European Commission's earlier refusal to grant the Agreement exemption under Article 85(1), on the grounds that – among other things – they had failed to consider the UK–Irish book market as a 'common language area', while permitting a broadly similar system of retail price maintenance for this reason for books in the German–Austrian common language area. Ironically, in the light of the comfort letters given to the German and Austrian publishing industries, it is not impossible that the Net Book Agreement would ultimately have been granted exemption under Article 85(3), and might still gain such exemption if it or anything like it is ever re-introduced in the UK. At the time of writing, however, this prospect seems unlikely.

The effect on inter-state trade must be appreciable and not insignificant: the Commission in its most recent guidance Notice, held the view that goods and services accounting for less than 5 per cent of the relevant product market (in that part of the common market affected by the agreement) and also not exceeding turnover of 300 million ECU, do not generally fall under the prohibition in Article 85(1). In calculating this turnover, the group turnover of all parties to the agreement, or any network of agreements of which it forms part, has to be taken into account. This guidance is not legally binding and is dependent upon an accurate definition of the relevant product market, which is notoriously difficult.

Exemptions and block exemptions

Individual exemptions

Parties may apply to the European Commission for an agreement (or decision, or concerted practice) to be exempted from Article 85(1) but they must prove four things:

1 that the agreement contributes to improving the production or distribution of goods or to promoting technical or economic progress;
2 that it allows consumers a fair share of the resulting benefit;
3 that it does not impose restrictions which are unessential for achieving those objectives;
4 that it does not make it possible to eliminate competition altogether in a substantial proportion of the product market concerned.

Thus a licensing agreement – with restrictions which are anti-competitive – may nevertheless be exempted if overall it encourages more efficient distribution or stockholding, or enables costs to be held down via higher discounts, or provides a stable trading base for increased research and development.

Block Exemptions

To save time, the European Commission has issued block exemptions to whole categories of agreements: agreements in the relevant categories do not need to be individually notified to the Commission, and are automatically valid without separate exemption provided all the terms of the particular block exemption are met. Block exemptions are interpreted narrowly.

The two block exemptions most relevant to publishing are those relating to exclusive distribution and exclusive purchasing agreements; there are also block exemptions covering a number of other areas, including franchising and patent and know-how licensing agreements. The last two block exemptions are in the process of being replaced, from April 1996, by a new Technology Transfer block exemption. Although there is as yet no block exemption for software licensing, it may sometimes be possible for some widely distributed software products to take advantage of the block exemption for certain exclusive distribution agreements.

Exclusive distribution agreements

The economic advantages of 'vertical' agreements which grant exclusive distribution rights – for example in enabling a distributor to achieve a better market penetration – often far outweigh the disadvantages. Both UK and EU law recognise this. Exclusive distribution agreements may often escape the need for registration under the Restrictive Trade Practices Act 1976 – if, for example, only one party accepts restrictions – and if they are properly drafted they may equally benefit from the block exemption from Article 85(1).

The block exemption covering exclusive distribution agreements is contained in EU Regulation 1983/83. It applies to agreements:

- for the distribution of goods (but not services, or agreements which are predominantly licensing agreements);
- between only two undertakings;
- under which one agrees to supply exclusively to the other goods for resale within the whole EU or a defined area of it.

Restrictions on the supplier

The supplier may be restricted from supplying any other distributor in the contract territory, and may also be restricted from selling directly to end users itself. However, it is *not* permitted to attempt to prevent the supplier from selling into other territories from which parallel imports into the contract territory may occur, where this involves all or part of an EU member state or some other country with which the EU has an association or free trade agreement: any such restrictions are absolutely prohibited. So a UK publisher entering into an exclusive distribution agreement with a distributor in France may agree not to supply anyone else in France, but may *not* agree not to supply into say Belgium or Luxembourg, if the intention is to prevent parallel imports back into France. It is very important to appreciate that an exclusive distributor is not given absolute territorial protection.

Restrictions on the distributor

The distributor may be restricted from doing the following things:

- selling (or manufacturing) competing goods, during the life of the agreement;
- buying the contract goods from any other source;
- seeking customers for the goods outside the territory (or establishing a foreign branch or distribution depot).

It is *not* permissible to impose any kind of export ban, for the same reasons that prevent restrictions on parallel imports.

Positive restrictions may also be imposed on exclusive distributors. The following obligations are generally regarded as permissible, and will be covered by the block exemption:

- to purchase complete ranges of goods (for example, a series, or possibly an entire list), or minimum quantities;
- to sell the goods under particular trade marks, or packed and presented according to particular specifications;
- to advertise and promote the goods;
- to maintain a sales network or stock of goods;
- to provide customer and guarantee services;
- to employ staff with specialised or technical training.

Agreements with restrictions not covered by the above list will fall outside the block exemption.

It will also not cover *reciprocal* exclusive distribution agreements between manufacturers of identical or equivalent (that is, directly competing) goods. Non-reciprocal agreements between such manufacturers will only be allowed if one of them has an annual turnover of less than 100 million ECU. Finally, the block exemption will not apply where users have no alternative sources of supply, or where one or both of the parties to the agreement make it difficult for them to obtain the goods elsewhere. This will be the case, for example, if any attempt is made to restrict parallel imports.

Purchasing agreements

EU Regulation 1984/83 governs exclusive purchasing agreements, where a dealer purchasing goods for resale agrees to buy them only from one supplier and not from anyone else. Unlike an exclusive distribution agreement, there is no corresponding restriction preventing the supplier from supplying anyone else in the territory.

The block exemption applies only to agreements between two undertakings – and for periods no longer than 5 years. The reseller may agree to purchase only from the supplier, 'from a connected undertaking, or from another undertaking which the supplier has entrusted with the sale of his goods'.

Restrictions on the supplier

The supplier may not be prevented from supplying the contract goods to other dealers or resellers in the territory, at least 'at the reseller's level of distribution', but may be prevented from distributing direct to users.

Restrictions on the purchaser

As well as the primary restriction on buying from anyone else, the purchaser may be restricted from manufacturing or distributing goods which compete with the contract goods. The purchaser may be made subject to the same positive restrictions as are permitted under exclusive distribution agreements, for example to purchase minimum quantities, or advertise and promote the goods (see above, p. 278).

The block exemption will not cover reciprocal exclusive purchasing agreements between manufacturers of identical or equivalent goods, and non-reciprocal agreements will only be allowed if at least one manufacturer has annual turnover below 100 million ECU. The exemption also does not apply to agreements for more than one type of (non-connected) goods, or for agreements lasting for more than 5 years or for an indefinite period. Agreements which are automatically renewable are regarded as being indefinite, and so not within the scope of the block exemption.

Agency agreements

There is no block exemption as such for agency agreements. This is because an agreement which is regarded as an agency agreement for the purposes of EU competition law is generally not within the scope of the EU competition rules. Labels can be deceptive. As in other aspects of EU competition law it is the economic *effect* of the agreement that is important, and not the label that is attached to it. A personal agency agreement – as, for example, between an author and a literary agent – will not be regarded in itself as anti-competitive or objectionable under Article 85 since it will have no effect on competition: in economic terms, one person is simply stepping into the shoes of another. In legal terms, true agents in any particular transactions act only for the people they are appointed to represent (their 'principals'). They may, for example, seek out and pass on orders for their principals' products, but the customers are at all times their principals' customers, not their own, and their role is purely that of an intermediary. They accept no commercial risk in performing their transactions.

However, more general agency agreements where agents do more than simply represent their principals and also operate on their own account as independent traders, might well have competition implications and might well be caught by Article 85, since the 'agent' will in such cases not be regarded as an agent for the purposes of EU competition law. They might also be caught under UK competition law, for example by the Restrictive Trade Practices Act 1976 or under the Competition Act 1980 (see above, p. 273).

Although not part of EU competition law it is worth noting that throughout the European Economic Area, there is now legislation regulating commercial agents. For this purpose a commercial agent is a person who has continuing authority to negotiate or accept orders for the sale or purchase of goods on behalf of, and in the name of, his or her principal. These rules have now been implemented in the UK in the shape of the Commercial Agents (Council Directive) Regulations 1993. The Regulations contain provisions governing remuneration, such as terms of commission and also minimum terms of appointment and (in particular) termination, including mandatory compensation payable on termination. It should be noted that a number of European countries have legislation which is more extensive than that in the UK, often extending to services provided by an agent. In most cases the law of the country in which the agent is based does not allow contracting out.

Key factors which will determine whether an agreement is a true agency agreement for the purposes of EU competition law, or is a more arm's-length commercial arrangement between two separate business entities liable to have competition law implications, include the following:

- Does the 'agent' bear an independent commercial risk in relation to the transaction?
- Does the 'agent' hold substantial stock?
- Does the 'agent' determine pricing and marketing strategy?
- Does the 'agent' provide an independent customer service?

If the answers to any of the above questions are 'yes' it is likely that the agreement is not a true agency agreement for the purposes of EU competition law and might well have competition law implications under EU law. If the relationship relates to goods then the EU and UK rules on Commercial Agents may also apply.

ARTICLE 86: ABUSE OF A DOMINANT POSITION

While Article 85 covers anti-competitive agreements between two or more persons or companies, Article 86 regulates behaviour by single entities alone. It may happen that one major company or key information provider comes to acquire a position of such market dominance that it can effectively ignore its competitors (if it has any). The normal checks and balances of free market competition then cease to apply, and there is a danger that it will behave monopolistically, such as by controlling the supply of goods or information, favouring some customers or suppliers against others, or excessive or predatory pricing. A major book publisher may find itself in this position in some markets, or a collective licensing body, or in some cases an individual licensor such as a quango or government department if it controls vital information or intellectual property not available elsewhere.

Article 86 provides that:

> any abuse by one or more undertakings of a dominant position within the common market or in a substantial part of it shall be prohibited as incompatible with the common market insofar as it may affect trade between member states.

Let us look at some of these terms a bit more closely.

Undertakings

As in Article 85 (see above, p. 275) an undertaking can include any legal entity that carries on activities of an economic nature in the market concerned. This has been held to include not only individual persons and companies, but trade associations and collecting societies, privatised state enterprises (such as British Telecom), and government departments which trade commercially. The Spanish post office and the German federal employment office have both been held to be undertakings – similarly bodies in the UK which engage in commercial activities, such as the Ordnance Survey or HMSO would probably also be covered, particularly if they control access to information not available elsewhere.

Dominant position

How powerful do you have to be in order to be 'dominant'? The term is not defined, but a company or organisation which can effectively operate without any need to pay attention to its competitors or customers is very likely to be treated as occupying a dominant position. Market share is clearly going to be relevant (although there may be other factors, such as exclusive ownership of key rights or technology). A company with only 30 per cent of any given market can be regarded as dominant if it holds key intellectual property or other rights, and with a market share of 40 per cent or more the risk is considerably increased.

The relevant market must be defined accurately and is likely to be quite narrow: the European Court of Justice has repeatedly rejected attempts by undertakings to define markets widely so as to appear to reduce their market share. In disputes about bananas the relevant market is the banana market, not the entire fruit market – similarly, in any dispute about, say, children's books the relevant market would be likely to be a specific market sector such as children's educational books (rather than children's books generally) and certainly not the whole book market. The most useful test in determining the relevant market is likely to be whether goods are truly interchangeable, so that customers would accept one in place of the other – if they are, they are probably in the same market. If not, they are probably not. The approach would be the same in any specialist market, such as on-line information services for professionals like doctors or lawyers. A publisher might therefore arrive at a dominant position in a relevant market without necessarily being a major international corporation, and the competition implications of trading behaviour should always be borne in mind, even by enterprises which operate primarily in one member state.

It is important to appreciate that market share is only one factor in assessing dominance. A very high market share may be decisive. However, especially in the case of publishers, the holding of key copyright or other intellectual property rights, such as the benefit of a well-known brand name, will be relevant.

The dominant position must be held either in all, or a substantial part, of the common market.

Abuse

Holding a dominant position is not objectionable in itself – it is what you do with it. Article 86, which is general in its application gives four examples of common abuses of a dominant position:

1 *Imposing unfair prices or conditions*. This may be done directly or indirectly. Charging excessive prices or licence fees, not in any way related to the economic value of the goods or information supplied, would be an obvious example of an abuse. Equally, deliberate under-pricing for some favoured customers may be an abuse, such as loss-leading designed to force out competitors from the market.

2 *Limiting production, markets or technical developments*. This may well be an abuse if done to the prejudice of consumers. A refusal to supply straightforward orders from one particular customer, or class of customer, may have the effect of limiting the market, and therefore be an abuse. Indeed, for a company occupying a dominant position, any refusal to supply can be dangerous – especially if the goods or information are not available elsewhere. Insisting on the use of an established production or distribution system may equally limit technical development.

3 *Applying dissimilar conditions to equivalent transactions*. To do this so as to place other trading parties at a competitive disadvantage will be regarded as abusive behaviour if the undertaking is in a dominant position. Discounts for bulk orders, or for regular business are normally regarded as acceptable business practice, but in such cases the transactions are not 'equivalent'. In other cases, where the conditions ought to be the same, conditions which are

imposed in order to discriminate against certain trading partners are very likely to be treated as an abuse.

4 *Tying contracts to supplementary obligations.*
Imposing supplementary conditions or obligations not naturally connected with the order itself may also be considered an abuse – for example, tie-in sales, where it is a condition of acquiring one product that the customer has to purchase another, economically unrelated, product.

In the publishing sector particular care is needed to ensure that a company in a particular market does not abuse that position by strengthening its position in a neighbouring market.

It is important to remember that a company which holds a dominant position in a particular market owes a special responsibility to others operating in that market or wishing to enter it. Thus in defending its position it may react, but only in a reasonable and proportionate manner.

Abuse of copyright ownership?

A recent decision by the European Court of Justice has confirmed that even the exclusive rights of copyright owners to license (or refuse to license) who they please must be read in line with Article 86. In the *Magill* TV listings case, finally decided in 1995, a refusal by the Irish State TV and radio company RTE and others who held the copyright in TV listings, to supply details of the basic information on programme scheduling, in which they held a dominant position, to a new market entrant which wished to publish a weekly TV guide was held to be an abuse of a dominant position. This was despite the fact that RTE owned a copyright in its programme listings, and argued strongly that it was under no obligation to license them. The Court of First Instance and the full European Court both decided, on the contrary, that RTE's behaviour 'clearly went beyond what was necessary to fulfil the essential function of copyright as permitted in Community law' – which the European Court defined somewhat narrowly as being 'to protect the moral rights in the work and ensure a reward for creative effort, while respecting the aims of, in particular, Article 86'. Important features of this case were that *Magill* was seeking to enter a market for which the court found that there was clearly a demand and in which RTE was already present through its subsidiary. RTE, which owned the copyright in the TV listings, was attempting to use that copyright to protect its position in the downstream market of weekly TV guides, by refusing access to the raw material which was indispensable for the compilation of a weekly TV guide. All this supports – and extends – an important principal of EU law which is that while ownership of restrictive intellectual property rights such as copyright does not of itself create a dominant position and is not in itself anti-competitive (it is actually protected, with other forms of 'industrial and commercial property', in Articles 36 and 222) the *use* of those rights may be.

ARTICLE 30: FREE MOVEMENT OF GOODS

Just as copyright ownership or licensing – though protected as such – must not be exercised in an anti-competitive way, or in abuse of a dominant position, so it must also not be allowed to interfere with the free movement of goods. The free movement of goods provisions of the Treaty of Rome are contained in Articles 30 to 34, and prohibit any 'quantitative restrictions' on imports or exports between member states. Put another way, there must be no internal barriers in the single common market: there must be free movement of goods within the EU (and, equally, free movement of services and information). Goods lawfully on sale in one member state may not be prevented from entering any other member state. This clearly outlaws quantitative restrictions imposed by states themselves, but it equally restricts geographical market divisions within Europe imposed by individual rights owners. This is of considerable significance to UK publishers, particularly in relation to English-language co-editions which will be on sale not only in the UK but elsewhere in Europe. The ownership of intellectual property rights is clearly incompatible with the principles of free movement, and in a number of recent decisions of the European Court of Justice national copyright protection, and the exercise of intellectual property rights generally, has increasingly given way to the overriding free movement of goods provisions of Article 30. Despite the fact that Article 36 specifically exempts 'the protection of industrial and commercial property' from the full effect of Article 30, this is subject to a proviso in Article 36 itself that restrictions on the free movement of goods shall not be allowed to constitute 'a means of arbitrary discrimination or a disguised restriction on trade between Member States'.

Territories in Europe

Under co-publishing deals between, say, a UK and US publisher (see chapter 5), a schedule of world territories would normally be agreed: some would be exclusive to either side, and the rest would be 'open' markets, where either edition may sell. The US publisher would usually want exclusive rights to publish in North America, and the UK publisher might have asked for exclusivity in the UK and other territories of the former Commonwealth. Traditionally, most of the rest of the world would have been regarded as an 'open market' – including (until now) European countries such as Holland or Belgium. In view of the free movement of goods provisions of Article 30, such an arrangement is now highly unsafe, and the UK exclusivity is almost certainly unenforceable against parallel importation of US (or any other) editions lawfully on sale in Holland or Belgium – or in any other member state.

Once the US edition is lawfully on sale in (for example) Holland, there is nothing the UK publisher can do under Article 30 (or Article 36) to prevent its importation into the UK. Our own Copyright Designs and Patents Act 1988, in fact, expressly guarantees this under section 27(5) – nothing in that Act will prevent the importation of any article:

> which may lawfully be imported into the UK by virtue of any enforceable community right.

If UK co-publishers wish to achieve effective exclusivity for their own edition in the UK, therefore, they will now need to consider negotiating exclusive rights to the whole of the EU and EEA. Such agreements will still of course need to be permissible generally under EU competition law.

Exhaustion of rights

It seems appropriate that the last topic in a law book should be the doctrine of exhaustion. The free movement of goods provisions of Article 30 apply to goods lawfully on sale in any member state – in the case of copyright goods such as books, it might have been possible under Article 36 to argue that books licensed by the copyright owner for territory B only, but then re-imported via parallel importation back into territory A without the owner's consent, would be infringing copies in territory A and could still be excluded. However, in a leading 1971 case involving *Deutsche Grammophon*, the European Court of Justice decided that once copyright goods have been put on the market in any EU member state by the copyright owner or licensor, or with their consent, then their intellectual property rights restricting the distribution or circulation of those goods are 'exhausted'. Local, national, copyright cannot thereafter be used to prevent parallel importation from one member state to another. It is superseded by Article 30.

Exhaustion only applies *within* the EU, however, and where the owner has *consented* – there is no exhaustion of rights if goods are marketed outside the EU (for example, in a third country such as the USA) and then imported into the EU. Similarly, if goods are released onto the market inside the EU without the owner's consent – for example via a compulsory licence in one member state – the rights will probably not be exhausted. In the case of *EMI v. Patricia* in 1989, the European Court of Justice held that records released lawfully marketed in Denmark not with the consent of the copyright owner but purely because the term of local copyright protection expired, could be prevented from entering the German market, where copyright protection still remained in force. If the Danish recordings had been produced with the owner's *consent*, however, their rights would have been exhausted.

EU COMPETITION LAW: SUMMARY CHECKLIST

- Is this an anti-competitive agreement under Article 85?
- Is it between undertakings, and does it affect trade between member states?

- Does it have as its object or effect the prevention, restriction or distortion of competition within the EU?
- Might it be individually exempted from prohibition, or is a block exemption available?
- Is there a dominant position under Article 86?
- Has it been abused?
- Are we within the free movement of goods provisions of Article 30?
- Should we be seeking exclusivity across the whole EU?
- Have we exhausted our rights?

Appendix A:
A to Z glossary of legal terms

Action | A legal action in a court of law, normally commenced by the issue of a writ. A 'letter before action' is often designed to avoid the need for this.

Applicable Law | The law which applies, for example to a contract, and which will govern any dispute arising under it.

Assignee | Person to whom rights are assigned.

Assignment | Formal transfer of ownership, for example in copyright. Assignments of copyright must be in writing and signed, by or on behalf of the copyright owner.

Assignor | Person assigning rights to another (called the assignee).

CIF (Cost Insurance and Freight) | Delivery terms under which the price includes delivery to the buyer's own designated port of entry (but not normally all the way to the buyer's own warehouse) (compare FOB).

Common Law | A body of English law based on decided cases and developed by the judges over many centuries. Actions for breach of contract or negligence are common-law actions. It is no longer the primary source of new law in the UK, which largely now arises from statutes.

Condition | Fundamental term of a contract, which goes to the root of the whole contract. Breach of a condition by one party normally entitles the other party to terminate the contract.

Consideration | Something of value, usually given in return for a promise or undertaking: to be legally binding, most contracts must be supported by some valuable consideration.

Covenant	A binding undertaking, often limiting future activity (such as a restrictive covenant).
Damages	Remedy normally available to a successful Plaintiff. Awards of damages may be liquidated, to compensate for specific losses, or general, or sometimes punitive if the Defendant's behaviour has been particularly blameworthy.
Defendant	The party being complained about in a legal action; they must defend themselves against one or more Plaintiffs (see below).
Directive	An EU law, adopted by the EU Council of Ministers following circulation of a draft or proposed Directive by the EU Commission. Directives do not as a rule have direct effect as law in member states, but member states are required to implement them within a specified time limit.
Estate	Means of holding and administering property (for example, an author's, including any copyrights) after death: any property is normally vested initially in executors, for the benefit of any beneficiaries: if there are no designated beneficiaries, there are complex statutory rules on entitlement to any assets.
Equity	A traditional body of law developed over the centuries by English judges, parallel to the common law, concentrating less on formal procedure and more on fairness and justice to the parties. Injunctions are mainly equitable remedies. An equitable interest or other entitlement may arise where legal ownership has not formally been transferred (via an assignment, for example) but where it is clear that it was intended to create an interest or it is fair to do so (perhaps where the price or part of it has already been paid).
Exclusive Licence	Licence where the person granting the licence undertakes not only that there will be no other licensees, but also that there will be no rival exploitation by the licensor itself. Exclusive licences must be in writing and signed by or on behalf of the copyright owner.
FOB (Free on Board)	Delivery terms under which the price paid does not normally include freight or insurance costs of transport to the buyer's warehouse or port of entry (compare CIF) but is normally based on delivery to the buyer's agent or shipper at the seller's port of shipment: traditionally legal title to the goods, and risk in them, was not transferred from the seller to the buyer until the goods 'passed the ship's rail'.

Grantor	One who grants, for example, a publishing licence or sub-licence.
Indemnity	A term in a contract under which the party giving it agrees to bear all the risks arising out of any breach of specified warranties and compensate the other party fully for any losses, damage, costs or expenses which may be incurred.
Indictment	Formal criminal charge before a Crown Court.
Injunction	A Court Order, either ordering someone to do something or ordering them to stop (or not to start).
Insolvency	The condition of being unable to pay current or outstanding debts as they fall due. Insolvency of individuals (as opposed to companies) is commonly referred to as bankruptcy.
Libel	A defamatory statement published in written or permanent form.
Licence	A grant of rights, normally limited to a specific period of time (or limited in other ways, for example, territorially or to particular languages or formats or subject to other conditions). Licences may be sole, exclusive or non-exclusive. Licences may normally be revoked, for example for breach of their terms.
Minor	Person under the age of 18. Contracts entered into by minors may be voidable under some circumstances.
Novation	Fresh execution of contracts (for example, where a new owner of a publishing business wishes to re-confirm existing author contracts).
Plaintiff	The complaining party who seeks a remedy via a court action. The party being complained about is called the Defendant. If the case goes to appeal, the party appealing is the Appellant and the party resisting is the Respondent.
Prima Facie	At first sight, or on the face of it.
Reversion	Rights granted (for example, under a licence) may revert to the person granting them if a specified term comes to an end, or if the terms are breached.
Slander	A defamatory statement made verbally, and not in permanent (for example, printed) form.
Sole Licence	A licence in which the person granting the licence (the licensor) agrees that there will be no other licensees, but that the licensor itself may reserve the right to exploit the rights concerned (compare exclusive licence).

Specific Performance	A court may in some circumstances make an Order of specific performance, ordering one party to perform one or more of their obligations under a contract, for example ordering a publisher to publish a book. The courts are reluctant to oversee the performance of contracts in such a direct way, where damages are an alternative.
Statutes	Acts of Parliament: now the primary source of UK law (compare common law above). Statutory measures may include Statutory Instruments (SIs) and other Orders made under Acts of Parliament.
Summary Conviction	Conviction for a criminal offence by a magistrates' court. Penalties are normally lower than those following conviction on indictment before a Crown Court.
Tort	A civil wrong (as opposed to a criminal wrong which is a crime). Examples of torts include negligence, defamation or passing off. Actions for tort may be commenced in the civil courts by the aggrieved parties (unlike crimes which are prosecuted by the authorities through the criminal courts). The most common remedy sought is an award of damages: in appropriate circumstances injunctions may also be granted.
Title	Legal ownership, for example of specific goods or property.
Ultra Vires	Beyond the given authority – an agent or an employee acting *ultra vires* is acting beyond his or her authority and the actions concerned may be challenged or declared void later (although authority may be implied in some circumstances).
Void	Of no legal effect.
Voidable	Liable to be declared void.
Warranty	A term of a contract under which the party making the warranty gives certain guarantees, for example, that the subject of the contract (for example, a manuscript) is not defamatory or does not infringe any copyright or is not otherwise illegal. Breach of a warranty usually gives rise to an action for damages, and may sometimes entitle the other party to terminate the contract.
Work	A literary, artistic or other creation, such as a novel or a photograph or a computer program. Most, but not all, original completed works of UK citizens, or first published in the UK, will qualify for copyright protection in the UK.

Writ   Issue of a writ of summons is the normal method of
                 commencing an action (usually accompanied by a statement
                 of claim).

Appendix B:
Useful addresses

Advertising Standards Authority
2 Torrington Place
London WC1 7HW

Association of Authors' Agents
c/o 5th Floor, The Chambers
Chelsea Harbour
London SW10 0XF

Book Packagers Association
93A Blenheim Crescent
London W11 2EQ

British Copyright Council
Copyright House
29–33 Berners Street
London W1P 4AA

Copyright Licensing Agency
90 Tottenham Court Road
London W1P 0LP

Copyright Tribunal
Hazlitt House
45 Southampton Buildings
London WC2A 1AR

Data Protection Registrar
Springfield House
Water Lane
Wilmslow
Cheshire SK9 5AX

Design and Artists Copyright Society Ltd (DACS)
2 Whitechurch Lane
London E1 7QR

Directory Publishers Association
93A Blenheim Crescent
London W11 2EQ

Educational Recording Agency Ltd (ERA)
33 Alfred Place
London WC1E 7DP

The Independent Publishers Guild (IPG)
25 Cambridge Road
Hampton
Middlesex TW12 2JL

Office of Fair Trading
Field House
Breams Buildings
London EC4A 1HA

Patent Office (Including Trade Marks Registry)
(Department of Trade)
25 Southampton Buildings
London WC2A 1AY

Performing Right Society
29–33 Berners Street
London W1P 4AA

The Publishers Association
19 Bedford Square
London WC1B 3HJ

Registrar of Public Lending Right
Bayheath House
Prince Regent Street
Stockton on Tees
Cleveland TS18 1DF

Society of Authors
84 Drayton Gardens
London SW10 9SB

UNESCO
7 Place de Fontenoy
75700 Paris
France
(UCC Convention)

US Copyright Office
Register of Copyrights, Library of Congress
Washington DC 20559

The World Intellectual Property Organisation (WIPO)
34 Chemin des Colombettes
1211 Geneva 20
Switzerland
(Berne Convention)

Writers Guild of Great Britain
450 Edgware Road
London W2 1EH

Index